The Politics of Race in Panama

University Press of Florida
Florida A&M University, Tallahassee
Florida Atlantic University, Boca Raton
Florida Gulf Coast University, Ft. Myers
Florida International University, Miami
Florida State University, Tallahassee
New College of Florida, Sarasota
University of Central Florida, Orlando
University of Florida, Gainesville
University of North Florida, Jacksonville
University of South Florida, Tampa
University of West Florida, Pensacola

The Politics of Race in Panama

Afro-Hispanic and West Indian
Literary Discourses of Contention

SONJA STEPHENSON WATSON

University Press of Florida
Gainesville/Tallahassee/Tampa/Boca Raton
Pensacola/Orlando/Miami/Jacksonville/Ft. Myers/Sarasota

Library of Congress Cataloging-in-Publication Data
Watson, Sonja Stephenson.
The politics of race in Panama : Afro-Hispanic and West Indian literary discourses of
contention / Sonja Stephenson Watson.
pages cm
Includes bibliographical references and index.
ISBN 978-0-8130-4986-1 (cloth: alk. paper)
ISBN 978-0-8130-5401-8 (pbk.)
    1. Panamanian literature—History and criticism. 2. Blacks—Panama.
3. Race awareness in literature. 4. Panama—Race relations. I. Title.
PQ7520.5.W38 2014
860.9'97287—dc23   2013044105

University Press of Florida
15 Northwest 15th Street
Gainesville, FL 32611-2079
http://www.upf.com

This book is a part of the Latin American and Caribbean Arts and Culture publication initiative, funded by a grant from the Andrew W. Mellon Foundation.

To Jermaine, Solomon, and Samson, Latin lovers

Contents

Acknowledgments   xi

**Introduction: Race, Language, and National
Identity in Afro-Panamanian Literary Discourse**   1

1   **National Rhetoric and Suppression of Black
    Consciousness in Poems by Federico Escobar
    and Gaspar Octavio Hernández**   17

2   **Anti–West Indianism and Anti-Imperialism in
    Joaquín Beleño's Canal Zone Trilogy**   42

3   **Revising the Canon: Historical Revisionism in
    Carlos "Cubena" Guillermo Wilson's Trilogy**   69

4   **West Indian and Caribbean Consciousness in
    Works by Melva Lowe de Goodin, Gerardo Maloney,
    Carlos Guillermo Wilson, and Carlos E. Russell**   94

5   **Beyond Blackness? New-Generation Afro-
    Panamanian Writers Melanie Taylor and Carlos
    Oriel Wynter Melo**   128

    Conclusion: Forging Afro-Panamanian Identity?   144

Notes   149
Bibliography   161
Index   171

Acknowledgments

This project would not have come to fruition without the invaluable assistance I received while I was in Panama. I express gratitude to the Society of Friends of the West Indian Museum of Panama (the Sociedad de Amigos del Museo Afro Antillano de Panamá, or SAMAAP), which is the organ of the black community in Panama. Through SAMAAP, I came to know Melva Lowe de Goodin, Jerónimo Escala, and Inés V. Sealy, who shepherded me throughout this journey, whether it was directing me to the Biblioteca Nacional de Panamá or the Free Zone in Colón. To Miss Inés and Mr. Cecil Reynolds, I greatly appreciate our biannual visits to Gamboa and the Feria Nacional de Artesanía. I wish to acknowledge the support of Carlos E. Russell, who engaged me in person about Panamanian-Caribbean racial identity politics and whose enthusiasm conveyed to me that I was on the right path.

I wish to express my gratitude to the University of Texas at Arlington for the support of the Research Enhancement Grant, which allowed me to return to Panama to complete this manuscript. I also acknowledge the program in African and African American Studies at Washington University in St. Louis for granting me a two-year postdoctoral fellowship from 2005 to 2007. While there, I benefited from the expertise of numerous scholars, including Tim Parsons, who read initial versions of the book prospectus. I also wish to acknowledge the support of Michael Handelsman, who witnessed this project from the beginning.

In the final stages, the book benefited from timely suggestions made by Antonio D. Tillis and an anonymous reader for the University Press of Florida. I am most appreciative of the editorial support of Sian Hunter at the University Press of Florida, who made herself accessible at all costs.

This book would not have been possible without the support and encouragement of my husband, Jermaine, who read the entire manuscript from start to finish; my parents, Willie and Millie Stephenson; my sister Becky L. White; and my young sons, Solomon and Samson. I wish to extend thanks to colleagues and friends who supported me throughout this journey including Lori Celaya, Dawn Duke, and Antonio D. Tillis.

I would like to thank Marveta Ryan for providing me with a copy of Federico Escobar's rare poem "Chispas," which she obtained from the José Martí National Library while in Cuba. I express gratitude to Carlos E. Russell for permission to reproduce ample portions of an interview that I conducted with him in 2010 and the poems that appear in chapter 5. A portion of chapter 1 has been revised from an earlier version that appeared in *Afro-Hispanic Review*. I would like to acknowledge Rossy Toledo for translating the following works by Federico Escobar and Gaspar Octavio Hernández: "28 de noviembre," "3 de noviembre," "Nieblas," "Canto a la bandera," "El culto del idioma," and "Visión nupcial." Additionally, I appreciate Inés V. Sealy's help translating select prose from Joaquín Beleño's novels, which I acknowledge in the second chapter. Unless otherwise indicated, all other translations are my own.

Introduction

Race, Language, and National Identity in Afro-Panamanian Literary Discourse

On June 9, 2009, *Parecen noticias* [Looks Like News], a popular weekly program in Panama that satirizes politics, parodied Panama's recently nominated minister of education Lucy Molinar in a segment called "Yo quiero a Lucy" [I Love Lucy]. The program created a caricature of Molinar using the stereotypical image of a gorilla. The association of Molinar with a gorilla is offensive because she is black. Appointed by President Ricardo Martinelli (2009–14), Molinar is one of the few visible blacks who had a presence on Panamanian television, as former anchorwoman of TVN's (the national television network) Channel 2 morning-news program. Although Molinar did not respond publically to the parody, in a letter to present-elect Martinelli, the president of the Society of Friends of the West Indian Museum of Panama [Sociedad de Amigos del Museo Afro Antillano de Panamá, or SAMAAP] requested that Martinelli make racism and discrimination a priority in his current administration in light of the recent event. In the same fashion that civil rights leaders in the United States reacted and continue to react to racial injustices, West Indians lambasted the news organization for its racist characterization. The protests by SAMAAP resulted in a public apology broadcasted on the show as well as one generated in person by the show's producers at one of their weekly meetings, which I attended. This event is significant because it dispels age-old myths about racial democracies in Latin America and the nonexistence of racism in Panama. The fact that members of the West Indian community were the first to denounce this stereotypical portrayal is no surprise, because as they saw it, it was an attack on the entire black community, unveiling discrimination toward Panama's dark ancestors. What is also interesting is that members of SAMAAP and Lucy Molinar represent two different black ethnic groups in Panama, respectively: West Indians (black immigrants) and Afro-Hispanics (descendants of slaves in Panama). Yet their common African heritage tells the story of Afro-Panamanian race relations of the present and the past. Despite their cultural differences, they are united around a common ancestry. The literature by African descendants in Panama illustrates that the journey to this union was marked by intraethnic tensions as well as racial and cultural politics shaped by ideologies of *mestizaje*, or race mixing, and blackness.

Black literature in Panama falls into two general categories—the writings of Spanish-speaking blacks (Afro-Hispanics[1]), direct descendants of enslaved Africans in Panama, and the writings of West Indians, who are part of the community who migrated primarily from the Anglophone Caribbean to work on the Panama Railroad (1850–55) and the Canal (1904–14). While Afro-Hispanics have "assimilated," older generations of West Indians have not, and they continue to assert their black consciousness over their Panamanian nationality. This conflict has strained race relations between West Indians and Panamanians because the former vehemently challenge the racial (Hispanic), linguistic (Spanish), and religious (Catholic) components of Panamanian nationality. While Afro-Hispanics promote their cultural and national affiliation with the nation, West Indians spurn all three national tenets because they are black, English speaking, and Protestant. The cultural and linguistic distinctions between Afro-Hispanics and West Indians, and the overt national discrimination directed toward the latter, have divided the two populations according to perceived cultural and linguistic differences despite their common African heritage. Thus, the articulation of race, language, and nation is problematic within Panamanian literary discourse because it is tied to a national imaginary that emphasizes *panameñidad*, or Panamanianness, and, by extension, *hispanidad*, or Spanish nationality.

National rhetoric coupled with *mestizaje* discourse stymied black consciousness and further marginalized West Indians. Not only did the national ideology exclude Africanness, it also spurred intraethnic tensions between Afro-Hispanics and West Indians, a racial dynamic that is unique to Panama. Inevitably, national ideological tensions arose between "Spanish" Afro-Hispanics and "black" West Indians. Until now, critical works on the black experience in Panama have focused on either Panama's West Indian heritage or the Afro-Hispanic component. None has examined the dynamic, evolving, and often-tense relationship between the two groups and what it means to be black in Panama. *The Politics of Race in Panama: Afro-Hispanic and West Indian Literary Discourses of Contention* explains cultural divisions and intraethnic tensions that complicate Panamanian identity and persist today.

The Politics of Race is the first to conceptualize Afro-Panamanian identity by viewing it as a product of various diasporas and by exploring the black community's quest to become Panamanian after centuries of slavery and decades of postcolonial migration. Critical works on the black experience in Panama primarily focus on the West Indian component and the works of Carlos Wilson, Panama's most prolific writer of African descent. Smart's *Central American Writers of West Indian Origin: A New Hispanic Literature* (1984), as the title suggests, centers on the West Indian experience in Panama (Joaquín Beleño, Gerardo Maloney, and Carlos Wilson) and Costa Rica (Quince Duncan). Birmingham-Pokorny's *Denouncement and Reaffirmation of the Afro-Hispanic Identity in Carlos Guillermo Wilson's Works* (1993) examines the perception of women and identity conflict in Wilson's works. Zoggyie's *In Search of the Fathers: The Poetics of Disalienation in the Narrative of Two Contemporary Afro-Hispanic Writers* (2003) analyzes the works of Wilson from a postcolonial perspective and compares him to the Afro-Colombian novelist Manuel Zapata Olivella. Indeed, the West Indian influence has garnered more attention. The 2009 special issue of *Latin American and Caribbean Ethnic Studies* (*LACES*) edited by Nwankwo spotlighted Afro–Latin Americans of Anglophone Caribbean ancestry. The *LACES* special issue, "African Routes, Caribbean Roots, Latino Lives," attests to this continued interest and the ways in which English-speaking Caribbean populations complicate Hispanic identity in the Americas, and particularly in Panama, which two of the four featured articles addressed. While a majority of other works have focused on West

Indians, Webster's 2003 analysis, *En un golpe de tos sintió volar la vida: Gaspar Octavio Hernández—Obras escogidas* [In a Fit of Coughing Life Passed Him By: Gaspar Octavio Hernández—Selected Works], of Afro-Hispanic Gaspar Hernández's poems, offers a welcomed addition to the field of Afro-Panamanian Studies. These works have viewed the Afro-Hispanic and West Indian populations in isolation. I conceive the population as a new racial identity while considering its particular historical, geographical, and linguistic (English versus Spanish) differences. This book expands on previous scholarship in that it interrogates the problematic relationship between Afro-Hispanics and West Indians, delineates how blacks have been historically excluded from the national imaginary, and incorporates Afro-Panamanian discourse into Latin American and Caribbean discourse on nationalism and national identity.

Similar to other Latin American countries, the concepts of race and nation in Panama are interconnected and exclude people of color by reinforcing national discourses of homogeneity. Studies have illustrated that discourses of nationality supersede those of race, culture, or ethnicity; that is to say, when it comes to national identities, nation and culture are synonymous (Gellner, Gilroy, Wade). As the philosopher Gellner notes, "Nationalism is a political principle which maintains that similarity of culture is the basic social bond" (3). This national discourse of homogeneity and similarity affects the integration of blacks into the national milieu throughout the African Diaspora. The discussion of race alone is problematic in Latin America since "race is a social construction" (Wade 3). Thus, the classification of Latin Americans varies according to class, color, and complexion. To complicate the racial ambiguity, as Davis notes, racial status in Latin America "depends more on social class than on color or other racial traits" (99). However, this does not mean that racism is nonexistent, because the darkest Latin Americans often form part of the lowest socioeconomic group (Davis 103). This polarized racial construct fails to recognize the complexities of Latin America as a multicultural and multiethnic continent. In fact, this same plurality complicates the articulation of race and ethnicity in Latin America, and particularly in Panama, where indigenous and African components of the nation were eclipsed by race mixing. Cultural plurality complicates racial identification in Panama. As Craft Alexander notes in her study on blacks in Panama, the range of terms employed to identify African descendants is multiple and complex: *afrocolonial* [Afro-colonial], *afroantillano* [Afro-Antillean], *afrodescendiente* [Afro-descendant], *afrohispano* [Afro-Hispanic], *afrolatino* [Afro-Latino], and *afropanameño* [Afro-Panamanian] (124–25). Throughout this study, I use the term *Afro-Hispanic* when discussing blacks in Panama whose ancestors were enslaved on the isthmus. I prefer the use of *Afro-Hispanic* as opposed to *Afro-Latino*, for example, because it refers specifically to populations in Panama who speak Spanish and not to Anglophone Caribbeans or African descendants in the United States from Latin America or the Hispanic Caribbean. Furthermore, the use of the term *Afro-Hispanic* as opposed to *Afro-colonial*, also permits comparisons to other black populations in Hispanic territories. By contrast, I use *West Indian* to reference black immigrants from the British Caribbean (Jamaica, Trinidad, Barbados) in Panama. The term *West Indian* carries with it myriad significations, one of which is a connotation of blackness (Smart, *Central American* 12). Indeed, the term *West Indian* most often refers to the English-speaking populations of the "Caribbean," because "to be West Indian is to be Anglophone and black" (Mosby 21). Thus, the use of *Afro-Hispanic* and *West Indian* is reserved for populations in Panama of known African ancestry and/or who identify as "black" or "brown." I reserve the term *Afro-Panamanian* to discuss the collective group of Afro-Hispanics and West Indians in order to reference the process of both populations of becoming black and Panamanian. *Afro-Panamanian* is a more inclusive term that denotes the union of one's Panamanian and African heritage and the reconciliation of race, nation, and identity in the nation-state.

The process of becoming (Afro-)Panamanian involves the recognition of the fact that the nation comprises multiple diasporas, which lends itself to the creation of hybrid cultural identities. Hall explains these cultural identities in terms of "similarity" and "difference," positing that the former defines cultural identity as a shared, collective one, whereas the latter points to "deep and significant difference which constitute 'what we really are' or rather 'what we have become'" (225). The identity of Afro-Hispanics and West Indians resides at the intersection of these two conceptual frameworks of identity formation. Afro-Hispanics historically have identified with the national foundation of the nation, which has excluded Africanness from its conceptual framework. By contrast, West Indians consolidated around what Gilroy and Craft Alexander call "black internationalism," aligning themselves with other diasporic displaced African populations (27, 127). As diaspora subjects, both Afro-Hispanics and West Indians share a common African heritage that is rooted in heterogeneity, diversity, and difference. Becoming Afro-Panamanian recognizes this shared experience as a product of diversity but also as one that is constantly in transformation. The recognition of this shared African identity in Panama is problematic because blackness is anathema to the national foundation of the nation. Gilroy's work on nationalism, blackness, and identity are important to this study because it illustrates that the emphasis on culture causes nationalism and racism to coalesce (27). This fusion obliterates race and racism from the national imaginary, a phenomenon that characterizes Panama. The literary discourse exemplifies that the problematic of identity suppressed racial discourse on the one hand and created intraethnic tensions on the other.

National pride and the negation of blackness are the subject of the first chapter, "National Rhetoric and Suppression of Black Consciousness in Poems by Federico Escobar and Gaspar Octavio Hernández," which conveys how the poets Escobar and Hernández promoted nationality over race. In the few poems that evince racial consciousness, the writers primarily subordinate their blackness to either spirituality or whiteness. In the essay "El culto del idioma" [The Cult of Language], Hernández expresses disdain for West Indians who refuse to learn and/or speak Spanish. He also criticizes them for trying to be North American instead of Panamanian, because of their ties to the Canal. Hernández distinguishes West Indians from Afro-Hispanics on the basis of linguistic and cultural differences, illustrating that tensions heightened between the two groups as a result of perceived distinctions of nationality. Escobar is most intriguing because, while a majority of his poetry manifests a patriotic discourse, in a few poems he sharply criticizes his fellow Panamanians for the inferior status held by blacks and exhibits a racial pride uncharacteristic of nineteenth- and early twentieth-century Panamanian verse.

The construction of the Canal inspired literature that was critical of the U.S. occupation of the Canal Zone. The United States not only took over construction of the Canal but also transformed all aspects of Zone life by imposing a racial hierarchy that differed from the Latin American model, which categorized blacks according to appearance or skin color. The Latin American racial model contrasted with the "one drop rule" of the United States in which anyone with one drop of African blood was considered black. This proved problematic, since nineteenth-century Panama was already a nation characterized by racial diversity in which blacks represented a significant portion of the population. In the second chapter, "Anti–West Indianism and Anti-Imperialism in Joaquín Beleño's Canal Zone Trilogy," I focus on Beleño's trilogy (*Luna verde* [Green Moon], *Curundú*, and *Gamboa Road Gang*), which objects to racial injustices against Panamanians in the Canal Zone. Beleño differentiates West Indians from Afro-Hispanics and other Panamanians to thwart North American imperialism. Although Beleño protested U.S. racism, he failed to see himself as a supporter of the racist national discourse against West Indians that pitted Panamanians against them as well as other immigrant groups.

In chapter 3, "Revising the Canon: Historical Revisionism in Carlos 'Cubena' Guillermo Wilson's Trilogy," I highlight the novels of Panama's best-known writer of West Indian ancestry, Carlos Guillermo Wilson (1941-2016), known in literary circles as "Cubena." I argue that Wilson's works merit entry into the Panamanian literary canon for what the canon critic Brown considers "informative content," because his novels give a voice to the Panamanian West Indian who has been silenced since he or she ventured across the Atlantic more than a century ago. His trilogy, which includes *Chombo* (a term of disrespect directed toward West Indians), *Los nietos de Felicidad Dolores* [The Grandchildren of Felicidad Dolores], and *La misión secreta* [The Secret Mission], is historical and rewrites the national discourse that has erased blackness from the national paradigm.

Black movements in Panama mobilized solidarity between Afro-Hispanics and West Indians through the establishment of the unified National Committee of Black Organizations. One of the issues that continue to promote dissention among Afro-Hispanics and West Indians is the use of the term *Afro-Panamanian* to describe all African descendants in Panama. For many West Indians the term signifies a denial of their British Caribbean ancestry; for Afro-Hispanics, it conflicts with their Hispanic heritage. The fourth chapter, "West Indian and Caribbean Consciousness in Works by Melva Lowe de Goodin, Gerardo Maloney, Carlos Wilson, and Carlos E. Russell," revisits the theme of national identity and examines the role of black movements in the aid of Afro-Panamanian consolidation. Specifically, it considers the writings and political activism of Panamanian West Indian writers who address the issue of Afro-Panamanian identity from disparate geographical spaces— the United States and Panama. The subjects of this chapter, Melva Lowe de Goodin (Panama), Gerardo Maloney (Panama), Carlos Wilson (United States), and Carlos Russell (United States), represent third-generation Panamanian West Indians, and their works illustrate the complexities of being both West Indian and Panamanian from the 1970s to the present. Lowe de Goodin incorporates West Indian consciousness through history and ethnic memory, whereas Wilson problematizes his racial identity as a black Panamanian, Latin American, and Caribbean. Writing from inside the Panamanian nation-state, Maloney's works often privilege Afro-Panama over his Anglophone Caribbean heritage. By contrast, his contemporary Russell promotes a Caribbean heritage through a consciously racialized discourse. Recent works by both Maloney and Russell, however, convey a Caribbean consciousness, which further complicates yet enriches our understanding of blackness in Panama.

The final chapter, "Beyond Blackness? New-Generation Afro-Panamanian Writers Melanie Taylor and Carlos Oriel Wynter Melo," engages the respective feminist and postmodern literature of Taylor and Wynter Melo, who are both of Panamanian and West Indian ancestry. Born after 1970, both writers clearly identify as black, yet this racial identification does not manifest in their literary repertoire. Short stories by Taylor and Wynter Melo interrogate black identity in twenty-first-century Panama and provide a road map to racial consolidation and the forging of Afro-Panamanian identity and unity.

Nineteenth-Century Panamanian Nation Building

In 1789, free blacks or slaves comprised 63 percent of the total Panamanian population (Rout 273). Moreover, the percentage of free blacks in Panama City jumped from 7.8 percent of the population in 1575 to 65 percent by 1794 (Priestley and Barrow 228). Panama's large Afro-descended population contributed to its reputation as a black province in the nineteenth century. The African presence troubled the Panamanian criollo oligarchy during the early nineteenth century, especially in light of the Haitian Revolution (1789–1804), which intensified the oligarchy's fear of its black, indigenous, and mixed populations on the one hand, and its own minority status on the other (Szok 19).[2] Haiti's occupation of the Dominican Republic and its expulsion of Santo Domingo's European population would alter the construction of race in the Dominican Republic, which later defined itself as a Spanish-speaking nonblack nation (Derby 7). Haiti would later serve as a model that was not to be followed in Latin America. Representing only 12 percent of the Panamanian population, the criollos feared that Panama would turn into "another Haiti," a country of blacks (Szok 19). As a result, Panama's large black population influenced the oligarchy's decision to join Simón Bolívar's Gran Colombia (present-day Colombia, Ecuador, Panama, and Venezuela) after it gained independence in 1821. Bolívar frequently expressed concern over Haiti and its rebellious blacks, and he stressed that it was an example that Latin America should avoid if at all possible (Geggus 48–49). In fact, Bolívar was already preoccupied with Colombia's large African population in the coastal region of Cartagena, where free people of color constituted the majority of the population (Helg, "A Fragmented Majority" 161).

The fear of Panama's omnipresent dark population contributed to the nineteenth-century literary portrayal of the nation as non-black, as Pulido Ritter explains in *Filosofía de la nación romántica* [Philosophy of the Romantic Nation]. The essay "El Orejano" [Countryman] (1882) and the letter "Carta a un amigo" [Letter to a Friend] (1904) by the president Belisario Porras (1856–1942) defined Panamanian nationality in opposition to the terminal cities of Colón and Panama, which were heavily populated with West

Indians and North Americans.[3] Porras defined Panama on the basis of its indigenous heritage, rooted in the interior provinces of the nation (Veraguas, Coclé, Chiriquí). Similar to *Enriquillo: Leyenda dominicana* [Enriquillo: A Dominican Legend] (1882), which rewrote Dominican history on the basis of its indigenous roots and excluded the large African population, these texts are fundamental nation-building works that served to eliminate blackness and West Indianness from the national imaginary (Stinchcomb 86). The Dominican Republic redefined itself as a nation of *mestizos*, or mixed race, and *indios*, or indigenous peoples, distancing itself simultaneously from its African past and Haiti. Like the Dominican Republic, Panama also rejected any meaningful identification with its large Afro-Hispanic and West Indian population. After Panama's independence in 1821, the term *negro* "became politically charged . . . because of its identification with slavery" (McGuinness, *Path of Empire* 22). Instead, the oligarchy chose to use the phrase *gente de color* (people of color) to describe the black and *mulato* masses that comprised a majority of the population in Panama City and Colón. Despite the nation's efforts to hide the African majority, it became increasingly more difficult because of the burgeoning West Indian population that had migrated to Panama during the mid-nineteenth and early twentieth centuries.

West Indian immigrants, however, were essential to Panamanian autonomy and to Panama's establishment as an independent republic. Panama grew tired of its status as a dependent republic. Coupled with its distance from Colombia and its geographical ties to South America instead of Central America, the nation fought for independence and complete autonomy. Nationalists such as Justo Arosemena began to articulate Panamanian nationalism and the country's desire to become a sovereign nation. This sovereignty became contingent on Panama's geographic position as a pathway between the Americas. During the federalist period (1855–85), Panama realized its dream of becoming what Szok calls a "Hanseatic Republic," "a place of international transit, and community traditionally dependent on its close interaction with foreigners" (121). Panama's "Hanseatic" dream commenced in 1850, a year that marked an important milestone in Panamanian history, with the abolition of slavery and the construction of the railroad. From 1850 to 1855, thousands of black West Indians

migrated to Panama in search of better opportunities and economic prosperity. During this period, more than 45,000 Jamaicans came to the Isthmus of Panama, along with workers from
Grenada, England, Ireland, France, Germany, Austria, India, and
China. The attempted construction of the French Canal from 1880
to 1889 would bring 84,000 more Jamaicans to Panama. After
France's construction failure, the United States intervened, with
the agreement to complete construction of the Canal and supported Panama's independence from Colombia. On November 3,
1903, Panama seceded from Colombia and became a protectorate
of the United States. The United States remained on the Isthmus
of Panama from 1904 to 1914 during the arduous construction of
the Canal and imported as many as 19,900 workers from Barbados and a small number of workers from Martinique, Guadeloupe,
and Trinidad.

After the Panama Canal was completed in 1914, Latin America,
as well as other countries, perceived Panama as a U.S. territory
devoid of its Hispanic heritage. Panama reaffirmed its *hispanidad*
by utilizing neocolonial architecture; constructing a monument of
Cervantes in 1923; and naming its currency the *balboa*, in honor
of its conquistador, Vasco Núñez de Balboa (Szok 99). All of this
was done with the hope that the outside world would recognize
Panama as a unified Hispanic nation. Moreover, *hispanidad* became a major tenet of Panamanian nationalism, which aimed
to whiten Panamanian culture (Szok 94). Panamanian nationalists desired to rid themselves of anything that did not reflect a
nationhood of common people, that is, a mestizo, Catholic, and
Spanish-speaking republic. Religion, language, and Hispanic culture marked the major differences between West Indians and Panamanians, including Afro-Hispanics. Indeed, West Indians presented
a threat to the unity that Panamanian nationalists and intellectuals
desired. The thousands of Protestant English-speaking West Indian immigrants who came to Panama during the nineteenth and
early twentieth centuries to help build the nation were viewed as
a threat to the nation-building project. In the eyes of many nationalists, West Indians were not willing to assimilate, that is, to
speak Spanish and intermarry, as many Afro-Hispanics had done
centuries before. The fact that they continued to speak English,
to construct Protestant churches, and to maintain high rates of

intermarriage confirmed that West Indians were a threat to the mestizo nation and the project of *mestizaje*.

In Latin America, national constructions of homogeneity excluded the African masses because of the emphasis on *mestizaje*. During the Panamanian nation-building project, racial particularities were de-emphasized, and the intellectual discourse of *mestizaje* permitted a unified nation based on a "common" group of peoples. As Juan de Castro notes, "The discourse of *mestizaje*[] thus became a way for the three numerically dominant races living in the Americas—white, Amerindian, and black—to become incorporated into the same national project" (19). *Mestizaje* discourse in Panama strengthened national ties. As Spanish speakers, Afro-Hispanics expressed national solidarity through shared traditions, customs, and rituals associated with the interior provinces of the nation. By contrast, West Indians were immigrants who resided in the peripheral Canal Zone, which became synonymous with "foreigner," "the United States," and "outsider." Consequently, the classification of many Panamanians of African descent ranges from *mulato* to *mestizo*, *moreno*, and *negro*, depending on their complexion and presence or absence of African features. Even though the term *mulato* generally refers to the mixture of whites and blacks, *mestizo* is commonly used to designate any combination of the white, indigenous, and African populations and, therefore, ignores racial differences. The terms *moreno* and *negro* refer to people of visible African ancestry but differ on the basis of the visibility of people's African characteristics. The classification of a person of African ancestry as *moreno* or *negro* depends on one's proximity to whiteness or blackness in terms of both color and physical features. Afro-Hispanics often identify as *moreno*; depending on the presence or absence of African features and their position within the color spectrum, they, too, can be considered *negro*. Obviously, the use of these terms remains ambiguous. In Panama, the term *negro* continues to generate negative connotations that are associated with slavery, Africa, and the West Indian population. When Afro-Hispanics identify as *negro*, they often use the clarifier *negro colonial* [colonial black] to distinguish themselves from *negro antillano* [black West Indian]. As a result, many black West Indians are almost always referred to as *negro* because they are more visibly black and speak English. In turn, for many

Afro-Hispanics, to be called *negro* is an insult and aligns them with the denigrated West Indian population. The use of *negro colonial* versus *negro antillano* exemplifies cultural differences between the two groups and the resulting intraethnic tensions. Moreover, the stigmatization of the term *negro* reflects the burgeoning national anti–West Indian sentiment prevalent in Panama during the early twentieth century.

National Anti–West Indian Sentiment

The first decades of the twentieth century commenced with a fierce anti–West Indian sentiment. As Andrews explains, "Panama's delegate to the 1919 meeting of International Labor Organization protested bitterly the presence of 'tens of thousands of Antilleans who are intellectually and racially inferior to the Panamanians, whose religion and customs differ from ours, speaking a language different from ours'" (140). In the same manner, Alfaro's *El peligro antillano en la América Central* [West Indian Danger in Central America] (1924) articulated the anti–West Indian sentiment and the difference(s) between Afro-Hispanics and West Indians. Alfaro wrote: "Es evidente que hay gran diferencia entre el negro antillano y el hombre de color desarrollado dentro de la civilización Indo-Americana, no solamente por su status en las vecinas colonias inglés así donde su situación económica es deprimente y sus salarios ridículos, sino también por el ambiente de respeto de que en nuestras sociedades disfrutan las razas de color, consideraciones que les han sido acordadas por la nobleza de su carácter y su asimilación a nuestras más altas virtudes morales" [It is evident that there is a large difference between the black West Indian and the man of color raised in the Indo-American civilization, not only because of his status in the neighboring English colonies, where his economic situation is depressing and his salaries ludicrous, but also because of the respectable environment in which our colored races enjoy, considerations that have been accorded because of their noble character and assimilation to our most moral virtues] (7). In other words, Afro-Hispanics were Hispanic, Catholic, and Spanish speaking, whereas West Indians were black, Protestant, and English speaking. The Panamanian oligarchy promoted West Indian assimilation and encouraged West Indians to leave Panama after the completion of the Canal in 1914. Law 13 (1926) and Law 26 (1941) prevented West Indians from entering the country and made citizenship contingent on speaking Spanish. West Indians finally achieved full citizenship in 1946 under the new Constitution (Herzfeld 151). However, as Law 26 had previously mandated in 1941, the 1946 Constitution promoted cultural assimilation since many feared that the Anglophone West Indian's Protestant religion and native English language would alter the cultural paradigm of Panama. Many West Indian leaders believed that the success of West Indians in Panama rested solely on their ability to assimilate and adopt the major tenets of Panamanian nationality: language, culture, and religion. As a result, prominent West Indian leaders such as George Westerman (1910–88) encouraged other West Indians to assimilate in order to be accepted into Panamanian culture. Not surprisingly, Westerman did not focus on cultural or racial differences between West Indians and Panamanians. Instead, he promoted assimilation and celebrated the West Indian's intellect and economic contributions to Panama. Westerman encouraged West Indians to obtain an education and called attention to unfair practices in the Canal Zone.[4] His foundational text *Los inmigrantes antillanos en Panamá* [West Indian Immigrants in Panama] (1980) chronicles the importance of West Indians to the national foundation of the isthmus.

Panamanian intellectuals had promoted the myth that West Indians posed a problem because of cultural distinctions instead of racial ones. By contrast, the Afro-Hispanic population was fully integrated. Biesanz noted the cultural problem that West Indians posed to the nation. He wrote: "It is not simply visibility that marks out the 'chombos,' but biological visibility in combination with cultural differences, the chief of which is language" (776). While West Indians were discriminated against because they were culturally different from Panamanians, Biesanz failed to recognize that the discrimination also stemmed from racial prejudice. That is, although Biesanz viewed racial discrimination exclusively as a cultural issue, the cultural differences created the impetus for Panamanians to racially discriminate against West Indians. Biesanz's assertion was common. It was believed that Afro-Hispanics' low economic status was due to class distinctions that were independent of racial problems, and that discrimination against West Indians stemmed from their cultural and national incompatibility (Barrow and Priestley 187). Although he was an integrationist, Westerman also understood that the problem of the West Indian was principally one of color (*Un grupo* 26). Despite Westerman's hopes for the West Indian population in Panama, the harsh reality was that Panamanians rejected the group not only because they spoke a different language but also because they were black. Thus, many Panamanian West Indians repudiate Westerman's assimilation thesis and strive to incorporate West Indians into the Panamanian social and political matrix while maintaining their Caribbean heritage. Panama's national resistance to cultural and racial heterogeneity is recuperated in the writings of Lowe de Goodin, Wilson, Maloney, and Russell, who object to the national anti–West Indian sentiment and make an effort to integrate the Anglophone Caribbean into the national discourse of *panameñidad*.

Black movements have continuously helped to forge Afro-Panamanian identity, unity, and relations between Afro-Hispanics and West Indians. The new millennium ushered in new organizations and new perspectives in the black community in Panama. The platforms of these organizations echo internal debates within the West Indian community about racial identification and the Afro-Panamanian community at large. While *West Indian* refers to Anglophone Caribbean descendants in Panama, *Afro-Panamanian* is a more inclusive term that denotes the union of one's Panamanian and African heritage. With regard to Afro-Panamanian unity and identity, neither term adequately describes Afro-Hispanic populations or West Indians without accentuating a component of their identity with the risk of excluding or reinforcing another. For Afro-Hispanics, the very term *Afro-Panamanian* bolsters an Afro identity over their Hispanicized identity and counters the official discourse of *panameñidad*. For West Indians, the term remains problematic because *Afro-Panamanian* reinforces a Hispanic heritage that many feel silences and excludes their Caribbean one. Furthermore, the term *Afro-Panamanian* is rarely used in everyday speech, which gives way to the more colloquial terms of *negro colonial*, *negro*, and *negro antillano*, a fact highlighted by the 2010 Panamanian census, which for the first time asked Panamanians "Do you consider yourself: 'negro colonial,' 'negro antillano,' 'negro,' other or none of the above."[5] The term *Afro-Panamanian* has been a widely disputed label and became the subject of a debate at the Congreso del Negro Panameño, or Black Panamanian Conference, a conference series held in 1981, 1983, and 1988 that discussed the use of the term and other issues confronting the black community. The conference was organized primarily by black Panamanians on the isthmus. Although not a principal organizer of the initial conference, the conference reflects the more inclusive views of Panamanian West Indian Gerardo Maloney with regard to identity (Priestley, "Antillean-Panamanians" 63).[6] These different views and representations of blackness underlie the problematic of racial identity and identification in Panamanian literary discourse that commenced with the writings of nation-building poets Escobar and Hernández.

1

National Rhetoric and Suppression of Black Consciousness in Poems by Federico Escobar and Gaspar Octavio Hernández

Black writers in Panama during the period 1880–1920 promoted a nationalistic unity based on an imagined and deracialized cultural homogeneity. Instead of focusing on racial differences, writers such as Federico Escobar (1861–1912) and Gaspar Octavio Hernández (1893–1918) worked in the name of *panameñidad* [Panamanian cultural nationalism]. As Omi and Winant, and Kymlicka, have argued, cultural nationalism views the nation as a common culture with a shared sense of community, identity, and "peoplehood" (*Racial Formation* 40; *Politics* 243). This brand of Panamanian nationalism characterizes the writings of Afro-Hispanics who viewed themselves as an integral part of the Panamanian nation-state. Thus, these writers' focus on *panameñidad* emphasized their cultural, national, and patriotic affiliation with Panama and dismissed the need for any emphasis on race. Because *panameñidad* was understood in terms of the customs, habits, religion, and language that Panamanians shared, there was no need to acknowledge racial differences. The Afro-Panamanian journalist and economist Armando Fortune noted the connection between *panameñidad* and culture: "La panameñidad es, ante todo y sobre todo, la peculiar calidad de la cultura panameña. En términos corrientes, es condición del alma, del espíritu; es complejo de sentimientos, ideas y actitudes" [Panamanian nationalism is, above and beyond all, the peculiar quality of Panamanian culture. In popular terms, it is the condition of the soul, of the spirit; it is the complex of feelings, ideas, and attitudes] (294).

Panama's emphasis on culture and nation at the expense of race is consistent with that of other Latin American countries. Race and nation have remained inseparable concepts in Panama that have excluded people of color by reinforcing national discourses of homogeneity. Because the nation viewed Afro-Hispanics as culturally compatible with their Panamanian counterparts, their racial and ethnic differences were de-emphasized and their allegiance to the nation was stressed. Thus, throughout the period of nation building, black leaders and writers in Panama sacrificed a racialized discourse for a patriotic one. Leaders such as Juan B. Sosa (1870–1920), a prominent figure in Panama's Partido Liberal de Negros [Black Liberal Party], and Carlos A. Mendoza (1856–1916), Panama's first black president, "did not serve as forceful advocates for their own race but instead worked for national unity within the framework of *hispanidad*" (Szok 101).[1]

The leaders' nationalistic politics resonate with that of other black trailblazers throughout the African Diaspora who set aside their personal or racial agenda in favor of the nation. For example, Martín Morúa Delgado, one of few Afro-Cuban elected officials at the turn of the twentieth century, spearheaded a law that declared "illegal any racially-defined political party," thus putting an end to the race-based agenda of the political platform of the Partido Independiente de Color [Independent Colored Party] in 1910 (Fuente 210).[2]

The nationalistic agenda colored the writings of Afro-Hispanic poets as well. For example, the Panamanian Afro-Hispanic poet José Dolores Urriola (1834–84) participated in political movements during this period and served as the secretary of the civil jury in 1861 (Miró, *Cien años* 35). Urriola's poetry was both popular and satirical, and it characterized national concerns of the nineteenth century. Although known as "El Mulato," Urriola wrote as a national or romantic poet by centering his discourse on current political problems and other nonracial material. Despite his African heritage, he chose to write for his country and avoid racial identification in his works. This nationalistic discourse of exclusion influenced writers of African and non-African descent in Panama from the mid-nineteenth to the early twentieth century, and it is evidenced in the writings of Escobar and Hernández, who wrote primarily as national poets.

Furthermore, poems by Escobar and Hernández form part of the emerging *negrista*, or poetic negrism, movement that piqued in the early decades of the twentieth century with the publication in 1930 of the Afro-Cuban Nicolás Guillén's *Motivos de son* [Son motifs]. The *negrista* movement flourished during the 1920s and 1930s in the Hispanic Caribbean and was a pseudoblack poetry that focused on physical elements of the black, sexual prowess, and propensity toward music (Cartey 67). *Negrista* poets such as Luis Palés Matos (1898–1957), Emilio Ballagas (1910–54), and Manuel del Cabral (1907–99) appropriated poetic devices such as onomatopoeia, repetition, rhythm, and rhyme to portray African culture. Although this poetry was concerned with the black image, it was primarily a movement of white intellectuals who objectified the black literary subject. As a result, the movement has often been viewed as the "exploitation of black culture by white writers" (Cartey 41). Poetic negrism writers portrayed blacks and African culture as sensual, exotic, and sexual, without any psychological profundity. The black literary image that materialized during this period was often superficial and rarely focused on the sociohistorical and socioeconomic factors that plagued black America, such as poverty, discrimination, and racism. Although poetic negrism is often associated with the stereotypical portrayal and sexual exploitation of the black (female) corpus by white male Caribbean writers (Palés Matos, Ballagas, del Cabral) on the one hand and the onomatopoeic verses of Guillén on the other, poetic negrism also colored the writings and intellectualism of late-nineteenth- and early twentieth-century black literary thinkers. These "pre-*negrista*" writers leaned toward national affiliation and the homogeneous projects of whitening and *mestizaje*. For example, the Afro-Colombian poet Candelario Obeso (1849–84) is considered a "legitimate precursor of black poetry," yet he presented the nation as a utopia to fortify nationalistic pride.[3] Thus, Hernández and Escobar's focus on nationalism at the expense of racial identity is a tenet found in other black literary thinkers and exemplifies pre-*negrista* literature and nation-building rhetoric.

The works of the Afro-Hispanic poets Federico Escobar and Gaspar Octavio Hernández illustrate the tension that race created in writing during the formation of the new republic. These early writers were of colonial descent and represent Hispanicized blacks who were descendants of slaves. Their references to, or subordination of, their own blackness demonstrate the complex nature of being black and of writing during the height of the nationalistic movement. As writers of the new republic who were fighting for independence, they constantly felt the need to sacrifice their own ethnicity for the well-being of the nation. Although each dealt with blackness in his own way, their treatment of blackness, whether absent or visible, reveals much about being black during Panama's quest to establish itself as an independent nation. Jackson has analyzed Escobar and Hernández as poets who openly discussed their blackness or were escapists, respectively (*Black Writers in Latin America* 63); I illustrate that both were plagued by blackness and society's perception of race. Their works demonstrate the extent to which concepts of race and nation were intertwined during this period. Indeed, it was a constant struggle for these writers to affirm their blackness in their poetry and to maintain their national identity and acceptance by other Panamanians during the formation of the new republic.

"The Black Bard": Federico Escobar

Federico Escobar was committed to the national project but also expressed racial awareness in his writings. Escobar remains an important figure to study because he is the first writer of African ancestry in Panama to acknowledge his blackness and foreshadows the racial ambiguity inherent in the poetry of his contemporary Gaspar Hernández. Born José del Carmen de los Dolores Escobar, the poet was a carpenter by trade who worked twenty years for the French Canal (1880–99) (Miró, *Cien años* 64). Escobar lost his parents at a young age and sustained himself through his work as a carpenter, a profession he mastered under the tutelage of his uncle José Manuel Escobar. Escobar attained little formal education but managed to teach himself and become one of the leading poets of the nationalistic cause in the late nineteenth and early twentieth centuries. As one of the major poets of the era, he wrote a newspaper column titled *Caricaturas a la pluma* [Written Caricatures], which detailed aspects of quotidian Panamanian society (Escobar, *Patrióticas* 21). Escobar published several works during his lifetime, including three volumes of poetry—*Hojas secas* [Dry Leaves] (1890), *Instantáneas* [Snapshots] (1907), and *Patrióticas* [Patriotic Poetry] (1909); two pamphlets, *El renacimiento de un pueblo: Oda a Cuba* [The Rebirth of a Town: Ode to Cuba] (1902) and *Oda al 28 de noviembre* [Ode to November 28] (1899); and two theatrical works, *La ley marcial* [Martial Law] (1885) and *La hija natural* [The Natural Daughter] (1886). These published pieces represent only a fraction of his collection, as a result of a fire that burned several of his unpublished poems in 1880. Despite his two race poems that will be analyzed at length later, the overarching themes of Escobar's poetry reflect an escalating national climate due to Panama's quest for independence from Gran Colombia. Highly patriotic poems such as "28 de noviembre" [November 28] and "3 de noviembre" [November 3] commemorate Panama's independence, whereas his race poems, "Nieblas" [Fog] and "Chispas" [Sparks], reveal an Afro-Hispanic identity mired in racial contradiction.

Patrióticas (1909) is composed of several poems dedicated to Panama's celebration of independence. "28 de noviembre" (1889) is a highly patriotic poem that recounts Panama's tumultuous history and pursuit of independence from Spain in 1821. The poet-speaker recalls the years of rule and domination by Spain. The verse "tres centurias gemiste bajo el yugo de la opresión ibera" [you moaned for three centuries under the burden of Iberian oppression] evokes Panama's years of suffering during the colonial period under Spanish rule, which made Panamanians invisible and "relegated them to oblivion" (Escobar, *Patrióticas* 11). Reflecting on the importance of Panama's independence, the poet-speaker recognizes the evils of colonial rule, including slavery and oppression. In the third section, he reminisces, "El saber escribir era un delito en el esclavo" [the ability to write was a crime for the slave] (Escobar, *Patrióticas* 15). However, the recognition of the evils of colonialism and slavery are subordinated to the poet-speaker's patriotism and are viewed as elements of the past, thus eliminating any discussions of racial problems in Panama.

Like many other romantics of the nineteenth century, Escobar spoke of nationalism and celebrated his country's succession from Spain. Furthermore, Escobar's veneration of Panama demonstrated a burgeoning nationalistic spirit, despite the country's political ties to Gran Colombia. The presence of the French in Panama heightened his nationalistic spirit in light of the French "invaders." In 1889, the year when Escobar wrote the poem, the French had descended upon Panama and had already begun construction of the Canal. As history informs us, their project would later be taken over by the United States and completed in 1914. Thus, the fifth section of the poem expresses Escobar's fear of the French presence and occupation of Panama. In commemoration of the anniversary of Panama's independence from Spain, the poet-speaker urges his fellow compatriots to "guardar la integridad de nuestro suelo [para] continuar la jornada del progreso" [keep the integrity of our land [in order to] continue the journey of progress] (Escobar, *Patrióticas* 19).

Escobar returns to the theme of national independence in "3 de noviembre," a patriotic poem that expresses joy over Panama's independence from Colombia in 1903. Composed of twenty-two stanzas, "3 de noviembre" not only announces Panama's independence from Colombia but also establishes the poet's relationship to his homeland. In the first stanza, he reaffirms his *panameñidad* by exclaiming:

> Con qué número y metro yo pudiera
> cantarte ¡oh dulce e idolatrada Patria!
> ¿en tu fecha solemne? Yo no encuentro
> en este instante el verso delicado
> digno de ti ¡oh tierra de mis padres,
> en donde se meció mi triste cuna!

> [With what number and meter could I
> praise you sweet and idealized country!
> On your solemn day?
> I can't find in this instant the
> appropriate verse worthy of you
> Oh, land of my parents, where
> my sad birthplace was laid!] (Escobar, *Patrióticas* 20)

Escobar defines Panama as his *patria* because it is "el cielo donde vimos por la primera vez el solar astro," "la tierra idolatrada do corrieron los años de la infancia," and "el dulce arrullo del hogar . . . do nuestras madres nos dormían con músicas de besos" ["the sky where we saw our first sun star," "the idealized land where our childhood was spent," and "the sweet home lullaby . . . where our mothers put us to sleep with music-filled kisses] (22). Escobar continues to defend his country, and in the final two stanzas he describes Panama as a "crisol de razas," or melting pot, where "todas las razas se dan cita" [all the races come together] (28). His description is a utopia where racial harmony and economic prosperity exist for everyone, which leads him to describe his country very proudly as a "Cosmópolis" [cosmopolitan area] with "gente de diversas razas" [people of diverse races] (28). Similar to Candelario Obeso's "Expresión de mi amistad" [Expression of My Friendship] (1877), Escobar creates an idealistic vision of the nation in which races are equal (Prescott, *Candelario* 86). By 1906, not only were there a significant number of black West Indians in Panama, there were also other ethnic groups, though small in number, from China, England, France, Germany, Austria, and India. Escobar recognizes this cultural and ethnic diversity, yet he idealizes the situation when he proclaims, "No hay pueblo, ni aldea, ni villorrio sin escuela en el Istmo" [there is not a town, village, or shantytown on the isthmus without a school] (*Patrióticas* 28). García noted that during Colombia's rule, education was limited to Panama's elite (*Medio siglo* 15). It is doubtful just three years after Panama's separation from Colombia that educational opportunities were accessible in every Panamanian province. Clearly, Escobar's vision of Panama is subordinated to an idealism that is overshadowed by nationalistic pride for his country's victory over Colombia and its status as an independent nation-state.

Escobar's most anthologized poem, "Nieblas," expresses black awareness. The poem forms part of Rodrigo Miró's canonical *Cien años de poesía en Panamá* [One Hundred Years of Poetry in Panama] (1966). Despite the fact that Miró anthologized "Nieblas," its inclusion does not acknowledge the literary establishment's interest in promoting blackness or racial awareness. In the introduction that precedes Escobar's poems, Miró identifies the poet as a man of "piel oscura," or dark skin, but that is the only reference to his race

(64). Much like the nomenclature "the black bard," the emphasis on blackness is devoid of racial consciousness and context, and Escobar was "read" primarily as a representative romantic poet who treated national concerns. Furthermore, the poem diminishes the poet's Afro identity by conveying the importance of his shared cultural and national identity. Escobar opens "Nieblas" with an epigraph from "Negro nací" [I Was Born Black], a poem he attributes to the Afro-Colombian poet Candelario Obeso (1849–84).[4] "Negro nací" was written not by Obeso but by the nonblack Mexican poet Joaquín Villalobos, but the poem expresses an affirmation of blackness and provides Escobar with the inspiration to declare his own Afro-Latin identity. Escobar's choice of the poem he attributed to Obeso, a fellow compatriot and black man, reflects his awareness of Afro-Hispanic writers outside of Panama. Already in the nineteenth century, Escobar demonstrated a sense of "diaspora consciousness," which suggests, then, that racial identity transcended national boundaries. The following epigraph precedes "Negro nací" and prepares the reader for Escobar's poem on black identity:

> ¡Negro nací! ¡La noche aterradora
> trasmitió su dolor sobre mi cara;
> pero al teñir mi desgraciado cuerpo
> dejó una luz en el cristal del alma!
>
> [I was born black! The terrified night
> transmitted its pain into my face;
> but while it painted my unfortunate body
> it left a light in the crystal of the soul!] (Miró, *Cien años* 65)

Escobar commences "Negro nací" by declaring his blackness but concludes by presenting images of whiteness as the ideal:

> También negro nací; no es culpa mía . . .
> El tinte de la piel no me desdora,
> pues cuando el alma pura se conserva
> el color de azabache no deshonra.
> Hay en el mundo necios que blasonan
> de nobles por lo blanco de su cara;

que ignoran que en la tierra sólo existe
una sola nobleza: la del alma.
¿Qué importa que haya seres que se jacten
de nobles porque tienen noble sangre
si practican el vicio? . . . Nada importa;
que ellos son nada ante el Eterno Padre.
¡Negro nací; pero si Dios Supremo
ha teñido mis pieles con la tinta,
me ha dado lo que pocos hombres tienen:
un corazón virtuoso y una lira.
¡Negro nací, no importa! Mi conciencia
me dice que conservo pura el alma,
como las puras gotas de rocío,
como la blanca espuma de las aguas.
Y si la noche con su oscuro manto
logró cubrir mi cuerpo aun en la cuna,
una luz internó dentro mi pecho
y en mi mente una chispa que fulgura.

[I was also born black; it is not my fault . . .
the tint of the skin does not tarnish me,
because when the pure soul is preserved
the jet black color does not dishonor.
There are in the world fools that boast
nobility because of the white of their faces;
but ignore that on earth
only one nobility exists: that of the soul.
What does it matter that there are ones who brag about
nobility because they have noble blood
if they have a bad habit? . . . It does not matter;
they mean nothing to the Eternal Father.
I was born black; but if God
has tinted my skin with ink,
he has given me what very few possess:
a virtuous heart and a lyre.
I was born black, it does not matter! My conscience
tells me that I conserve a pure soul
like the pure drops of morning dew,
like the white foam of the waters.

And if the night with its dark cloak
managed to cover my body while still in the crib
a beam penetrated my chest
and in my mind a sparkle glows.] (Miró, *Cien años* 65)

Although Jackson identified Escobar as a writer who openly accepted his blackness, as opposed to Hernández, who was noted
for his racial ambiguity, a closer reading of Escobar's poem "Nieblas" shows that he, too, wrestled with the literary declaration of
his blackness (*Black Writers in Latin America* 64). Jackson notes
that Escobar "was the most unashamedly black of the Panamanian
group and the most straightforward in his approach to himself, to
his trade, and to his country" (64). To Jackson's credit, he envis-
aged Escobar as a poet who informed us about black identity in
nineteenth-century Panama and who openly identified as black, as
evidenced by his pen name and the incorporation of the epigraph
to "Nieblas." However, while Escobar identifies with his African
heritage, it is evident that his blackness plagued him just as much
as it did his contemporary Hernández. Escobar reveals some contradictions in his affirmation of blackness. It is evident that when-
ever Escobar makes reference to his race, it is in opposition to his
spirituality. He is superior because he has a "corazón virtuoso y
una lira" [virtuous heart and a lyre]. In the first stanza he insists
that "[el] tinte de la piel no me desdora, pues cuando el alma pura
se conserva el color de azabache no deshonra" [the tint of the skin
does not tarnish me, because when the pure soul is preserved the
jet black color does not dishonor], and in the fifth stanza he continues, "[y] si la noche con su oscuro manto logró cubrir mi cuerpo
aun en la cuna una luz internó dentro mi pecho" [and if the night
with its dark cloak managed to cover my body while still in the
crib, a beam penetrated my chest]. Finally, he compares his soul to
"las puras gotas de rocío" [the pure drops of morning dew] and
"la blanca espuma de las aguas" [the white foam of the waters].
Escobar's legitimacy stems not from his racial identity but from
his spirituality. His heart, soul, and ability to write poetry enable
him to transcend the racial boundaries of discrimination. Furthermore, Escobar's spirituality is described through images of whiteness: "alma pura" [pure soul], "luz internó dentro mi pecho" [light
beamed into my chest], "las puras gotas de rocío" [the pure drops

of morning dew], and "la blanca espuma de las aguas" [the white foam of the waters]. These images of whiteness contrast with the darker images that the poet uses to describe himself: "el color de azabache" [the jet-black color] and "oscuro manto" [dark cloak]. Although Escobar begins his self-portrait affirming his blackness, as evidenced by the first verse ("también negro nací" [I was also born black]), the poet elevates his status as a black man by demonstrating that his spirituality, characterized by white images, is what distinguishes him and has earned him a place in society. Thus, Escobar's poem results in elevating whiteness over blackness.

In the second stanza of "Nieblas," he insists that only one nobility exists, that of the soul. In the remaining stanzas, he mocks those who feel they are superior because of their affluent lineage. Escobar retorts that he is superior because of his spirituality ("el alma pura" [pure soul]) and his position as a poet ("una lira" [a lyre]). Clearly, Escobar's insistence on his spirituality as opposed to his racial characteristics is understood. Escobar espoused the *mestizaje* rhetoric of the era and defended his blackness, which was not valued by elevating his spiritual qualities.

While "Nieblas" minimizes the poet-speaker's black consciousness, Escobar's lesser-known poem "Chispas" is perhaps his most overt attack against society's racism toward blacks and their social status. It is worth mentioning that the poem was published in the Cuban newspaper *La igualdad* [Equality] (1893), and to my knowledge is unavailable in Panamanian national archives.[5] If "Nieblas" vacillates between upholding whiteness and declaring a black consciousness, then "Chispas" reacts to a nationalistic rhetoric of whiteness and black exclusion. The tone of "Chispas" is one of a disgruntled poet-speaker who feels oppressed by a white elitist society. He notes, "¿Por qué me arrojan sus sangrientos dardos algunos seres de la gente blanca? / ¿Por qué me insultan y abatirme intentan?" [Why do some members of the white race throw their bloody darts at me? / Why do they try to insult me and knock me down?]. The poet-speaker engages in dialogue with his fellow brothers throughout the African Diaspora and attacks the literary establishment of the era and its desire to suppress the articulation of black national identity. Escobar clearly illustrates the dilemma of black writers during this period who agonized over expressing their blackness and being censored by the white literary establishment, as evidenced in the verse "¿Quieren matar la voz en mi garganta?" [Do they want to kill the voice in my throat?]. The poet-speaker denounces the literary establishment for denying artists the articulation of a black identity and a place in Panamanian society and politics. He laments, "¡Si canto, soy un negro miserable! / ¡Cantar un negro, condenable audacia!" [If I sing, I'm a miserable black! / A black man who sings, reprehensible audacity!] As in "Nieblas," the poet-speaker insists that valor, talent, and dignity remain the core measures of goodness and symbolize one's spirituality. However, the poet-speaker delineates the evils of whiteness: "el vulgo inepto de la gente blanca [y] blancos que tienen negra, corrompida el alma" [the incompetent mob of white people (and) whites with black, corrupted souls]. Whiteness does not always equate goodness, and in some instances, it amounts to spiritual corruption. The poet-speaker utilizes the opposition between lightness and darkness to elevate blackness and deviates from the cult of whiteness. In this poem, whites have dark, corrupted souls and white tombs bear decay deep within, meaning that whiteness embodies darkness and a lack of spirituality. This contrasts with "Nieblas," where whiteness corresponds to righteousness and liberates the black from the stain that he inherited from birth. However, in "Chispas," the poet-speaker does not completely break from the white aesthetic. Black tombs contain mother-of-pearl, and blacks have hearts made of snow. For example, "De ébano hay urnas negras y lucientes en do se encuentran perlas nacaradas / así hay sujetos de color moreno que corazones, como nieve" [There are black and bright urns made of ebony where one finds mother-of-pearl / likewise there are dark-colored subjects whose hearts (are) like snow]. Thus, both "Nieblas" and "Chispas" vacillate between upholding whiteness and affirming blackness; "Chispas" further complicates this dichotomy (blackness–whiteness) by vacillating between positive and negative images of blacks and whites. "Chispas" conveys the dichotomous relationship between blackness and whiteness by demonstrating that it remained difficult to articulate black identity without the representation of white images. The mere mention of blackness in relation to whiteness exemplifies that neither poem breaks completely with extolling whiteness.

Although a majority of Escobar's poetry treats the national question, "Nieblas" and "Chispas" tell much about Panamanian race relations and the reception of blacks and a black racial consciousness in Panama. "Nieblas" recognizes his blackness and his reference to Obeso, despite the attribution error, and confirms his conscious connection to a broader, black literary diaspora. Escobar attempted to legitimize himself in a nation that adored whiteness, abhorred blackness, and desired to dilute the latter into oblivion. Both poems reflect a racist nineteenth-century Panamanian society, but "Chispas" further challenges the national rhetoric of exclusion of the era by addressing the issues of difference, identity, and racism.

"The Black Swan": Gaspar Octavio Hernández

Known in Panamanian literary circles as "El Cisne Negro" [the Black Swan] for the sensuality and sentimentalism that are transmitted in both his poetry and prose, Gaspar Octavio Hernández is perhaps the most widely known Afro-Hispanic poet of Panama's nation-building period. Born Octavio Hernández Solanilla in 1893, he later became known in literary circles as Gaspar Octavio Hernández, taking the name of Gaspar Núñez de Arce, a nineteenth-century Spanish poet. His published works include two volumes of poetry, *Melodías del pasado* [Melodies of the Past] (1915) and *La copa de amatista* [The Amethyst Glass] (1923), as well as *Iconografía* [Iconography] (1916), a collection of short stories, prose poems, essays, and national eulogies. Like Escobar, Hernández experienced a life of poverty. Abandoned by his father at a young age, he became an orphan after his mother passed and was forced to abandon school after three years of formal education. He became a sweeper at a local construction company, eventually becoming a cashier, and worked there until his death in 1918. As a young adult, Hernández suffered from alcoholism and lived a bohemian lifestyle that lacked financial or familial stability, leading him to father two children out of wedlock. Despite his troubled childhood, Hernández sustained himself early on with odd jobs and began publishing his poetry in weekly newspapers such as *El nacional* [The National] and then began directing the literary journals *Nuevos ritos* [New Rituals], *Esto y aquello* [This and That], and *Memphis* (Figueroa Navarro 12). Despite his literary success, he found that he was unable to support himself as a journalist or a poet, and a year before his death, he sold a large portion of his library collection to provide for his family (Figueroa Navarro 13). The loss of his mother at a young age contributed to his melancholic existence. Hernández's poem "Melodías del pasado" [Melodies of the Past], from the volume of poetry of the same title, expresses his childhood of suffering without his mother and captures the void that her absence left in his life and heart. "Melodías" is a longing for the distant memories of the past that the poet can attain only through the recollection of his mother's lyrical voice. Throughout the eight-stanza poem he repeats the phrase "inolvidable canto materno" [unforgettable maternal song], a song that he longed for after his mother's death. His melancholic childhood foreshadows his untimely death; he died in a fit of coughing from the effects of tuberculosis on November 13, 1918. His death is memorialized annually in Panama on this date in celebration of his life in journalism and literature.

Hernández is best known nationally for "Canto a la bandera" [Flag Song] (1916), a patriotic lyric that continues to be one of the most anthologized poems in Panama today. Along with "Patria" [Fatherland], by the nationally revered poet Ricardo Miró, "Canto a la bandera" is considered Panama's poem of nationality and independence, and it confirms Hernández's nationalism in opposition to U.S. imperialism. Published in 1916, "Canto a la bandera" marks the celebration of Panama's independence from Colombia in 1903 and the completion of the Canal in 1914. In the epigraph to "Canto a la bandera," the poet-speaker evokes his patriotism through the "mancebo," or youth: "el mancebo sientóse inquieto entusiasmo: el entusiasmo le hizo poeta y le inspiró este cantar" [the youth felt a restless enthusiasm: the enthusiasm made him a poet and inspired this song] (Miró, *Cien años* 190). The youth exclaims:

> ¡Ved cómo asciende sobre el mar la enseña
> que refleja en sus vívidos colores
> el mar y el cielo de la patria istmeña!
> ¡Mirad! . . . ¡Es la bandera panameña,
> vistosa cual gentil manto de flores!

[Look how the ensign ascends over the ocean
and on its vivid colors reflects
the sea and sky of the isthmian fatherland!
Look! . . . It is the Panamanian flag,
as colorful as a gentile flower mantel!] (Miró, *Cien años* 190)

The flag and the sea symbolize liberty, independence, and national autonomy. The poet-speaker expresses his exuberance by employing the use of exclamation marks and by setting the scene in the sea. The second stanza provides a vision of a marine celebrating his country's freedom while sailing across the sea with Panama's flag. The ascension of the flag in the first and second stanzas parallels the "canciones de alegría," or songs of happiness, sung by the marine (Miró, *Cien años* 190). The flag affects not only the sailor but also "los hombres duros" [the strong men] and "las mujeres bellas" [the beautiful women] who, in the fifth stanza, "se inflaman por las estrellas" [become inflamed by the stars] (Miró, *Cien años* 190). "Canto a la bandera" echoes Escobar's poems "28 de noviembre" and "3 de noviembre" in that it pays tribute to Panama's independence.

While "Canto a la bandera" rejoices over Panama's independence, Hernández's brief essay "El culto del idioma" [The Cult of Language] (1916), expresses disdain for West Indians who refuse to learn and/or speak Spanish. Hernández seems angered not only by the U.S. presence but also by the presence of foreign workers who migrated to Panama to construct the railroad and the Panama Canal. What disturbs Hernández most is that many of these foreigners, who have become permanent citizens, refuse to speak Spanish. He criticizes them for trying to be North American instead of Panamanian. In "El culto" he argues that West Indians "se pirran por norteamericanizarse . . . prescinden descaradamente de su lengua madre y se ufanan de expresarse a menudo en incomprensible y tosco *patois* anglo-yankee" [long to North Americanize themselves . . . disregard their mother tongue, and boast of expressing themselves in an incomprehensible and rouge Anglo-Yankee patois] (112). Hernández demonstrates that the anti–West Indian sentiment intensified with U.S. intrusion. Because a large number of West Indians still communicated in their native languages

(English or French), many Panamanians, including Hernández, viewed them as a threat to the Catholic, *mestizo*, Spanish-speaking nation. Therefore, English-speaking West Indians who constituted a majority of Anglophone Caribbean immigrants were perceived as allies of North America. Hernández's sentiments foreshadow those of Panamanian *negrista* poet Víctor Franceschi (1931–84), who in his 1959 essay "El hombre blanco en la poesía negra" [The White Man in Black Poetry] claimed, "El negro de la colonia yace más asimilado a nuestra nacionalidad, son más criollos y por lo tanto difieren bastante" [the colonial black is much more assimilated to our nationality, they are more native and therefore are very different (from West Indians)] (135).[6] Franceschi's assertion reinforces the myth that colonial blacks (Afro-Hispanics) assimilated into Panamanian culture and that West Indians did not. The distinctions made by Hernández and Franceschi between Afro-Hispanics and West Indians affected the reaction of Panamanian West Indian writers Carlos Wilson, Gerardo Maloney, Carlos Russell, and Melva Lowe de Goodin who seek to redeem these myths and negative portrayals in their works.

Clearly, Hernández was an integrationist and believed that black West Indians and other immigrants should renounce their native cultural and linguistic affiliations for those of their new homeland. In other words, they were to speak Spanish, convert to Catholicism, and intermarry. For Hernández and other Panamanians, *West Indian* signified "foreigner," as the group was identified with North Americans because of their language and perceived economic advantages. In Hernández's essay, we begin to see the seeds of racial tensions between Afro-Hispanics and West Indians. Thus, Hernández's essay anticipates the anti-imperialistic and anti–West Indian literature that forms the basis of the social protest literature of the 1930s and 1940s, which I examine in chapter 2.

Despite the nationalistic focus of "Canto a la bandera" and "El culto del idioma," Hernández's poetry stands out for the well-known *modernista* images of swans, swallows, and jasmine that are employed to venerate whiteness and to convey the despair inherent in the *modernista* aesthetic. These images of whiteness come to fruition in "Visión nupcial" [Nuptial Vision], which also appears under the title "Vida nupcial" [Nuptial Life] in *La copa de amatista.* "Visión nupcial" describes a woman adorned in garbs of white:

> Siempre que hacia la torre de mis penas
> el dulce vuelo tu recuerdo arranca,
> te miro toda blanca, toda blanca
> de azahar, de jazmines, de azucenas.

> [As long as the sweet flight of your memory
> pulls toward the tower of my sorrows,
> I see you so white, so white
> of orange blossom, of jasmines, of white lilies].
>   (Hernández, *La copa* 50)

Again, the images pointed out before of jasmines and white lilies evoke the cult of whiteness inherent in *modernista* poetry and the poet's overriding preoccupation with white images. The bride described in "Visión nupcial" is not one of man but of God, which makes her purity everlasting. The poet envisions this virgin, who is an angel of God, as a bride with folded arms who taunts him:

> Vistes la inmaculada vestidura
> de las que van a desposarse . . . y tiendes
> los bracitos en cruz, porque pretendes
> crucificar en mi tus desventuras.
> [se va] raudamente . . . como un vuelo
> hacia el azul, cual si del tenue velo
> de virgen novia [se] nacieran alas.

> [You wear the immaculate dress
> of the ones who will get married . . .
> and you stretch out your tiny arms crossed,
> because you intend
> to crucify me in your misfortunes.
> (she leaves) swiftly . . . like a flight
> toward the blue, as if from the fine veil
> of virgin bride wings would sprout].
>   (Hernández, *La copa* 50)

The poet-speaker identifies the virgin as an angel of God who ascends into heaven toward an infinite, ethereal place ("el azul"). The poet's emphasis on the virgin's whiteness and the continuous use of white images throughout the poem have earned Hernández the reputation of being an escapist, not only from exterior reality but also from his black consciousness (Jackson, *Black Writers in Latin America* 66). Further readings of Hernández's poems contest notions that he was merely an escapist; the poems illustrate that Hernández attempted to conform to a white aesthetic.

"Visión nupcial" is not the only poem that reflects Hernández's literary fixation on the white female subject; several of Hernández's poems in his canon venerate white women: "Vespertina" [Evening], "Nupcias" [Nuptials], "Venus del trópico" [Venus of the Tropics], and "Afrodita" [Aphrodite]. In "Vespertina," the poet-speaker describes the effect of the woman's whiteness and beauty. "Avanzaba y . . . me detuve cuando tú, maravillosa visión de clámide blanca, coronada de jazmines y de rosas coronada, pusiste tus pies de nieve" [I moved forward and . . . I stood still when you, a marvelous vision of white cloak, crowned of jasmines and of crowned roses, you placed your feet of snow] (Webster 33–34). The female subject in "Afrodita," the Greek goddess of love, has "trenzas blondas," or blond braids (33). In "Venus del trópico," a woman appears "cantando barcarolas desnuda, blanca y tímida" [singing barcaroles, naked, white, and timid[7]] (Hernández, *La copa* 17). In "Nupcias," the poet colors not only the bride's exterior with whiteness but also the bride herself. He urges the music to break in song "cuando veáis pasar su cuerpo blanco, blanco de tules, de azahares, que es como lirio en clara noche plenilunar" [when you see her white body pass by, white of reeds, of orange blossoms, that is like a lily in the clear light of the full moon] (37). Although one might argue that Hernández's use of white images and veneration of white women are typical of *modernista* poems, the reading of Hernández's poetry becomes psychologically telling with respect to whiteness when one notes that he privately obsessed over white women. The Panamanian poet Demetrio Korsi (1899–1957) confirms Hernández's infatuation with white women:

[Octavio Hernández] loved women, and he loved them with the singular and delectable love of a true poet. He dreamt of oriental harems. For this reason all of his poems are saturated with evocations of flesh white as snow, of alabaster bodies, of breasts small and pure as fresh lilies. Blonds attracted him like magnets with supernatural powers; blonds from Scandinavia, blue-eyed ones of German descent, or the spiritual daughters of our beloved Paris. An idealization of whiteness, very lyrical indeed, plucked the chords of his harp, which was always filled with white swans, mother-of-pearl-skinned princesses, immaculate orange blossoms like cotton on branches and perfect ivory. (Cited in Jackson, *Black Writers in Latin America* 67)

His veneration of whiteness is consistent with other Afro-Hispanic poets who, as Piedra suggests, "wrote white" to avoid racial difference.[8] The women celebrated in many of Hernández's poems are often Anglicized, described as having "cabello de oro" [golden hair] and "tez de nieve" [snow skin]. The detailed descriptions of the white female subjects that color his poetic repertoire contrast starkly with three poems where he depicts the black female subject. With the exception of the poems "Claroscuro" [Chiaroscuro] and "Cantares de Castilla de Oro" [Songs of Golden Castille], as well as the prose poem "Coincidencia" [Coincidence], all of the women that he portrays are white dressed, white bodied, and white spirited. Hernández describes in a lackluster fashion the women in "Claroscuro," "Cantares de Castilla de Oro," and "Coincidencia" as *morenas*. In "Cantares de Castilla de Oro" the poet-speaker sings praises to a "morenita, morenita de pollera colora" [little brown girl, little brown girl of a colored *pollera*[9]], but he offers no other development of her physical characteristics (*La copa* 61). Similarly, in "Coincidencia," the female subject is "alta y morena, tenía los negros cabellos en cortos bucles trenzados sobre la nuca y rodeados de fino ceñidor blanco" [tall and brown, her hair was in short curly braids over the nape of her neck and was surrounded by a fine white sash] (Hernández, *Iconografía* 134). Thus, these poems lack the exotic description of the *morena*'s beauty and physical characteristics as evinced in the poems that center on white women. His use of the term *morena* to describe dark female subjects also conveys a less racially stigmatized black female corpus. Furthermore, it is not clear that Hernández is describing someone of African ancestry, since in Latin America *morena* is often used to describe someone who has dark features or dark-brown hair and not necessarily someone who is black.

Possessing the most extensive description of a dark woman in Hernández's poetry, "Claroscuro" differs from both "Cantares de Castilla de Oro" and "Coincidencia" in that it depicts a dark woman with African features. The title expresses the tension between light and dark that provides the structural and thematic framework of the poem. Blackness can exist only in relation to whiteness and, therefore, in relation to what it is not. Hernández defines the *morena*'s beauty by negation:

> Ni albor de mirto, ni matiz de aurora,
> ni palidez de nardo, ni blancura
> de cera encontraréis en la hermosura
> de su faz que a los reyes enamora.

> [Neither white myrtle flowers nor tint of dawn
> neither spikenard's paleness, nor the whiteness
> of wax can be found in the resplendence
> of your face, that the kings love.] (Webster 41)

The repetition of *ni* and *ni* [*neither* and *nor*] insists on the absence of whiteness, defining her blackness through negation. Hernández ends the poem by elevating the female subject's features:

> Como a la Sulamita encantadora
> que hizo del Rey de Oriente la ventura,
> hacen más adorable a su figura
> sus rizos negros y su tez de mora.
> Así la presintió mi fantasía . . .
> bella hermana del príncipe del día,
> hija del sol y de la noche, aduna
> y en la complejidad de su belleza
> las pompas de la tarde y la tristeza
> de un tranquilo y sutil claro de luna.

> [Like the enchanting Shulamite
> who gave the eastern monarch fortune,

your Moorish skin and black curls
make your figure more lovely.
My fantasy sensed . . .
a beautiful sister of the prince of dawn,
child of day and night, combined
in the complexity of her beauty
the splendors of the afternoon and the sadness
of a quiet and subtle moonlight]. (Webster 41)

In the second stanza, the poet recognizes beauty in the woman's blackness. In effect, Hernández challenged the cult of whiteness of the era by daring to mention the beauty of a woman with African features, exemplified by her "rizos negros" [black curls] and "tez de mora" [Moorish skin]. Moreover, she is not only beautiful; she forms part of the poet's fantasies. The poet found it difficult to describe her because of the "complejidad de su belleza" [complexity of her beauty]. This forces one to question whether the woman's beauty is complex, or whether the poet lacks the language to describe a black woman's physical characteristics. Given that the poet appropriates typical *modernista* images to describe what the *morena* is not, it is evident that language posed a problem. Indeed, color was complex during this period, and the *morena*'s beauty did not conform to the white aesthetic. One must bear in mind that Hernández was speaking to a white audience, and thus politically, he had to demonstrate to his audience that this woman did not possess the features typically associated with whiteness and, by extension, beauty. Language and time period were not the only determining factors that presented challenges for Hernández. His private obsession with whiteness and his personal struggles with his own identity shed light on his poetic elevation of the white aesthetic.

Perhaps Hernández's poem "Ego sum" [I am] (1915) best reflects his interior struggle with blackness. "Ego sum" is structurally and thematically similar to "Claroscuro." As Jackson asserts: "Both of these poems suggest blackness by contrast rather than through direct mention, as if the poet could not bring himself to confront it" (*Black Writers in Latin* 74). In the first stanza, Hernández, turning once again to the *ni-ni* [neither-nor] framing, describes himself first in terms of what he is not:

> Ni tez de nácar, ni cabellos de oro
> veréis ornar de galas mi figura;
> ni la luz del zafir, celeste y pura,
> veréis que en mis pupilas atesoro.

> [Neither pearly skin, nor golden hair
> will you see adorns my countenance to the finest;
> neither sapphire's light, celestial and pure
> in my eyes you will see that I treasure].
>   (Cited in Miró, *Cien años* 187)

The words *nácar* [mother-of-pearl], "luz del zafir" [sapphire's light], "celeste" [celestial], and "pura" [pure], which evoke beauty and purity, contrast dramatically with the next stanza, in which the poet fatalistically describes who he really is: a black man with African features:

> Con piel tostada de atezado moro;
> con ojos negros de fatal negrura,
> del Ancón a la falda verde oscura
> nací frente al Pacífico sonoro.

> [For I was born with skin of Moorish blacks,
> with black eyes of fatal blackness, upon
> the dark green hillside of Ancón,
> I was born against the sonorous Pacific].
>   (Cited in Miró, *Cien años* 187)

Hernández describes himself not only as black but of a fatal blackness. He establishes the white-black, pure-unpure, and light-dark dichotomies with the contrast between the "tez de nácar" and "piel tostada" [pearly skin and dark skin] and "ojos celestiales" and "ojos negros" [celestial eyes and black eyes]. Although he identifies himself as black in this poem, it is with reluctance and in relation to not being white. The language that Hernández appropriates presents the problematics of identity that the black writer faced during this period. As in "Claroscuro," he appropriated the language of the *modernista* aesthetic that proved inadequate to describe himself or the complexities of his race and ethnicity. Hernández's appropriation of the *modernista* aesthetic resulted in the poet describing himself in terms of what he was not. Ironically, to affirm his identity, he had to first negate who he really was. Reluctantly, he used the language of the colonizer and that of the *modernista* aesthetic to reach his audience, to identify himself, and to establish a niche in Panamanian literary circles. He defined himself by appropriating the language of the colonizer, since he already knew, as evidenced by the repetition of *neither*, that it was not adequate to articulate his Afro-Panamanian identity.

Therefore, "Ego sum," which could be an affirmation of his identity as a black Panamanian, concludes by being a negation of identity. In effect, it demonstrates the poet's internal dilemma and struggle with society's image of beauty. Ironically, "Ego sum," as the poem's title suggests, is not an affirmation of his identity or his blackness. Hernández's polarized description (white-black) seems to evoke Fanon's assertion that in the collective unconscious of the "Negro," everything that is opposite of white and is black remains negative when blackness equates to "ugliness, sin, darkness, and immorality" (192). Clearly, Hernández's poetic sentimentalism and negative self-image stem from his internal suffering as a black man in a white world. Of course, his internal suffering and self-realization is not uncommon. As Nkosi notes, "Black consciousness really begins with the shock of discovery that one is not only black but is also non-white" (cited in Olliz Boyd 65). The Panamanian literary critic Roque Laurenza confirms Hernández's preoccupation with his blackness and obvious fixation with whiteness when he notes: "tuvo siempre como obsesión la blancura . . . se evadió de la realidad y vivió siempre en un completo autoengaño" [he was always obsessed with whiteness . . . he escaped reality and always lived in a complete state of self-deception] (cited in Figueroa Navarro 16).

"Ego sum" and "Claroscuro" illustrated not only the problematic that language posed for Hernández but also that he was conflicted because of his blackness and Panama's reaction to it. According to the Panamanian literary critic Ismael García, Hernández's color was a hindrance to his literary success, which was not fully recognized until after his death (*Historia* 69). For example, when discussing the literary generation of the republic (1903–20), Laurenza acknowledges that Ricardo Miró, and not Hernández, is more representative of the literary movement of his era.[10] He points out that Miró is the only "authentic" poet of this generation, as Peña acknowledges (114). One might argue that Hernández lacks authenticity according to Laurenza because he is a poet of African ancestry or because he chose to write about his blackness, albeit with some hesitation. Hernández avoided racial identification in a majority of his works because the nation at large neither valued nor accepted blackness. Laurenza recognized that Hernández's blackness pained him, which led the poet to escape from reality (cited in Figueroa Navarro 16). However, he found a way to transcend his melancholic existence and his plight as a black man in Panama through verse, which was praised posthumously. Thus, he suffered as a young poet because he did not know how to negotiate both his blackness and nationalism in Panamanian literary circles.

Hernández's racial ambiguity, escapist tendencies, and self-portrait are related to his nationalistic identity and focus on his *panameñidad* instead of his race. As Jackson suggests: "The pressures that propelled the poet on the one hand into evasive flights toward whiteness and on the other toward the depths of melancholy, in part because of the futile nature of these flights, are the same pressures that made him opt for a patriotic stance rather than a racial one. He chose the greater glory of a nationalistic identity over a purely ethnic one, certainly over one that was black, considering the low esteem in which blackness was held—even by the poet himself—at that time" (*Black Writers in Latin America* 70). Jackson is correct in his analysis of Hernández's nationalistic focus as opposed to a racial one. The above-mentioned statement could also be applied to Hernández's literary contemporary Federico Escobar. However, Hernández, who has been perceived as an escapist, was very much aware of the reality of Panamanian society and the population's views on blacks. He was cognizant of the negative perceptions of blacks in Panama and alluded to them in his homage to the black journalist, Edmundo Botello, when he lamented, "Todavía persiste en algunos pseudos antropólogos la idea de que la raza negra es miserable manada de imbéciles, dignos tan sólo de habitar en sucias viviendas bajo el inclemente sol africano" [There still persists among some false anthropologists the idea that the black race is a miserable group of imbeciles, only worthy of

inhabiting dirty neighborhoods underneath the harsh African sun]
(Hernández, *Obras selectas* 417). Indeed, Hernández was cognizant of racial problems in Panama. Therefore, Hernández's apparent ambiguity toward his racial awareness is a testament not only
to his struggle with his blackness but also to society's ignorance of
black culture and quest for nationalism, which eliminated racial
differences whether absent or present. Hernández challenged the
racial paradigm that elevated whiteness over blackness by emphasizing that he was defined by both his race and his cultural nationalism, that is, by his blackness and his *panameñidad*.

The poets Federico Escobar and Gaspar Hernández challenged
the national discourse of *panameñidad* by representing themselves
as black, albeit with a bipolar racial consciousness. Their poetry
elucidates how the imaginary of the nation affected late-nineteenth-
and early twentieth-century Afro-Panamanian discourse and identity politics. Both toiled with varying degrees of success and failure
under the complexities of the color line, where many writers (un)-
consciously furthered the national agenda by negating or dimin-
ishing their own Afro-Latin identity in order to be identified with
the national foundation of the nation. It is important to remember
that while Hernández's poetry is nationally revered because it is
patriotic and nationalistic, Escobar's poetry was less accepted because it "served much to awaken the government of Panama to the
trend of unjustifiable practices of the time" (Barton 207). Escobar
and Hernández should not be remembered as poets who stressed
their *panameñidad* over their blackness, but instead as poets who
emphasized their nationality from their position as black writers in
a Hispanicized territory. Escobar's "Nieblas" and "Chispas" plant
the seed for black awareness, and Hernández further problematizes this black consciousness in his poem of identity "Ego sum."
Moreover, both men challenged the national paradigm by attempting to portray themselves in a society that desired to be viewed
as a mestizo nation with little visible African heritage. They were
the first writers of African descent in Panama to leave behind published works and to provide insight into the trials and tribulations
of being black and Panamanian during the height of the nationalistic movement. This nationalistic trend is recuperated in Joaquín
Beleño's Canal Zone trilogy, which bolsters Panamanian identity
by attacking West Indians, and which I discuss in the next chapter.

2

Anti–West Indianism and Anti-Imperialism in Joaquín Beleño's Canal Zone Trilogy

Es más bien el Canal, abierto gracias al ingenio del hombre, el que ha constituido hasta ahora el medio básico de nuestra vida. La república nació por obra del Canal y ha venido derivando de esta obra de dominio de las fuerzas telúricas, la razón de su existir.

[It is the Canal, open thanks to man's genius, that until now has constituted the basic means of our existence. The Republic of Panama was born because of Canal labor and has continued to derive from this dominion workmanship of telluric strengths, the reason for its existence].

—Ismael García, *Historia de la literatura panameña*

While Federico Escobar and Gaspar Hernández wrestled with the literary declaration of their blackness that opposed the Panamanian nation-state, Afro-Hispanic writers such as Joaquín Beleño (1922–88) became the mouthpiece for all Panamanians against U.S. imperialism, which was buttressed by the construction of the Panama Canal (1904–14). Beleño targeted the by-product of the Canal, the West Indian, who symbolized everything that Panama abhorred: imperialism, blackness, and foreigners. The aftermath of the construction of the Canal and Panama's fear of being labeled a "black nation" bolstered tensions between Panamanians and West Indians. In Hernández's essay "El culto del idioma," we witnessed the seeds of intraethnic tensions between Hispanicized blacks and West Indians. These tensions are played out in Beleño's Canal Zone trilogy, a genre that became a metaphor for the cultural, racial, and linguistic plurality that characterized Panama during this era and continues to typify Panama today.

The Canal is a contradiction that represents economic promise and hope on the one hand and geographical exploitation and (neo) imperialism on the other. At the same time that the Canal gave Panama economic independence, it also subordinated the country to a hegemonic regime that further transformed Panama's national foundation. Thus, since 1903, when the United States helped Panama achieve independence from Colombia and assumed control of the Canal Zone, the Panama Canal has been a major theme in Panamanian literature. More writers turned away from the nation's autochthonous interior and concentrated on urban Panama as Panamanians grew increasingly hostile to and resentful of U.S. occupation and domination. Writers who focused on life in Panama's cities, especially Panama City and Colón, were the first to recognize not only that *panameñidad* existed in the country's interior, as José Isaac Fábrega illustrated in *Crisol* (1936), but also that these urban areas were a vital part of Panamanian culture.[1] The interest in urban Panama led to the fruition of the Canal Zone novel, a novel that centered on the complexities of the Canal as a catalyst for social change and conflict in Panama. Novels that followed this pattern include Rodolfo Aguilera Jr.'s (1909–89) *50 millas de heroicidad* [50 Miles of Heroism] (1941), Renato Ozores's (1910) *Puente del mundo* [Bridge of the World] (1951), Gil Blas Tejeira's (1901–75) *Pueblos perdidos* [Lost Towns] (1963), and Yolanda Camarano de Sucre's (1915–2000) *La doña del paz* [The Madam of Peace] (1967).[2] While these novels focused on the historical and economic aspects of the construction of the Panama Canal, the Canal Zone novels of Beleño served as a platform for him to vehemently denounce U.S. racism, imperialism, and exploitation. The Canal Zone is presented in Beleño's works as the contemporary plantation, and it demonstrates the omnipresence of the United States along with subsequent threats to a Hispanicized nation.

The Canal Zone represented what Greene calls empire building for the United States and brought the promise of independence for Panama that resulted in a cultural and racial transformation that Panamanians eventually grew to hate.[3] The United States not only took over construction of the Canal but also transformed all aspects of Zonian life by imposing a racial hierarchy that differed from the Latin American model, which categorized blacks according to appearance or skin color and not the so-called one-drop rule.[4] This proved problematic since nineteenth-century Panama was already a nation characterized by racial diversity where blacks represented a significant portion of the population (Smart, *Central American* 10). Not surprisingly, the racism imposed by the United States was based on a polarized racial system, that is, black versus white, with no variations in between. The polarized racial system led to the enforcement of Jim Crow practices—which were prevalent in the North American South—in the Canal Zone.[5] Many U.S. soldiers deployed in the Canal Zone were raised in the racially segregated South and were highly influenced by the racist climate of the period. In the United States, the practice of Jim Crow led to segregation laws that banned interracial marriages and called for separate public facilities for blacks and whites. These laws deprived African Americans of their civil rights by defining them as inferior to whites. U.S. soldiers and workers in Panama internalized this racist mentality, and regardless of skin tone, everyone of African descent was considered black.

Because the United States could not legally enforce Jim Crow laws in Panama, it created a pay system for Canal Zone workers that reflected Jim Crow practices. The pay system classified workers as "gold roll" and "silver roll" employees. Those designated as gold-roll employees were primarily whites from the United States, and those on the silver roll were "colored" Panamanians, black West Indians, Europeans, and Colombians (Conniff 32–36; Greene 127).[6] Gold-roll employees earned twice as much as silver-roll employees for the same position. The Isthmian Canal Commission (ICC) further discriminated against West Indians by classifying their labor as different from that of other silver-roll employees. For example, the ICC classified the workmanship of West Indians as "artisans," whereas a white U.S. worker who performed the same job would be called a skilled mechanic (Greene 127). This created a social and racial stratification within the Canal Zone that undeniably was based on race and U.S. prejudice toward blacks and West Indians. Panamanians and West Indians were not only paid less, they were also not allowed to use the same facilities as those used by U.S. soldiers (e.g., the commissary, restrooms). In effect, the Jim Crow system in Panama maintained an imperialistic society that reinforced racism and inequality (Conniff 35).

The Jim Crow system failed to recognize the diversity of the racial and ethnic composition of Panama and, by extension, of Latin America. Because the strict racial paradigm in the United States did not allow for Panama's racial ambiguities, it relegated all people of color to rigid categories that oscillated between *blanco* and *moreno*. As a result, a dual racial hierarchy formed in Panama during the early twentieth century: the one found in the Canal Zone and the other in the regions of the interior. While the Canal Zone's racial hierarchy was patterned after the binary model of the United States, the one in the interior followed the Latin American mestizo model. Because Panamanians had always prided themselves on not being black, those who were now considered *negro* began to harbor deep resentment against the United States and West Indians.

Consisting primarily of white Panamanian elites, the Panamanian oligarchy manipulated the United States' binary racial code to subordinate nonwhite Panamanians to the category of "blacks." Conniff explains this as follows: "White Panamanians, who had been aware of American racism from the start, learned how to manipulate it for their own benefit. . . . Since Panamanian prejudices were milder than American ones, the net effect was less disadvantageous to the native mestizos and blacks than to the West Indians, who had to contend with racism in the Canal Zone and chauvinism in Panama. Panamanians rarely admitted to race prejudice, and when they did, they could blame the Americans for having introduced it" (42–43).

Obviously, racial discrimination in the Canal Zone did not stem solely from the prejudices of U.S. soldiers. However, the nature of imperialism provided Panamanians with an easy scapegoat for their own racial prejudices. Threatened by the increasing number of blacks in the nation, color-conscious upper-class Panamanians did not protest the unfair treatment of the Canal Zone; rather, they blamed the United States for the social injustices (McCollough 576). While white Panamanians manipulated the racist paradigm to their advantage, which allowed them to maintain their status as minority elites, colored Panamanians found ways to distinguish themselves from blacks as well. In effect, Panamanians of color had already begun to internalize this racist paradigm, which taught that people of color were second-class citizens. Because the U.S. categorization did not racially differentiate Panamanians from West Indians, Panamanians distinguished themselves from the West Indian population on the basis of cultural and linguistic differences. In effect, this dual racial hierarchy, along with nation-building rhetoric, inadvertently pitted Panamanians against West Indians.

These cultural and racial tensions are reflected in Joaquín Beleño's Canal Zone trilogy. The populations depicted in Beleño's novels represent Panama's multiplicity, marked by people of African, indigenous, and Hispanic descent. Beleño was born in the humble Panama City neighborhood of Santa Ana, to a Panamanian mother and a Colombian father from Cartagena de Indias. He was not only a novelist but also a prolific journalist who contributed to the newspapers *La hora* [The Time] and *La república* [The Republic] (Strom 4). Beleño received his college degree in public and business administration from the University of Panama; he also participated in the student movement of 1940 and worked as a laborer in the Canal Zone, where he kept a diary, which served as a major resource for his Canal Zone trilogy (Strom 3; Padrón 15). He published four novels, including the trilogy, which are discussed in this chapter: *Luna verde* [Green Moon] (1951); *Curundú* (1956, but written in 1946); and *Gamboa Road Gang*, published simultaneously under the title *Los forzados de Gamboa* (1961).[7] Beleño's last published work was *Flor de banana* [Banana Flower] (1965), a novel that condemned the United Fruit Company for its discriminatory practices.[8]

Beleño's trilogy not only deals with problems of U.S. imperialism and discrimination in the Canal Zone but also introduces intraethnic tensions between Afro-Hispanics and West Indians. Beleño became familiar with the West Indian population as a Canal Zone worker in 1940. His characterization of Afro-Hispanics and West Indians brings to light the issues of race and identity as they affect life in the Canal Zone on the one hand, and his own racial identity on the other. While Sepúlveda, Smart, Strom, and Pérez-Venero do not classify Beleño as a "black" writer, the Panamanian writer Justo Arroyo is one of the few who considers him to be of African descent.[9] He notes that "Beleño, a Black writer, shows, as a 'colonial' Black, how the distrust and distancing produce a form of internal racism" (158). Edison also recognizes Beleño's African heritage, stating that his mother was a "colonial" black (317). To add to the uncertainty and ambiguity of his racial background, Beleño himself does not mention any racial affiliation in his one-page autobiography published in 1960 in the Panamanian literary journal *Revista lotería*. Beleño's neighborhood in "colored" Santa Ana consisted of *negros, zambos, mulatos, mestizos,* and poor whites. Santa Ana formed part of the *arrabal,* or the "outskirts" or "slums" (McGuinness, *Path of Empire* 25), and it "was known by Panamanians and foreigners alike as the part of the city where people of color predominated" (McGuinness, "Searching" 93). This racial ambiguity highlights the dilemma of the Afro-Hispanic writer in Panama, who often feels pressured to adopt a national ideology that proclaims "todos somos panameños" [we are all Panamanians], and therefore avoids any ethnic or racial identification. As discussed in chapter 1, this trend was also evidenced in the writings of Escobar and Hernández, who, as poets writing during the nationalist project, were torn between representing their country or their race. For the purposes of this study, Beleño's African ancestry is considered and analyzed as an example of an Afro-Hispanic writer who chose a nationalistic and imperialistic agenda over a racial one, a trend established by Hernández and Escobar during the nation-building period. These factors and the various classifications of his own racial background are important when examining his treatment of Zonian racial discrimination in the Canal Zone trilogy as well as his representations of Afro-Hispanics and West Indians.

Luna verde (1951), *Curundú* (1956), and *Gamboa Road Gang* (1961) are individual testimonies of Canal Zone workers and prisoners that serve primarily to protest North American empire building. The Canal Zone trilogy chronicles the personal quests of Ramón de Roquebert (*Luna verde*), Rubén Galván (*Curundú*), and Atá (*Gamboa Road Gang*), who all perish tragically while struggling to find the meaning of life and their place in U.S. imperial Panama. Beleño portrays "brown" Panama, and for this reason, the notable Panamanian literary critic Rodrigo Miró has criticized his characters for being of "discutible panameñidad" [disputable Panamanian heritage] (*La literatura* 193). Miró was obviously referring to the recent immigrants, the West Indian "diggers," who to him did not symbolize *panameñidad*. For him, the Canal Zone was clearly "una parte mínima de la realidad de Panamá" [a minimal part of Panamanian reality] (Miró, *La literatura* 193). Despite Miró's views on the significance of the Canal, and by extension, Panama's nonwhite populations, Beleño created a space for his characters who constitute an essential part of Panamanian society. Miró reflects the early twentieth-century Panamanian rhetoric that focused on Panama's Spanish roots, which for him and others was not reflected in Colón and Panama City, two cities with a large number of immigrants and Afro-Hispanics. *Panameñidad* was symbolized by a white minority of elites, and the Canal Zone revealed the darker populations of the nation that did not fit into the country's homogeneous image. For this reason, Beleño's texts are compelling because they present populations that up until this time period were either denigrated and/or unexplored in Panamanian literature.

Luna verde is the personal diary of Ramón de Roquebert, a Panamanian of French origin (non–West Indian), which transpires between 1942 and 1947. The novel chronicles the migration of Ramón from rural Río Hato to the urban area of Panama to work in the Canal Zone in Milla Cuatro. As a Milla Cuatro worker, he has an accident, returns to Río Hato, and eventually goes back to Panama to work in the Canal Zone, where he is killed during an anti-imperialist student demonstration that protested the signing of the Filós-Hines Treaty (1947), which granted the United States permission to construct military bases outside the Canal Zone.[10]

The second novel in the trilogy, *Curundú* (1956), documents the moral, spiritual, and physical decline of Rubén Galván (Ruiloba 83). Written before *Luna verde* in 1946, *Curundú* transpires at the beginning of World War II and was conceived during the summer of 1940, when Beleño worked at the Canal Zone's Fort Clayton military base. As an anti-bildungsroman, it chronicles the trials and tribulations of a youth who searches for the meaning of life.[11] *Curundú* describes the psychological effects that arise when one culture imposes its way of life on another. As an adolescent, Rubén has no effective way of dealing with this domination. The following passage suggests the psychological impact that the (neo) colonial regime had on Rubén: "Por encima de Rubén Galván existe un país agresivo que ha elaborado el concepto abstracto de la palabra democracia que no expresa ninguna idea clara en la mentalidad indisciplinada de un adolescente, en conflicto con su propia tragedia" [On top of Rubén exists an aggressive country that has elaborated the abstract concept of the word *democracy* that does not express a single clear idea in the undeveloped mind of an adolescent, who is in conflict with his own tragedy] (Beleño, *Curundú* 157). The phrase "por encima," or "on top," which is used frequently throughout the text, reinforces the idea that Rubén has no control over his environment, and thus falls prey to the hegemonic sociopolitical order that has destroyed everything native in Panama. Rubén forms relationships with other Canal Zone workers, including the Panamanian Lobo Guerrero and the West Indians Red Box, Tamtam, Liequí, and Salvador Brown, who are all silver-roll employees. Lured by high Canal Zone wages, at the age of sixteen Rubén spends his holidays working in Fort Clayton. Ultimately, he dies after being attacked in a church by U.S. soldiers.

The last novel of the trilogy, *Gamboa Road Gang* (1961), protests racial discrimination in the Canal Zone and U.S. imperialism by examining the search for identity of a black West Indian Panamanian, Arthur Ryams. *Gamboa* documents the story of Arthur, or "Atá," who is sentenced to fifty years in prison for the rape of a U.S. Zonian, Annabelle. Characters in the novel unite in prison (Gamboa), a place similar to the Canal Zone that symbolizes an imposed order. *Gamboa* is based on the real-life story of Lester León Greaves, who was accused of raping a white woman and sentenced to fifty years in prison. Beleño's examples of the social injustice of the *latifundio zoneíta* demonstrate that his primary objective in writing *Gamboa* is to attack U.S. imperialism as a disruptive force that has exacerbated past racisms.[12] At the same time, it has created social conditions that have transformed Panama and its national imaginary.

The trilogy possesses a shared mission to reject the U.S. occupation of the Canal Zone and culminates by evoking an anti–West Indian sentiment. Although the trilogy denounces imperialism and the United States' treatment of marginalized groups in Panama, the texts frequently exaggerate the sexuality of the *gringa* [white U.S. woman] or stereotype West Indians. Equally so, *gringas* exist primarily to satisfy the male sexual appetite and serve as vehicles to denounce imperialism. The overemphasized sexuality of the white female corpus is reminiscent of a trope inherent in *negrista* literature, which typically portrayed black women as seductive temptresses who destroyed their victims (Williams, *Charcoal* 69). Thus, the invention of the female stereotype of black sexuality and promiscuity on the one hand, and the purity and chastity of the white woman on the other, emerged as an expansion of *negrista* literature in the 1920s. Beleño substitutes this negative image of the black woman with that of the *gringa*. His descriptions of the *gringa* possess the same sexual attributes that *negrista* writers used to characterize the *mulata*, *zamba*, and *negra*. Thus, the descriptions of the *gringa* mirror those of the *mulata*, who dates back to nineteenth-century Spanish American literature and comes to the forefront in the 1920s during the apogee of the *negrista* period. In *Luna verde*, Ramón's description of a white woman equates that of a forbidden fruit: "Te amo, gringa-gringuita de piel sin carotén y xantofila; blanca de ausencia de mi sol, intocada de mi raza. ¡Oh fiesta de la raza de mi cuerpo y el tuyo! [. . .] Déjame olerte a gringa-gringa, déjame reír en tu boca, locamente, hasta que mi raza contagie tu raza, tu mandíbula ponderosa de sajona domi-nante" [I love you, *gringa-gringuita* without carotene or xantho-phyll skin, white absence from the sun, untouched by my race. Oh what a party between my race's body and yours! . . . Let me smell you *gringa-gringa*, let me laugh in your mouth, crazily, until my race corrupts your race, your ponderous jawbone made of Anglo-Saxon dominance] (Beleño, *Luna verde* 139). In *negrista* literature, exotic descriptions of the *mulata* provided folklore and primarily objectified the black female body. However, the exotic description of the *gringa* in this text serves a different purpose: to obtain re-venge against the United States. The passage strongly suggests re-taliation against the *gringa*, a retaliation that no doubt stems from Ramón's anger toward the United States. In effect, Ramón desires to corrupt the white race [*contagie tu raza*] by darkening it, and he uses the *gringa* as a weapon to stymie imperialism.

Interestingly enough, Beleño's texts do not merely idealize the *gringa* or *mulata*; they also romanticize the *mestizo*, *mulato*, and *chombo* of mixed racial ancestry, who are all described as exotic creatures. Beleño further appropriates the *negrista* discourse in the classification of Sandino, the half East Indian and half West Indian protagonist from *Luna verde*. "Sandino era uno de esos hombres raros y primitivos, producto de un fecundo cruce de razas exóticas" [Sandino was one of those rare and primitive men, product of a fertile mixing of exotic races] (Beleño, *Luna verde* 166). It is clear from the narrator's description that Sandino represents the "other": "Yo conocí a Sandino. Era un muchacho cruzado de hindostano y antillana. Tenía el cabello liso y negro. Sus rasgos eran del tipo caucásico; pero deformado por la imperceptible película de movimiento que siempre imprime la raza negra. Delgado, alto y muy elegante" [I met Sandino. He was a young man mixed with Hindu and West Indian. He had straight black hair. His features were Caucasian-like; but deformed by the imperceptible pellicle of movement that always oppresses the black race. Thin, tall, and very elegant] (Beleño, *Luna verde* 165–66). While the passage admires Sandino's height, physical stature, and appearance, it demeans his blackness. The word *deformado*, or "deformed," creates a negative tone that stems from racial prejudice based on perceived biological and social inferiority. While Sandino's European features are accentuated ("cabello liso," or straight hair), his blackness is viewed as a detriment to his physical appearance as well as to his character. The description inevitably values the white aesthetic and devalues the black one. Clearly, Sandino represents a new unwanted culture that characterizes Panama and the country's struggle to deal with the West Indian heritage that became an integral part of Panamanian society in the early twentieth century. In *Luna verde*, Ramón discovers that he is unable to accept the *antillanidad*, or "West Indianness," of a country that resembles the Caribbean instead of South America (206). He reaches the conclusion, "Quizá estemos más cerca de las Antillas que de Colombia y de allí la confusión de nuestras almas" [Perhaps we are more similar to the culture of the Antilles than that of Colombia, and there resides the confusion in our souls] (Beleño, *Luna verde* 266). In effect, he finds himself caught between two worlds, two cultures, and two languages. While he feels compelled to accept the *antillanidad* of Panamanian culture, he fears that doing so will signify a loss of *panameñidad* and, therefore, *hispanidad*.[13]

The description of Sandino enlightens the reader to the contradictions inherent in Beleño's novels and other early twentieth-century texts that portrayed minority populations as one-dimensional figures. Social protest novels such as *Huasipungo*, *Doña Bárbara* [Madame Barbara], and *Don Segundo Sombra*, for example, sought to restore the Andean region's indigenous past, but the texts often devalued the nonwhite aesthetic because the writers, similar to Beleño, were outsiders to the native populations that they were describing.[14] Furthermore, Beleño also forms part of this tradition. His character Ramón confesses that he is an avid reader of "revolutionary books," such as *Huasipungo* (1934), *En las calles* [In the Streets] (1935), *La vorágine* [The Vortex] (1924), *Los de abajo* [The Underdogs] (1916), *Don Segundo Sombra* (1926), *La trepadora* [The Climber] (1925), *Doña Bárbara* (1929), *Jubiabá* (1935), and *Cacao* [Cocoa Bean] (1933) (Beleño, *Luna verde* 88–89).[15] Like these writers of early twentieth-century Latin American literature, Beleño desires to denounce, attack, and give a voice to subaltern populations, yet he marginalizes the very characters that he seeks to voice.

Beleño's texts further denounce unfair wages paid under the silver and gold rolls, and they condemn treatment of Panamanian and West Indian women by the United States. Ramón's grandfather, Don Porfirio de Roquebert, abhors the United States' arrogance, as well as the soldiers' abuse of women in the Canal Zone (Beleño, *Luna verde* 224, 226). The lasciviousness of the U.S. soldiers who sexually take advantage of Panamanian women disturbs him the most. Consumed with hatred, he kills the North American who was in love with his daughter. Don Porfirio describes to his grandson, Ramón, what incited his hatred: "Odio a los gringos porque ellos tratan de humillar a todo cuanto ayudan. Ellos saben reír y saben dominar. Entonces se hacen dueños de todo cuanto quieren. Yo he visto morir a los hombres como arrieras en Culebra. . . . Ellos dicen que el canal es de ellos. Pero mienten porque allí trabajamos todos los hombres de la tierra; vinimos de Europa, de África, de Asia y de América. . . . Pero los gringos se han apoderado de esa obra y ellos exclusivamente pretenden ser los dueños absolutos. Y fue por eso por lo que lo maté" [I hate gringos because they try to humiliate everyone who they help. They know how to laugh and how to dominate. Then they become owners of everything that they desire. I have seen men die like mules in Culebra. . . . They say that the Canal belongs to them. But they lie because we men from all around the world work; we came from Europe, from Africa, from Asia, and from America. . . . But the gringos have taken possession of this task and they pretend to exclusively be the absolute owners. And it was because of that that I killed him] (Beleño, *Luna verde* 226–27). In effect, the relationship that Don Porfirio's daughter had with a U.S. soldier symbolizes the metaphorical rape of the Isthmus of Panama and the physical violation of the Panamanian woman.

Luna verde ends with the tragic death of Ramón, who fights against U.S. imperialism. Beleño recognizes that Ramón and other workers are victims of imperialism, but the text still demonstrates ambiguity toward West Indians. As Sandino and the *gringa* are repeatedly admired for their exoticism, they are also viewed with contempt because of the cultural and economic changes they brought with them. West Indians are viewed as allies to North American interests, particularly since they share the language of the new colonizer. Ramón's friend, Rodrigo, expresses this distrust: "Millones de dólares, miles de antillanos que piensan y sienten con las ideas y los sentimientos de las revistas norteamericanas que leen" [Millions of dollars, thousands of West Indians who think and share the same ideas and sentiments of the North American magazines that they read] (Beleño, *Luna verde* 240). Ramón concurs, asserting: "gringos [que] prefieren el jamaicano porque su lengua inglesa no sirve para contestar, que no para la protesta" [gringos (who) prefer the Jamaican because his English language serves neither to answer nor to protest] (41). The West Indian's success was attributed to his perceived submissiveness and indifference to racial inequities, as illustrated in *Luna verde* (122). Simply put, West Indians are traitors to the Panamanian cause because of their nationality, blackness, and language.

While *Luna verde* deals with the cultural and economic impact of neoimperialism, *Curundú* closely examines the religious differences between Rubén Galván and Salvador Brown, Afro-Hispanic and West Indian characters in the novel, respectively. Rubén and Salvador meet coincidentally when signing up to work in the Canal Zone and contrast spiritually, physically, racially, and culturally. When describing himself, Rubén proudly writes that he is "moreno" and not "negro" (Beleño, *Curundú* 19). Rubén has problems with all blacks, stemming from his paternal grandmother's prejudices.

His grandmother, who had always prided herself on being Hispanic, hated his father for marrying a black woman, a *morena* from Portobelo (80). As Andino observes: "Rubén Galván vive una contradicción: es oscuro, moreno, sin llegar a ser 'negro'" [Rubén Galván lives a contradiction: he is dark, brown, without being black] (86). As opposed to Rubén, Salvador is "moreno, azafranado, cabeza amplia, rasurada al rapé y boca redonda y sensual" [brown, saffron; broad-shaven head, with a round and sensual mouth] (Beleño, *Curundú* 23).

Although Beleño describes Salvador as *moreno*, he notes physical distinctions that align the protagonist more with his African roots than with his Spanish or European heritage. His "boca redonda y sensual" [round and sensual mouth], a stereotypical characteristic of African descendants, distinguishes him from Rubén's more European features, even though the latter may be of the same complexion. The narrator portrays the West Indian Salvador Brown as a religious zealot and derogatorily refers to him as "Kid Salva Cuatro," a pejorative term used to designate all Christians who are not Catholic (25). Appropriately named *Salvador*, or "Savior," he is frequently characterized as a religious fanatic who is not in touch with the social reality of the Canal Zone.

The religious dialogue between Salvador and Rubén demystifies some of the prejudices that both groups harbor against each other's religion. When speaking to Rubén and a group of workers, Salvador reminds the group, "En nombre de tu bonita religión católica, mataron a los indios y trajeron a los negros para esclavizarlos" [In the name of your wonderful Catholic religion, they killed Indians and brought blacks to be enslaved] (Beleño, *Curundú* 191). But Rubén reminds Salvador of the racial and ecclesiastical segregation in U.S. churches that prevented blacks and whites from worshiping together (192). Lobo Guerrero retorts: "Mentira, ustedes no creen en Cristo, sólo los católicos creemos en Cristo, en la virgen y en sus iglesias. . . . ¿Dónde has visto tú, alguna vez en tu vida, una iglesia protestante mejor que una iglesia católica?" [That's a lie, you guys don't believe in Christ, only we Catholics believe in Christ, the virgin, and in their churches. . . . Where have you ever seen in your lifetime, a Protestant church that was better than a Catholic one?] (Beleño, *Curundú* 187). The characters' youth and lack of knowledge of other cultures and religions lead them to such narrow conclusions. Although Beleño succeeds in exposing the myths that both groups have about each other's religion, he fails in his analysis by portraying Salvador as a marginalized and flawed character. In his contrast between Rubén and Salvador, Beleño often exaggerates the latter's religious convictions. For example, Brown is such a religious zealot that he relates learning English to learning about God (148). Even as Rubén searches to find true meaning in religion, he ends by returning to his Catholic roots. Salvador, no doubt, will continue trying to convert others to Protestantism, a religion that Panamanians associate with West Indians and the United States.

Religion, culture, and language divide Panamanians from all other racial groups in the Canal Zone. Language is a fundamental part of this trilogy and is especially examined in *Curundú*. While the characters often express disdain for West Indians because they speak English, they secretly admire them and wish that they, too, could communicate in the language of the new colonizer (Beleño, *Curundú* 147). In addition, Beleño makes a concerted effort to reproduce the English dialects (English-based Creole) in the Canal Zone.[16] Beleño transcribes the language of the Canal Zone, which is what the narrator describes as an "unharmonious mixture" of Spanish and English (136). The following language exchange between two West Indian Canal Zone workers, Tamtam and Liequí, demonstrates Beleño's ability to reproduce the effect of migration and linguistic hybridity in Panama. As the narrator acknowledges, the language of Tamtam and Liequí is "un nuevo idioma, hasta cierto punto, mezcla y aleación de inglés y castellano" [a new language, to a certain point, a mixture and alloy of English and Spanish] (135). Tamtam begins: "Tú ve Liequí, el vacilón es así, spar. . . . ¡El vacilón! Si tú te pones tof, tú te encuentras tu mamá y tu papá en la calle. Y esa boai! Tu sae bien a nosotro no guta vacilá aquí . . . y ram, ahuecamo pa onde otro pedazo de gallina que le guste el vacilón. Tú ve el vacilón . . . ? []Liequí afirma en silencio." [As you see Liequí, the joke is this way, *spar*. . . . The joke! If you get tough, you'll find your mother and father in the street. And that gal! You know very well, we don't like to joke here . . . and ram, we loosen up toward a piece of chicken (a person) who likes to joke. You see the joke . . . ? []Liequí silently agrees.[17]] (135–36). The language exchange between Tamtam and Liequí demonstrates the linguistic hybridity inherent in Panama that is representative of the cultural differences that typify cultures marked by plurality. Despite Panama's resistance to change and its unwillingness to accept West Indians as a legitimate part of the country, these changes have already taken place linguistically. The effect of English-based Creole is apparent today in Panamanian (Spanish) speech. The dialogue is composed of *panameñismos*, words that are characteristic of Panamanian speech such as *vacilón*, or "joke," and West Indian speech such as *spar* and *tof* (Padrón 18). Realizing that the reader will not understand certain words, Beleño glosses the terms *spar* and *tof*, which he translates respectively as "friend" and "tough." However, as Smart notes, Beleño's understanding of West Indian culture and language is limited. While he recognizes that *spar* is not Panamanian and resembles the English word *spark* and is used contextually to mean "friend," he does not realize that it comes directly from Jamaican Creole and is derived from the expression "sparring partner" (Smart, *Central American* 37, 127). Realizing that the Panamanian writer is an outsider to this culture, many of the terms are glossed at the end of the texts. However, Beleño, too, remains an outsider and has limited understanding, as this example suggests.

Beleño envisages West Indians as outsiders who have corrupted the Spanish language. As a result, they are further marginalized, which contributes to their image as intruders who are unwilling to assimilate into Panamanian society. After the interchange between Tamtam and Liequí, *Curundú*'s narrator reflects on the cultural significance that these new people and their language bring to the country: "Era la Mosca de Oro de la corrupción que transitaba desde el bajo fondo de una antillanidad envilecida y de un yanquismo degenerante del idioma que ascendía corrompiendo las formas de expresión" [It was the golden fly of corruption that passed from the bottom depths of a degraded West Indian heritage and a degenerating Yankeeism of language that ascended corrupting the forms of expression] (139). West Indian speech, just as the population itself, is viewed contradictorily. West Indians are admired for their exoticism and as economic assets to the country, yet they are also viewed with disdain.

The New Panamanian of West Indian Descent

The new Panamanian of West Indian descent who emerges in Beleño's works is one of mixed heritage, half West Indian and half North American, but not yet Panamanian. These characters are in search of their identity and fight to be recognized as gringos. *Curundú's* Red Box is a *gringo-chombo*, but he imagines himself as something different (Beleño, *Curundú* 167). Born to a North American father and a West Indian mother in Panama, Red Box strives to prove his whiteness in the Zone, which classifies anyone of color as black, regardless of skin tone. More disturbing, Red Box sees nothing but his whiteness and disdains anything associated with black people: "Quizás por eso no gustaba de ver su rostro en un espejo porque su faz rubicunda, esmaltada de pecas, no se conformaba armoniosamente lo que él mismo se imaginaba ser. Sus rasgos negroides, pronunciadamente belicosa su porte rubicundo, siempre le ofendieron de la misma manera que sus apretados cabellos duros; duros y rojizos que él acariciaba inútilmente, con un movimiento nervioso de sus manos, en un afán, de ondularlos con su contemplación" [Perhaps because of this he did not like to see his face in the mirror, because his red features, sprinkled with freckles, did not conform harmoniously to what he imagined it to be. His black features, aggressively pronounced his rubicund behavior, they always offended him in the same way that his curly nappy hairs, nappy and red that he caressed uselessly, with a nervous movement of his hands, with an eagerness to wave them with his contemplation] (167–68). Red Box's self-image fails to correspond to what he imagines it to be, a blatant reminder of Fanon's assertion that the black man who is a victim of colonization "is overwhelmed to such a degree by the wish to be white, it is because he lives in a society that makes his inferiority complex possible, in a society that derives its stability from the perpetuation of this complex" (100). Red Box's self-image is challenged when he tries to enter a church for whites only, to clean up after the incident. In this respect, Red Box foreshadows Charles McForbes, a West Indian protagonist in Quince Duncan's *Los cuatro espejos* [The Four Mirrors] (1973), who is in search of his identity and whose mirror image does not correspond to what he envisions. Like Charles, Red Box refuses to acknowledge his blackness, but unlike him, he never reconnects with his African roots.

Red Box attempts to assert his authority as a foreman, which he believes he deserves, not only because of his position in the Canal Zone but also because of his Anglo-American roots. Furious over not receiving a cold glass of water, he berates his subordinate Julio Quintano for not responding to him with such phrases as "Yes, Sir" and "No, Sir."[18] Red Box responds to Quintano's lack of respect and obliviousness to his own status as a gringo by venting: "I am an American citizen . . . My name, Red . . . Red Box The Killer . . . and you . . . negars (en inglés). Por eso tienen que obedecerme. Yo soy gringo" [I am an American citizen . . . My name, Red . . . Red Box the Killer . . . and you . . . n—— . . . (in English). Because of that you have to obey me. I am a gringo] (Beleño, *Curundú* 174). Red Box does not recognize that he too is a *chombo* or a "negar" in the eyes of many white Americans and to some Panamanians as well. During the protest, the priest does not allow him to enter the church because he is racially codified as black within the limits of the Canal Zone. Again, it is useful at this point to return to Fanon, who argued that racial oppression often made blacks turn against themselves and appropriate the racial discourse of the colonizer (192). In effect, the black utilizes the discourse of the colonizer against his own people and, by extension, against himself. As Red Box identifies others as *chombos*, he refuses to see himself as one of them.

After receiving his paycheck, Red Box decides that he wants to celebrate in a whites-only bar, the Clubhouse de Balboa. When Rubén and others warn him not to go, he ignores them, feeling that he will be allowed to enter because he is a gringo. When he enters the bar, a black West Indian waitress refuses to seat him for fear of reprisal from the other patrons; Rubén becomes enraged and gets into a fight with the white clients. As a result, he, Rubén, and Tamtam are fined for that week's earnings. Red Box's biracial identity is not permitted in the Canal Zone. Racial politics outside of the Canal Zone mirror those of other Latin American countries, which are based on color and complexion, as opposed to the United States' so-called one-drop rule, adopted in the Canal Zone. Red Box's struggle with his black identity foreshadows that of Atá, the principal protagonist in *Gamboa Road Gang*.

Gamboa Road Gang examines racial conflicts between West Indians and Panamanians and, similar to the former novels in the trilogy, derides the United States. The narrator reinforces that Panama was exploited because of its geographic location and Yankee imperialism. The most overt denouncement of U.S. imperialism is evident when *Gamboa*'s narrator compares the Canal Zone to a latifundio (Beleño, *Gamboa* 81). Beleño recuperates the dichotomous metaphor of the latifundio and the *terratenientes*, or landowners, omnipresent in social protest and *indigenista* literature of the 1930s.[19] His latifundio is the Canal Zone and the *terratenientes* are represented by the U.S. government. Coupled with anger against the United States was the Panamanian's distrust of the West Indian population; Panamanians viewed West Indians as new citizens of the country who were not totally committed to the national project (Beleño, *Gamboa* 140). Panamanians wanted the West Indian population to give up their cultural ties and patriotic allegiances to their homeland.

Although *Gamboa* attempts to expose discriminatory practices against Panamanians and West Indians, it often ends up contributing to the very same racial stereotypes that it intends to condemn. In fact, Beleño was criticized for his novels' derogatory remarks against West Indians. The Panamanian novelists Carlos Wilson and Justo Arroyo have both noted the anti–West Indian sentiment in Beleño's works (Birmingham-Pokorny, "Interview" 16, 158). For example, when describing Nelly's children, the narrator compares their blackness with "cordones eléctricos" [electric cords] (55). This statement objectifies their blackness and does not possess cultural awareness. Also, when describing the homes in a West Indian neighborhood, *Gamboa*'s narrator states that, contrary to what one may believe, the neighborhood is clean, and the people bathe regularly, brush their teeth, and practice good hygiene (Beleño, *Gamboa* 54).

Notwithstanding Beleño's attempts to dispel myths about the West Indian population, his discussion strengthens these misconceptions. Beleño's description is telegraphic and lacks an insider's perspective, that is, from within the West Indian culture. He reflects the racist stereotypes of the national imaginary and echoes the Panamanian national rhetoric. His tone is negative, and it is evident that he is an outsider to the population when viewing their bathing rituals as superstitious instead of as a vital part of their culture. It is no surprise, then, that Wilson cites this passage as one that infuriates him the most, because it demeans the West Indian population (Birmingham-Pokorny, "Interview" 16–17). Furthermore, according to Wilson, the novel is replete with stereotypical images of "chombas," that is, black West Indian women who are portrayed as exotic, spiritually misguided, uncouth, negligent, and too Africanized ("The image" 77).[20] He notes: "Joaquín Beleño has influenced me very much. Every time I read any of his trilogies, I become so angry because of the way he has portrayed 'chombos'—Afro-Hispanics[—]in his works. I am particularly angered by all the negative images and stereotypes he has presented in his works. As a result, I have tried to write and to present a more balanced and a more fair portrayal of 'chombos' and Afro-Hispanics" (Birmingham-Pokorny, "Interview" 16). The images of West Indians produced by Beleño illustrate what the Afrocentric critic Molefi Asante defines as an etic and emic approach to criticism. According to Asante, "Etic approaches to criticism are those methods that are from outside the discourse perspective, whereas emic approaches view the perspective from within the same culture as the discourse" (*Afrocentric Idea* 172). Beleño's incorrect linguistic analysis of the term *spar* previously analyzed in *Curundú*, as well as the stereotypes that plague his texts, supports the argument that he is an outsider to West Indian culture despite his experiences as a Canal Zone worker. Additionally, Beleño's negative representations of West Indians convey the degree to which he internalized the racial discourse of *mestizaje*.

Beleño's texts make disparaging remarks against African descendants that had been typically ascribed to blacks in the literature of the nineteenth century as well as that of the *negrista* period. Blacks are described uniformly as sensual and sexual beings who dance. Atá's alleged rape victim Annabelle Rodney wrote a thesis titled, "La contribución folklórica del negro americano en la cultura de los Estados Unidos" [The Folkloric Contribution of the American Black in the Culture of the United States]. The title reinforces that for whites in both Panama and the United States, blacks epitomize the anthropological. Annabelle's thesis supports the notion that her relationship with Atá was superficial and promulgated by curiosity and superficial interest.

The idea of a relationship between a black man and a white woman leads the narrator to ponder the motives of Annabelle's interest in Atá. He alludes to this when referring to the possibility of a relationship between Annabelle and Atá. He concludes that the only explanation for a relationship between a *gringa* and a black man is if the woman were under the influence of alcohol during Carnival. Not only are white women sexually promiscuous according to the narrator, their relationship with a black man can be explained only by the influence of outside factors such as alcohol and a dim setting. At night, tainted by alcohol and West Indian calypsos, the *gringa* has no control over her behavior, and her actions are dismissed as sexual whims.[21] Both the narrator and the inmate (August Mildred) reduce the relationship between Annabelle and Atá to a sexual adventure based on the former's sexual curiosity, simply because Atá is black.

Despite Beleño's diatribe against white women, he is outraged by the negative perception that U.S. soldiers have toward Panamanian women. The soldiers equally view brown and black women as sexual objects. Ironically, the protagonists do not question their derision of white women, yet evoke a sense of hatred when it comes to the sexual violation of Panamanian and West Indian women. Atá's girlfriend Perla is gang-raped by Bobby Rodney (Annabelle's brother) and his friends, who are seeking a black woman to avenge Annabelle's supposed sexual violation. The description of Perla's rape and its aftermath is one of Beleño's most poignant and artistic representations of Zonian crime and violence perpetrated by white Americans. The passage demonstrates violence as well as racial and gender inequities in the Canal Zone:

El cuerpo doliente y ardiendo en sus muslos. Las muñecas, los brazos y los pies, amoratados. Las uñas blancas se dibujaron clavadas en su carne barbadiense, color de té. La boca rota y la cara arañada. Como fue arrastrada sobre el llano, su traje de dacrón quedó entre zarzas y cadillos. Sus interiores rasgados por manos rubias que tiraron de ella igual que si arrancasen pellejos de una res muerta. A su pelo aplanchado estaban adheridas briznas secas del camino. Apestaba a gringos borrachos. Y le dolía el sexo por dentro. Cayeron ondulando sobre ella como buitres blancos sobre la morrina. Apretaron sus senos hasta arrancarle gritos de dolor en su larga pesadilla. . . . Los gringos cayeron sobre su cuerpo mientras tuvo fuerzas. Le cayeron encima, unos sosteniéndole las manos y otros los pies, como los condenados a descuartizamiento. Ella se rebeló y pateó, enardeciendo más a Bobby. . . . Cuando abrió los ojos había salido el sol y todo hallábase bajo la penumbra sombreada de la mañana. Estaba desnuda, inmóvil.

[The painful body and burning legs. Livid wrists, arms and feet. White fingernails encrusted in the Barbadian's tea colored skin. Burst mouth and scratched face. As she was being dragged through the plain, her Dacron dress was left between the bramble and burdock. Her insides torn by blonde hands that pulled at her as if they were stripping the hide from dead cattle. Her pressed hair held splinters from the road. She stunk of white drunkards. And her sex ached from within. They fell on her undulating like white vultures on a carcass. They squeezed her breasts until she screamed in pain in her long nightmare. . . . The white men fell on her body while she had strength. They fell on her, some securing her hands, others, her feet as those who are condemned to quartering. She rebelled and kicked, inflaming Bobby more. . . . When she opened her eyes, the sun had come up and everything was under the shadowy penumbra morning. She was naked, immobile[22]] (Beleño, *Gamboa* 132–33).

Like the corpse of an animal, Perla's body is attacked by mosquitoes. Raped and almost beaten to death, Perla is rescued by two other Panamanians and encouraged to go to the police. However, after a conversation about the social and racial inequities in the Canal Zone, she decides to return home and not report the incident, because Perla's rescuer reminds her that the justice system in Gamboa is for whites and not blacks. Her rescuer's statements make it clear that even if Perla were to go to the police, this heinous crime would go unpunished because of racial inequities in the Canal Zone's social justice system. In addition, Perla's gender prevents her from reporting the crime and underlines the double dilemma of a victim who is black and female. Clearly, if Perla were white like Atá's alleged victim, she would not fear reporting the crime. As a black woman, she is doubly marginalized because of her race and gender.

Atá's Double Consciousness

Like *Curundú*'s Red Box, *Gamboa's* Atá exemplifies the new Panamanian. Atá is a mestizo, born to a mother from Barbados and a
North American father. Although he represents the "[first] generation of children born to West-Indian immigrants and blends elements of the West Indies, the United States, and Panama," it is his
chombo heritage that proves problematic in the Zone (Conniff 68).
Atá is described as "un muchacho de cabellos rojos y atrasados, de
piel rubicunda y manchada de pecas. La primera impresión es la de
un negro albino, pero observándolo con familiaridad se descubre
enseguida que su madre es una legítima negra y su padre, un sajón
de pura cepa" [a redheaded boy, hair combed back, rosy skin and
covered with freckles. The first impression is that of a black albino, but upon familiar observation, right away one discovers that
his mother is a true black and his father, a true Saxon[23]] (Beleño,
Gamboa 43). However, Atá is also a "gringo-chombo, chombo-
bruto . . . gringo-pobre, chombo mallulón y chombo-blanco" [a
gringo *chombo*, a brute *chombo*[,] . . . a poor gringo, a big *chombo*,
and a white *chombo*] who wishes to only be a gringo (67). Atá attempts to *blanquearse*, or whiten himself, by straightening his hair
daily with Pomada Cuba and by having a relationship with a white
woman, Annabelle. From his viewpoint, he deserves to be with Annabelle because they are both white.

Atá refuses to accept his West Indian heritage and demeans the
other West Indian inmates. Speaking of the West Indian inmate
Wallai, Atá exclaims: "¡Ponlo en su lugar! Ninguno de estos chombos son gente. Yo los conozco. En su casa comen como puercos,
con la mano. Aquí es donde vienen a ser gente y a comer con tene-
dor y cuchillo" [Put him in his place! None of these chombos are
human beings. I know them. At home they eat like pigs, with their
hands. Here is where they learn to be human beings and to eat
with a fork and a knife] (Beleño, *Gamboa* 22). Atá's own self-
image is distorted to the extent that he does not recognize himself
as a member of the group that he so vehemently abhors. Furthermore, he has appropriated and internalized the national discourse
that views West Indians as second-class citizens. Because of his
self-hatred, Atá is despised by other West Indian prisoners. Wallai,

a West Indian who obviously views Atá as a traitor to his own race, mocks his attempt to be white and distinguishes himself from other prisoners because Atá received a fifty-year sentence for being with a "blue-eyed queen." The message of Wallai's mockery is evident. Atá has alienated himself from his West Indian ancestry and does not know his true identity. Ironically, it is in prison where Atá comes to this self-realization and finally identifies himself as black.

In prison, Atá distances himself from the other blacks and demeans them because they remind him of his own racial identity. Having internalized the racism, Fanon informs us that the black becomes "negrophobic" and turns against himself and other blacks (190–95). Atá has internalized this inferiority complex and evokes a self-hatred and self-loathing as a result of the colonizer's image of him. Similar to Red Box, Atá reflects Fanon's notion of a black inferiority complex: "Since in all periods the Negro has been an inferior, he attempts to react with a superiority complex. . . . It is because the Negro belongs to an inferior race that he seeks to be like the superior race" (213, 215). Atá is a victim because society has made him inferior and left him with no other option than to disdain his blackness and seek status as a white man.

Within the confines of the Canal Zone, the only thing that matters is Atá's blackness or whiteness. There is no room to be either Panamanian or West Indian. At first glance, it may seem to be a simplification to classify the problem of Atá's identity using the binary black-white paradigm (i.e., West Indian–Anglo-American). Clearly, the protagonist does not merely strive to be Panamanian or West Indian. Atá values only his Anglo American ancestry and ability to pass as a gringo. Atá emphasizes the *chombo-gringo*'s marginal status: "Los amigos míos que son negros no son panameños, porque ustedes no los quieren y los desprecian. No son gringos, porque aquí en la Zona no los aceptan. No son ingleses, porque la nacionalidad de sus padres no significa nada para ellos. Somos judíos. No tenemos patria. Somos lo que somos: gente que respiramos. Por eso yo quiero ser alguien. Quiero ser gringo. Soy negro. Soy gringo. Tú ves mi piel" [My friends who are black are not Panamanians, because you guys don't like them and despise them. They are not gringos, because here in the Zone they are not accepted. They are not English, because their parents' nationality does not mean anything to them. We are Jews. We do not have a country. We are who we are: people who breathe. Because of that I want to be someone. I want to be a gringo. I am black. I am a gringo. You see the color of my skin] (147). Beleño demonstrates the effect that migration and displacement have on an individual through the figure of Atá. As Smart notes, "His [Atá's] chombo blood inspires in him too a psychotic hatred for the only group that is willing and eager to accept him. This hatred is symptomatic of a presumed *chombo* inferiority and an equally unscientifically posited Yankee superiority. Like all of Beleño's *chombos*, he tends to be servile, and this is reinforced in his case by an absolute contempt for himself and his people" (*Central American* 18). Beleño identifies the ramifications of this polarized racial system by relating the historical account of Lester León Greaves through the problematic character of Atá. Throughout the novel, Atá receives letters from Annabelle and secretly hopes that she will prove his innocence by going to the Zonian police. After receiving Annabelle's last letter and discovering through the Zonian newspaper that she plans to wed, Atá finally realizes that Annabelle will never tell the truth, and more important, that his dream of liberation has come to an end. When she marries a captain in the United States, Atá's hopes are destroyed, and he basically commits suicide by attempting to escape from prison. The jail wardens have no other choice but to kill him when he crosses the line. Annabelle was not only "un símbolo de su libertad" [a symbol of his freedom] but also a symbol of his desire to become a gringo (119). His relationship with her (re)affirmed his status as a gringo because a white woman would never date a black man. Unable to deal with this realization, and still disillusioned about his identity, Atá yells while escaping: "Yo soy Atá. Yo soy blanco. Yo soy gringo. . . . Yo tengo un padre rubio y una novia azucena" [I'm Atá. I'm white. I'm a gringo. . . . I have a blond father and a white lily girlfriend] (170). Ironically, it is when Atá is close to committing suicide that he acknowledges for the first time that he is black, privately telling the narrator: "Annabelle y yo somos dos líneas paralelas. Negro y blanco" [Annabelle and I are two parallel lines. Black and white] (139). The two parallel lines, one black and the other white, are a metaphor for the relationship between Atá and Annabelle. Like these two lines, the two will never complete their union. Eventually, Atá is unable to deal with the reality of his blackness and escapes society's racism by fleeing to his death.

The conflict of *Gamboa*'s Atá and of *Curundú*'s Red Box, both of North American and Anglophone Caribbean ancestry, evokes the African American scholar W. E. B. DuBois's concept of double consciousness. It is worthwhile to return to DuBois's seminal work *The Souls of Black Folk*, written in 1903, in which he describes the problem of the twentieth century as that of the color line. He states: "It is a peculiar sensation, this double-consciousness, this sense of always looking at one's self through the eyes of others, of measuring one's soul by the tape of a world that looks on in amused contempt and pity. One ever feels his twoness, an American, a negro; two souls, two thoughts, two unreconciled strivings; two warring ideals in one dark body, whose dogged strength alone keeps it from being torn asunder" (5). Atá and Red Box are also plagued by this twoness, which has led them to deny their blackness in hopes of acceptance and social status. They do not know how to simultaneously embrace their West Indian and North American roots because society only values their whiteness. Thus, in the Canal Zone, they are both gringo and *chombo*, searching for an identity. Ashamed of their West Indian heritage, they seek status as gringos, but fail. This generation of West Indians, the first generation to be born in Panama, has not yet begun to accept or explore their *panameñidad*. Because of racial tensions in Panama, caused by problems stemming from the colonial period as well as problems brought by the United States, they struggle primarily as black subjects in a community that values whiteness. This is not unlike the future generations, who still struggle with this racial paradigm; however, the generation of Atá and Red Box has only begun to explore one facet of it.

Gamboa Road Gang is one of the most studied Panamanian novels inside and outside of Panama, because "for the first time a Panamanian author successfully portrays a man (Atá) struggling with himself and with his environment to belong to a human and social group which rejects him" (Smart, *Central American* 13). The struggle does not end with Atá; his girlfriend Perla has just given birth to another child, ironically fathered by her white rapist, Bobby. As Beleño warns us of the cyclical nature of history, the biracial baby will inevitably be "otro Atá, soñando con otra Annabelle" [another Atá, dreaming about another Annabelle] (Beleño, *Gamboa* 162).

The Canal Zone symbolizes the cultural, linguistic, and racial conflicts inherent in Panamanian society. The lives of the protagonists in the aforementioned trilogy end in destruction, caused by internal and external conflicts, those of Panama and the United States. Long before the United States began construction of the Canal in 1904 and assumed occupation of the Canal Zone, there were racial problems in Panama. However, the United States' presence exacerbated those racial problems by imposing a polarized racial construction on Panama that resembled the racial paradigm of the Southern United States. In effect, the Canal Zone has emerged as a microcosm of Panama, where racial conflicts and tensions affect relationships among Anglo-Americans and Panamanians, West Indians, Afro-Hispanics, and indigenous populations.

Beleño's novels succeed in presenting the effects of racial discrimination in the neocolonial and neoimperialist regime imposed by the United States. They also triumph in presenting the plight of the *chombo*, even though these texts, most apparently *Gamboa*, often reduce the latter's plight to essentialisms that inadvertently marginalize the West Indian characters. Moreover, Beleño's works show the effect that racial discrimination and classification have had on the Panamanian mestizo, as depicted in *Luna verde* and *Curundú*. *Luna verde* sees the hope in the mestizo as part of the solution to U.S. imperialism: "Serán los mulatos y mestizos enrubecidos que seguirán combinando esta ciudad que ya no tiene colores, sino un color: el del futuro" [It will be the blond mulattoes and mestizos who will continue intermixing in this city that does not have colors anymore, but one color: the one of the future] (185). Beleño's focus on the mestizo, *moreno*, and *mulato* reminds the reader how he was affected emotionally by the racial system that relegated nonblack Panamanians to the category of *negro*. Beleño views discrimination as a by-product of the Canal Zone, but he fails to recognize how Panamanians of non–West Indian descent were affected by the country's own racial problems and stigmas stemming from centuries of *mestizaje*. In effect, Beleño has internalized the racism, the discourse of *mestizaje*, and assimilation; therefore, he does not see himself as a proponent of this racist discourse. Beleño's works constantly emphasize that Panamanians were not the problem; rather, he fortifies the notion that the United States generated the racial complications. That is to say, while his trilogy protests racial discrimination, it does not view the racism perpetuated by Panamanians against West Indians as part of the conflict. The West Indian is portrayed as a conflicted character and is viewed as an outsider by Afro-Hispanics and other Panamanians. The third-generation West Indian writer Carlos Wilson recuperates the denigrated West Indian figure and redeems his literary and historical portrayal, which I turn to now.

3

Revising the Canon

Historical Revisionism in Carlos "Cubena" Guillermo Wilson's Trilogy

In a conversation with Seales Soley, the Panamanian West Indian writer Carlos "Cubena" Guillermo Wilson noted, "El principal tema de mis obras es el Canal de Panamá, la mayor fuente de mi felicidad y dolor, que ha tenido un impacto contundente en la vida de mis abuelos inmigrantes y en la consecuente odisea de los chombos" [the main theme of my works is the Panama Canal, the major source of my happiness and pain, that has had a forceful impact in the life of my immigrant grandparents and in the subsequent odyssey of the *chombos*] (68–69). A descendant of West Indian diggers who came to work on the Canal, it is no surprise that the Canal is a thematic contour in Wilson's works. The publication of Wilson's poems and short stories coincides with the 1977 signing of the Torrijos-Carter Treaty, which would transfer ownership and operation of the Canal from the United States to Panama. Hence, both *Cuentos del negro Cubena: Pensamiento afro-panameño* [Short Stories by Black Cubena: Afro-Panamanian Thought] and *Pensamientos del negro Cubena: Pensamiento afro-panameño* [Black Cubena's Thoughts: Afro-Panamanian Thought], both published in 1977, react to negative stereotypes of West Indians in Panama who ventured from the Anglophone Caribbean more than a century ago to work on the Canal. Wilson's reading of the Canal Zone and his inclusion of West Indian contributions to the monumental construction of the Panama Canal has led to his exclusion from the Panamanian literary canon. Through his portrayal of the

Canal, which permeates his literary corpus, he reinterprets Panamanian national history.

The Canal also forms the backdrop of Cubena's trilogy (*Chombo, Los nietos de Felicidad Dolores* [The Grandchildren of Felicidad Dolores], and *La misión secreta* [The Secret Mission]), three novels that rewrite, revise, and reenact Afro-Panamanian history as well as that of the African Diaspora. Cubena's trilogy spans three decades and discusses the cycle of black migration in Panama and the Americas from time immemorial to the present. Published respectively in 1981, 1991, and 2005, each novel tells the story of Afro-descendants in the diaspora and incorporates the Canal into its central narrative. *Chombo* takes place during the signing of the Torrijos-Carter Treaty of 1977; *Los nietos* takes place in 1999, the year when the operation of the Canal was transferred to Panama; and *La misión secreta* forecasts the hundred-year anniversary of the completion of the Canal in 2014. The novels collectively tell the story of West Indian migration, racial discrimination, black negation, intraethnic tensions, and Afro-American history. Wilson expresses this history by denouncing the conquistadors, Panamanians, and even his own Afro-Panamanian brothers and sisters of non–West Indian ancestry for slavery, ethnic cleansing [*mestizaje negativo*], and black negation and denial.[1] Thus, since the appearance of his first published works in 1977, Carlos Wilson has dedicated his works to voicing the experience of displaced African Diaspora figures in his poetry and prose. Until recently, however, his works have received very little attention in his native Panama.

Panamanian Literary Canon

In the first chapter, I noted that poets Gaspar Hernández and Federico Escobar suppressed a racial discourse in favor of a unified nationalistic one. Because of their patriotic stance, Hernández and Escobar are included in several anthologies as representative writers of *modernismo* and romanticism who contributed to Panama's national foundation. Rodrigo Miró's *Cien años de poesía de Panamá* [One Hundred Years of Panamanian Poetry] (1966) helped solidify their canonical status. Despite his international success, Cubena's works have not been well received in Panama, and only recently have his works been included in Panamanian literary anthologies. I surveyed several literary anthologies published about Panamanian and Central American writers, and Cubena was not published in many of them. He was not a part of *Cuentos centroamericanos* [Central American Short Stories] (2000), *Diccionario de la literatura panameña* [Dictionary of Panamanian Literature] (2002), *Antología de escritores del istmo centroamericano* [Anthology of Writers from the Central American Isthmus] (2003), or the recently published *Diccionario de la literatura centroamericana* [Dictionary of Central American Literature] (2007). The *Diccionario de la literatura panameña* is a compilation of Panama's most distinguished writers from the colonial period until 2002. Cubena's exclusion from the *Diccionario* is surprising because the anthology incorporates other black Panamanian writers such as Gaspar Hernández, Federico Escobar, Joaquín Beleño, Gerardo Maloney, and Carlos Oriel Wynter Melo. The editors noted that the purpose of the anthology, published a year before Panama's centennial anniversary, was to "fortalecer la identidad nacional" [fortify national identity] (Martínez Ortega 7). I thought initially that Wilson's exclusion was perhaps because he has lived in the United States since the 1950s. The anthologists acknowledged, however, that they also included international authors who treat Panamanian themes in their literary works (7). In their words, these writers who reside outside of Panama were included because their works "ficcionalizaron aspectos esenciales de la realidad panameña contemporánea" [fictionalized essential aspects of contemporary Panamanian reality] (7). These comments beg the question of whether Wilson was excluded because his works do not treat Panamanian reality, or at least a reality that Panamanians want to acknowledge.

Enrique Jaramillo Levi, one of Panama's most distinguished short-story writers and literary critics, does not include Wilson in his anthology *Poesía panameña contemporánea (1929–79)* [Contemporary Panamanian Poetry, 1929–79] (1980), which is surprising, since his poems were published in 1977. Jaramillo Levi also does not incorporate Wilson's short stories in his anthology *Panamá cuenta: Cuentistas del centenario, 1851–2003* [Panama Tells Short Stories: Centennial Short-Story Writers, 1851–2003], an anthology published in 2003 that includes sixty Panamanian short-story writers. In the introduction, Jaramillo Levi lists several short-story writers who have received international recognition for their work, but he fails to include Wilson, which is odd considering the reception that Wilson has received abroad. In the "Notes" section of his introduction, Jaramillo Levi includes Wilson among many writers who "también han publicado libros de cuento" [also have published books of short stories] (*Panama cuenta* 27). Unless readers were actually looking for Wilson's name, they would most certainly not find it. Furthermore, his inclusion of Wilson's works in the notes signifies that he is not one of the central short-story writers to be studied. Nevertheless, Jaramillo Levi incorporated Wilson into his short-story anthology *Sueños compartidos: Compilación histórica de cuentistas panameños, 1892–2004* [Shared Dreams: Historical Compilation of Panamanian Short-Story Writers, 1892–2004], published in 2005. He anthologizes Wilson's poem "El bombero" [The Fireman], which deals with racial prejudice in the United States during the turbulent 1960s by the Ku Klux Klan, a white supremacist group known for lynching blacks during the first half of the twentieth century. It is interesting that he includes a short story that deals with racial prejudice outside of Panama. The addition of "El bombero" as opposed to some of Wilson's other stories, such as "El niño de harina" [The Flour Boy], which deals with racism in Latin America, merely reinforces the myth of racial harmony in Panama. However, even with Jaramillo Levi's reference, Wilson still has not received the recognition that he deserves in his native Panama by literary critics. Much like other Afro-Hispanic writers, Cubena has gained more recognition outside of his *patria* than in his homeland.

Cubena's absence from literary anthologies is important, because they "create and reform canons, establish literary reputations and help institutionalize the national culture, which they reflect" (Mujica 203–4). Wilson's sharp criticism of Panama for its discrimination of West Indians and his "unapologetic didacticism," in the words of Jackson, clearly contributed to his lack of inclusion (*Black Writers and the Hispanic Canon* 79). Cubena's exclusion from Latin American literary canons is similar to that of other Afro-Hispanic writers in their native countries. Several studies have noted that Nicomedes Santa Cruz's exclusion from the Peruvian literary canon is race based and reflects the country's unwillingness to confront racial issues and its own black population (Ojeda 11; Jackson, *Black Writers and the Hispanic Canon* 100). I contend that Wilson's omission from the Panamanian literary canon is because his texts reveal decades of discrimination toward Afro-descendants and West Indians in Panama who helped shape the nation pre- and post-emancipation.

Cubena's Trilogy and the Canon

In the United States, Cubena's works have appeared in the Afro-Hispanic anthologies *Afro-Hispanic Literature: An Anthology of Hispanic Writers of African Ancestry* (1991) and *An English Anthology of Afro-Hispanic Writers of the Twentieth Century* (1995). Several monographs, articles, and dissertations have been written about Wilson's works, many of which I referenced in the introduction. However, the initial studies by Jackson and Smart helped congeal Wilson's canonical status as a must-read by any scholar of Afro-Hispanic studies. Jackson's analysis of Cubena's works in *Black Writers in Latin America*, published two years after the appearance of his collection of poetry and short stories in 1979, made everyone want to read the works of the new writer who professed a "West Indian rage," as Jackson characterized him. Five years later, Smart's groundbreaking text *Central American Writers of West Indian Origin* (1984) solidified Wilson as a West Indian who writes in Spanish, ranking him along with the Costa Rican Quince Duncan and Wilson's own compatriot Gerardo Maloney. Nearly two decades after his initial publication on Cubena, Jackson sealed the author's canonical status by including him in *Black Writers and the Hispanic Canon* (1997), which argues why fifteen writers of African descent should be a part of the Hispanic canon. Jackson's criteria for incorporating these writers into the Hispanic canon is both informative and descriptive. He notes, "I am only concerned, as in my previous work, with what Hispanic literature—and in particular, Black Hispanic literature—tells us about Blacks, about how we should treat others, and about how it can help us live our lives" (*Black Writers and the Hispanic Canon* xiii). In other words, Wilson was included for what he can inform us about what it means to be black and West Indian in Panama. Several other monographs have conveyed Wilson's importance in the field of Afro-Hispanic studies, including the previously mentioned books by Birmingham-Pokorny, Smart, and Zoggyie. Edison's doctoral dissertation, "The Afro-Caribbean Novels of Resistance of Alejo Carpentier, Quince Duncan, Carlos Guillermo Wilson, and Manuel Zapata Olivella," reads Wilson's works along with those of other Afro-Hispanic novelists. Finally, his works are offered in translation. Smart's translation of *Cuentos del negro Cubena: Pensamiento afro-panameño* [Short Stories by Cubena] (1987) ensured that his poems would be read by the English-speaking public. Needless to say, his works are well respected in the field of Afro-Hispanic studies by academics outside of his native Panama.

Wilson's mission to incorporate blackness, and specifically the West Indian experience, have contributed to his lack of recognition in Panamanian literary circles. Because West Indians were denigrated and portrayed negatively in Panamanian literature, Wilson's primary objective has been to redeem the literary image of the West Indian who was excluded from the Panamanian nation-building project. Wilson is committed to telling the untold story, revising history, and changing the perception of the West Indian that has been presented in Panamanian literature. Thus, he challenges national myths propagated during early twentieth-century Panama by presenting the West Indian as the central protagonist and, in turn, resignifies the national myth of Panama as Hispanic, Catholic, and Spanish speaking. Wilson's primary mission in writing is to bring awareness to the historical and cultural contributions of Afro-descendants in Panama, because they have been excluded from literary and historical texts, an oversight that he made known in his literary review essay "Sinopsis de la poesía afro-panameña" [Synopsis of Afro-Panamanian Poetry]. Wilson observed, "Llama la atención el hecho de que textos oficiales de la historia de Panamá hagan ocaso omiso de la presencia y sobre todo, del importante aporte de la gente de ascendencia Africana en Panamá" [It is notable that official texts about Panamanian history omit the presence and, above all, the important contribution of people of African descent in Panama] ("Sinopsis" 14). Wilson's novels aim to correct this historical omission.

In *Confronting Our Canons: Spanish and Latin American Studies in the 21st Century* (2010), Brown examined four intrinsic factors that lead to the canonization of works: a work's place in literary history as exemplary of something that is valued, its informative content, its perceived aesthetic superiority, and its ability to entertain or move the reader (144). Often, Afro-Hispanic writers are excluded from the canon because their texts do not fit into the established literary currents, and it remains difficult to read them along with other masters of the genre. Ojeda and Jackson have cited this as one possible reason for Santa Cruz's omission from the Peruvian canon. Thus, the place of Afro-Hispanic writers in literary history is difficult to solidify. Cubena himself noted in an interview, "Muy poca atención le he prestado al cosmopolitismo, cubismo, surrealismo, neorrealismo y otras técnicas del boom de la narrativa moderna, porque en mis obras lo más importante no es la experimentación, sino el mensaje que se pone de relieve en cuanto a la herencia de la africana en Latinoamérica" [I have given very little attention to cosmopolitism, cubism, surrealism, neorealism, and other boom literary techniques of modern narrative, because in my works what is most important is not experimentation but the message put forth about African heritage in Latin America] (Seales Soley 69). However, I along with other critics would argue that Afro-Hispanic texts can be read as exemplary of certain literary currents. In *Manuel Zapata Olivella and the "Darkening" of Latin American Literature*, Tillis analyzed the works of Zapata Olivella as exemplary of the boom novel that surged in Latin America during the 1960s (45). Tillis argued that Zapata Olivella's 1960s novels *La Calle 10* [Tenth Street], *En Chimá nace un santo* [A Saint Is Born in Chimá], and *Chambacú, corral de negros* [Chambacú, Black Ghetto] all possess "plots structured around incidents outside the Spanish-speaking world," a motif that unified boom novels (*Manuel Zapata* 45). Like the works of Gabriel García Márquez, Carlos Fuentes, and other boom writers, Zapata Olivella's works embody many boom aesthetics, such as experimental language, magical realism, and interior monologue. Likewise, Mosby found that many of Afro–Costa Rican Quince Duncan's novels stylistically possess innovative narrative techniques associated with the boom (121).[2] However, neither these novels nor their authors form part of the Hispanic canon.

The aesthetic superiority of a work and its ability to entertain are highly subjective and "poorly defined," as Brown suggests

(156). Nevertheless, "one indisputable requirement for canonicity is that a work of literature must be perceived as artistically superior" (Brown 156). In the past, works by black writers have been excluded for their unaesthetic appeal, meaning that they were either not written well or it was difficult to read them along with other canonical texts (because many Afro-Hispanic novels deal with the topic of racism against blacks in Latin America, it is often desirable to not analyze them with other canonical Latin American texts). However, the fact that the works were written by black writers may have been enough to exclude them. Quince Duncan proved this decades ago, in 1978, when he submitted his novel *Final de calle* [End of the Road] anonymously to be judged for the Aquileo J. Echevarría Prize, which is sponsored by Editorial Costa Rica. Duncan won. Clearly, his anonymous submission precluded any preconceived bias that may have hindered judges in their reading of his novel.

Many scholars have praised Wilson's works for their readability, use of humor and satire, and thus ability to move the reader. In the preface to *Sueños compartidos*, Jaramillo Levi noted that the criteria used for the selection of the writers and the short stories was "la búsqueda de calidad literaria" [the search for literary quality], which would apply to Wilson's selected work (xiv). Speaking of *Chombo*, Jackson noted, "the strength of *Chombo* lies in Cubena's well-defined characters" (*Black Literature and Humanism* 73). When discussing Wilson's short stories, Jackson indicated that Cubena "is an excellent storyteller who brings the reader quickly to the central focus of his tales, which almost always are on black awareness. If graphic inventiveness characterizes much of his poetry his stories are characterized by and punctuated with a final punch line worth almost as much as the entire story in its telling intensity" (*Black Writers in Latin America* 189). Wilson achieves this through the use of repetition, alliteration, humor, satire, and metonymy, which together make for a rich reading of the African Diaspora experience. Needless to say, Wilson's works are well written and of high literary quality.

Despite the fact that Wilson's literary works are well written, it is not my intention to argue the perceived aesthetic value of his novels. As Jackson informs us, "The very discovery of a black text makes it a readable item, and every critical reading, whether intentionally or not, is a celebration of the text's existence" (*Black Writers and the Hispanic Canon 5*). Thus, Wilson's works merit entry into the canon for not only how they are written but also for what they tell us about the black experience in Panama. I agree with Brown, who asserts that a "text that is valued for its informative content can . . . transmit knowledge about culture, history, the human experience, politics, ethics, and/or marginalized groups and minorities" (149). Wilson's novels, the focus of this chapter, inform us about the Afro-Panamanian experience and what it means to be black in a nation that is constructed around whiteness and, most important, nonblackness. His novels also exemplify what it means to be black and English-speaking in a nation of Spanish speakers. Finally, his works provide historical information not only on Panamanians and West Indians but also on African descendants throughout the diaspora. The content of his novels transmit knowledge about history, literature, culture, politics, and the marginalization of blacks in the New World, and specifically in Panama, where color, complexion, and culture are intricate.

In "*The Grandchildren of Felicidad Dolores* and the Contemporary Afro-Hispanic Historical Novel: A New Reading," I pointed out aspects of the Afro-Hispanic historical novel in Cubena's work *The Grandchildren*. I previously defined the Afro-Hispanic historical novel as "any novel written by a Spanish-speaking writer of African descent that reconstructs the past and incorporates historical vestiges with the aim to revise history" (Watson, "Changó" 72). The five characteristics of the Afro-Hispanic historical novel include orality, slavery and/or Middle Passage, historical revisionism, the incorporation of historical figures, and Afro-realism.[3] The Afro-Hispanic historical novel incorporates black Hispanics into the national dialogue on race, ethnicity, and identity. Afro-Hispanic writers emend historical omissions of African descendants from precolonialism to the present by appropriating an Afro-centered perspective. It is my intention not to analyze Cubena's trilogy as Afro-Hispanic historical novels, but instead to discuss how it merits entry into the Panamanian literary canon. Many aspects of the Afro-Hispanic historical novel inherent in Wilson's trilogy make his novels innovative, informative, and in my estimation, canonical. Wilson's novels rewrite, revise, and reinterpret the black experience from an Afrocentric vantage point. He achieves this historical revisionism through a diasporic focus that constitutes the Afro-American experience. As historical texts, the novels blend elements of fiction and reality to re-create the black experience. The novels become official textbooks of the Panamanian West Indian experience that contest falsehoods (e.g., West Indian antinationalism and cultural and linguistic incompatibility) propagated during the nation-building project (1880–1920).

Construction of an African Identity

The trilogy possesses a diaspora consciousness and incorporates thematically and structurally an African-derived consciousness. His novels render an Afrocentric approach to the re-creation of events and (re)position blacks and Africans within their native ancestral territory. This approach allows Wilson to (re)write, (re) interpret, and (re)analyze history from an Afrocentric perspective, defined as "placing African ideals at the center of any analysis that involves African culture and behavior" (Asante, *Afrocentric Idea* 6). Afrocentrism recognizes that the black experience in the Americas is a product of African history and culture, and it views the discourse of African descendants within this context and critical framework. In other words, for black writers and critics, Africa becomes the subject to be explored and analyzed, not an object to be exoticized. Afrocentrism has evolved since the 1960s as a critical tool for analyzing the black experience throughout the diaspora, and it is distinguished by the group's ties to Africa, their shared history of slavery, and experience with racism. However, the term *Afrocentrism* was popularized by Asante in 1980 with the publication of *Afrocentricity: The Theory of Social Change*, in which the author argues for the "centrality of Africans in post-modern history" (6). With respect to Afro-Hispanic criticism, Jackson's *Black Writers in Latin America* (1979), which responded to the "boom" of the study of black writing in Latin America during the 1970s, is one of the first major books to employ an Afrocentric theoretical framework as a critical tool for analyzing black writing in the Spanish-speaking Americas.[4] As Jackson explains, *Black Writers in Latin America* focuses "on the development of black self-awareness or the black as author from the controlled expression of the black writer of slavery times to the more assertive and aggressive black literature of our day" (xi). Smart continues this quest in *Amazing Connections: Kemet to Hispanophone Africana Literature* (1996), which utilizes an Afrocentric framework to discuss the writings of Duncan and Zapata Olivella and the "amazing connections" between Africa and the Spanish-speaking Americas, which are primarily rooted in religion. Although this perspective is beyond the focus of this study, Smart's analysis illustrates the importance of developing new tools to analyze what he calls "Hispanophone Africana literature" (*Amazing Connections* 4). Wilson constructs an African identity in his novels through a nonlinear structure, which defies European chronological time, and the construction of a matrilineal heritage originating in Africa, while also relating the diaspora figure's experience of displacement.

It was Wilson's interest in his African heritage that compelled him to take on the pen name "Cubena," the Hispanicized version of *Kwabena*, which is the Twi word for "Tuesday" in the Ashanti culture of Ghana. Born on a Tuesday, Wilson assumed the name *Cubena* because the Ashanti people of the Twi language have the custom of naming the male child according to the name of the day on which they are born. At the beginning of each of his literary works, the shield "Escudo Cubena" appears, with a seven-link chain, seven stars, a bee on top of a turtle, and a book, all followed by an explanation of their significance. Wilson explains that the seven-link chain represents the African cultures that were enslaved in the Americas; the seven stars represent regions where most Africans were enslaved, including Brazil, Cuba and Puerto Rico, Jamaica and Martinique, Panama, Peru and Ecuador, the Dominican Republic and Haiti, and Venezuela and Colombia; the bee represents the chains, lashings, injustices, and insults that Afro-descendant populations have suffered since 1492; the turtle symbolizes the type of character that Africans have developed during their odyssey throughout the Americas; and the book is a symbol of the principal tool used to combat mental slavery: education.

This shield is extremely important because it connects the author and his works to other displaced cultures of the African Diaspora. Wilson does not limit his experiences of exile and displacement to the Caribbean or to Panama, and he understands that it is one shared by other diaspora figures who are victims of dispersion and fragmentation caused by (neo)colonialism. In other words, Wilson demonstrates a diaspora consciousness that characterizes "displaced peoples [who] feel (maintain, receive, invent) a connection with a prior home" (Clifford 310). Wilson's identification with the diaspora resists Westerman's assimilation thesis, because Wilson remains connected to not only his Caribbean ancestry but also Africa. Whether real or imaginary, his ties to Africa can be easily interpreted as antinationalist. However, even though he resides in the United States, Wilson maintains his multiple allegiances to the Caribbean, Africa, and Panama. The shield that precedes each of his novels forecasts the Afrocentric focus of each narrative.

Chombo

The entire action of *Chombo* takes place in the background of the formal signing of the Torrijos-Carter Treaty in 1977. The title of the novel, *Chombo*, is a term of disrespect, of unknown origin, used against West Indians in Panama that evokes years of degradation and personal suffering. Similar to other terms used against West Indians, such as *jumeco*, derived from *Jamaican*, the term *chombo* can also carry positive connotations depending on the message and the messenger. Although the usage of the term by non–West Indian Panamanians is overwhelmingly negative, Wilson appropriates the dissenting image by naming his text *Chombo*. *Chombos* are the center of the action, and as a *chombo* himself, Wilson takes ownership of the expression and uses it to convey that West Indians in Panama are not ignorant, lazy, promiscuous, or uncouth. Instead, he makes it known that they are descendants of kings and queens who originated in Africa, survived slavery, and constructed the railroad and Panama Canal. *Chombo* narrates the history of the arrival of James Duglin (Papá James) and Nenén to Panama from Barbados and Jamaica; the story is told by an omniscient narrator, family members, and ancestors. The story begins with the main character Litó (Nicolás), a descendant of black West Indians who has recently returned to Panama from the United States. The signing of the treaty leads Litó and his mother to recall the history and the struggles of West Indians in Panama.

Their narrative focuses on a story about three gold bracelets that they trace to the arrival of West Indians to Panama. The bracelets appear and reappear throughout, and they evoke the history of Papá James and Nenén, Litó's grandparents who helped construct the Panama Canal. Nenén dies at the end of the novel, ironically before her voyage back to Jamaica. Finally, the characters discover that the three gold bracelets, which can be inherited only by female descendants of Nenén, have followed these generations of Afro-Panamanians from Africa to the West Indies to Panama.

Los nietos de Felicidad Dolores

The action of *Los nietos de Felicidad Dolores* (1991) commences in a U.S. airport in 1999 (the future), where West Indian descendants are reunited to return to Panama. For their pilgrimage, the families board a plane, and the narrator reminisces about Africa and reconstructs the arrival of blacks to Spain and the New World. Ironically, these Africans in Spain are related to the same West Indian "diggers" who constructed the Panama Canal, and thus they bring into question the extent to which West Indians are culturally different from Afro-Hispanics in Panama. The action of the novel advances to 1850, the year that the Panama Railroad was constructed, and it tackles the prejudices of two Panamanian families, those of Juan Moreno and John Brown, who are Afro-Hispanic and West Indian, respectively. The subsequent chapters of the novel deal with these families' prejudices toward one another, particularly those of Moreno, which are passed on to their descendants and prevent a romantic relationship between their children. The action then moves to 1941, the year when thousands of West Indians were asked either to adopt the native language of Panama or to leave. Throughout the novel, the characters attempt to discover the meaning of the word *sodinu*, which is *unidos*, or "united," in Spanish spelled backward. Because of the cultural fragmentation of the characters, they are unable to decipher the meaning of the word. Instead, Wilson, the author, inserts himself in the text and explains the meaning of *sodinu* in a letter in which he relates that Afro–Latin Americans are now united and, in fact, have always been, since the beginning of time.

La misión secreta

La misión secreta continues the cycle of Panamanian migration and history. There are several intercalated narratives in *La misión*. It tells the story of Papimambí, a black professor in California who teaches Afro-Hispanic and Hispanic Caribbean literature (strikingly similar to Cubena, the author). A descendant of West Indian immigrants and Felicidad Dolores, he longs to return to Panama for the hundred-year anniversary of the completion of the Canal in 2014. The novel could have easily been called *Sueños ancestrales* [Ancestral Dreams], because it combines Papimambí's dreams about his past African ancestors with events of the present. In these dreams he relives Afro-American history, literature, and culture. The story of Papimambí, his students, and the minor references to his former girlfriend Rosa serve as a conduit for Wilson to tell the real narrative, that of Afro-descendants in the Americas. Papimambí inherits the past through dreams and ethnic memory, which help him to recall the contributions of black slaves and conquistadors such as Estebanico, Juan Valiente, Nuflo de Olano, and Juan Garrido, who all inherit the secret mission. Specifically, the mission is passed from the African Obadelé (baptized in the New World as Juan Garrido) to future descendants of Felicidad Dolores. Both Juan Garrido and Papimambí are descendants of the African general Tarik, thus linking them to the African Diaspora. Garrido's secret mission is to protect four children—Bayano, Luis de Mozambique, Antón Mandinga, and Felipillo—all Afro-Panamanian maroons. Garrido must destroy and burn the colonialists' white bags in Santo Domingo to prevent the secret revenge of the Catholic monarchy: the enslavement of millions of Africans. The runaway slaves are essential to the survival of African descendants, freedom fighters, and all the black revolutions in the New World: the Haitian Revolution, the Independent Colored Party, and black participation in Cuban independence. The realization of these missions will allow them to achieve the final mission, to gain Afro-diasporic unity. In Cubena fashion, the novel ends on a positive note with the union of Afro-descendants throughout the African Diaspora.

Each novel possesses an Afrocentric perspective, and the structure of each reflects this perspective. *Chombo* is divided into seven chapters, each of which corresponds to a different day of the week. The novel begins on the day that Cubena was born, a Tuesday, and the names of the days of week are given in the Twi language of Ghana. Furthermore, an epigraph of a different Afro-Hispanic writer precedes each chapter. In the order that they appear in the novel, they include Spain's Juan Latino, Ecuador's Nelson Estupiñán Bass, Cuba's Nicolás Guillén, Uruguay's Virginia Brindis de Salas, Ecuador's Adalberto Ortiz, Peru's Nicomedes Santa Cruz, and Colombia's Edelma Zapata Olivella. These Afro-Hispanic writers prepare the reader for a voyage back in time. They not only encompass various countries of the African Diaspora but also represent different time periods, ranging from the sixteenth century to the present. Wilson's inclusion of these Afro-Hispanic writers demonstrates the importance of other writers of the African Diaspora and his desire to educate his readership about them.

Wilson further constructs an African identity in *Chombo* by incorporating the three gold bracelets into the story line, which in turn symbolize African heritage in Panama. This origin begins with the woman, and it must continue with her as the bracelets are passed on from generation to generation. The bracelets can be traced back to members of the African tribe Onítefos who were enslaved. Years later the bracelets reappeared in the Great River in Jamaica, and three centuries later they emerged in Panama, having arrived with the West Indian Canal Zone workers. Francis Wilson is a Jamaican descendant of the Onítefo tribe who inherits the bracelets, but she dies in childbirth en route to Panama. These bracelets, as well as the baby, are first discovered by Nenén, who passes them on to her female descendants. Abena Mansa Adesimbo (the daughter of Nenén and Papá James) is the first of Nenén's descendants to inherit them. In effect, the bracelets represent the African heritage that was lost as a result of slavery. In turn, the three gold bracelets become a floating signifier that links all the generations together.

One of Cubena's most compelling arguments and additions to (Afro-)Panamanian literature is his problematization of the Afro-Hispanic and West Indian polemic. *Chombo*'s Karafula Barrescoba is the major exponent of Afro-Hispanic prejudice, and she feels superior to West Indians because "su lengua materna era el castellano, su religión católica, y sobre todo porque el mestizaje le había robado algo de su africanidad" [her native language was Castilian Spanish, her religion Catholic, and above all because race-mixing had robbed some of her Africanness] (65).[5] She decides to hide her blackness so as not to be confused with a West Indian, one of the worst offenses in Panama. Her superiority stems from the ability to trace her lineage to the more Spanish elements of Panama. For example, she raves about being a descendant of blacks who witnessed the decapitation of conquistador Vasco Núñez de Balboa. Moreover, she stresses that she is *morena*, not *negra*, and not an "inferior" black West Indian like Nenén. Karafula abhors her own brother, appropriately named *Carbón*, which means "charcoal," for having nappy hair like the *chombos*. Fearing that his hair will cause others to mistake him for a West Indian, he proclaims in the Santa Ana plaza that he is a *moreno* and not a *chombo* (67).

In *Los nietos*, Wilson constructs an African identity through a nonlinear structure that defies European chronological time, the construction of a matrilineal heritage originating in Africa, and the use of *tremendismo negrista* to relate the horrors of slavery, the Middle Passage, and the exile's experiences of displacement.[6] *Los nietos* points to the contributions of Panamanian West Indians and strengthens unification among African descendants in Panama, one of Wilson's principal goals in his works. As in *Chombo*, form and content complement each other in *Los nietos*; the structure of the novel is cyclical, and it counters European chronological perception of time. There are eight sections in the novel, and three correspond to important Panamanian national historical events: the 1999 ownership of the Canal; the construction of the Panama Railroad; and 1941, the year when West Indians were denied citizenship. *Los nietos* is concerned with restoring Panama's African heritage, and the nonlinear time frame reflects this objective. As Howell suggests, "The lack of uniformity and or structure[] is a metaphor for slavery and the black experience" (41). Clearly, the novel's nonlinear structure reflects the black experience and that of slavery. Similar to slavery, the organization of the novel is chaotic and moves nonlinearly from one era to another. However, Cubena illustrates that, similar to the numerous slaves scattered throughout the diaspora, these characters are related not only through familial ties but also through diasporic ones, because they share a common African heritage. Thus, despite the chaos present in the novel, Cubena illustrates that there is unity among Afro-descendants.

The title of the novel, *Los nietos*, points to the origin of Afro-descended populations of this text who are descendants of Felicidad Dolores. Throughout the novel, she watches over her ancestors whether she is alive (she dies four times) or dead, and she hopes for the unity of all of her progeny. Felicidad Dolores represents Mother Africa, and she is the thread that connects all of the generations present in the novel. As Birmingham-Pokorny suggests: "Indeed, there is no doubt that Felicidad Dolores is the bridge that connects the entire history of the African race, linking the beginning in Africa to the beginning in America, and that as such, she is the future that holds the key that will ensure the future survival of the people of African descendants" ("The Afro-Hispanic" 122). Birmingham-Pokorny is correct in asserting that Wilson has created a new Afro-Hispanic woman in his works. In fact, Wilson resignifies the image of the black woman in Spanish American literature through the figure of Felicidad Dolores. She represents the hope and pain that African-descended populations have suffered and experienced. In addition, she symbolizes the common origin of Afro-Hispanics and West Indians. Instead of being described as Afro-Hispanic or West Indian, she is portrayed as African; as such, Felicidad Dolores is a reminder that colonization hindered the progress and unification of African-descended populations.

Because the four deaths of Felicidad Dolores do not occur chronologically, they reflect the African perception of death. She dies in 1968, 1926, 1955, and 1977. Her deaths correspond to pivotal moments in African American history: the death of Martin Luther King Jr. (1968); the signing of Panama's Law 13, which prevented West Indians from entering the country (1926); the signing of the Remón-Eisenhower Treaty, which resulted in West Indian expulsion from the Canal Zone (1955); and the signing of the Torrijos-Carter Treaty, which caused her final death (1977). Each of these events had a profound impact on the West Indian community in Panama. Wilson's inclusion of Martin Luther King Jr. symbolizes his awareness of other members of the African Diaspora, as well as the influence of the civil rights movement on the West Indian community and Wilson's own experiences in the United States during the 1960s and later. In addition, many West Indians feared that the Torrijos-Carter Treaty would contribute to the loss of jobs for many West Indians in the Canal Zone, as with the passage of the 1955 Remón-Eisenhower Treaty.

Intraethnic Tensions between Afro-Hispanics and West Indians

Wilson's exposure of Afro-Hispanic prejudice toward West Indians rejects the myth of racial solidarity among African-descended populations and illustrates the effect of migration and displacement. As Zoggyie notes: "By portraying this group as allies of the traditional villains, whites, Carlos Wilson not only exposes the magnitude of the problem of race in Panama; he also heightens the victim image he has assigned to the West Indian population" ("Subversive tales" 200). For this reason, Wilson goes to great lengths to trace the lineage of African-descended populations. The Afro-Hispanic and West Indian polemic inherent in *Los nietos* echoes the one in real life between Cubena and Joaquín Beleño, whose works were examined in the previous chapter. A champion of Panama's crusade against imperialism, Beleño vacillated in his characterization of West Indians, presenting the marginalized group as both victim and victimizer. The fact that Beleño's *Gamboa Road Gang* (1961) is required reading in Panamanian schools, and so part of the canon, deeply disturbs Wilson. Wilson reverses the literary and historical discrimination of the West Indian perpetuated by Beleño and the Panamanian nation.

As in *Chombo*, *Los nietos* aims to unite Afro-Hispanics and West Indians, and it brings to light the absurdity of their hatred of one another. This is evidenced by the familial feud between Juan Moreno, an Afro-Hispanic, and John Brown, a West Indian. Juan Moreno and John Brown are neighbors, separated by a room inhabited by Felicidad Dolores. Their names, which are merely Spanish and English translations of each other, represent their similarities in spite of their own perceived cultural and linguistic differences. A fruit salesman, Juan Moreno tries to distinguish himself from West Indians on the basis of his physical appearance. The feud forces Salvadora Brown, John Brown's daughter, to have a clandestine relationship with Aníbal Moreno, Juan Moreno's son. In the second section of *Los nietos*, we discover that West Indians were descendants of blacks in Spain, thus emphasizing their connection to Afro-Hispanics in Panama. Wilson acknowledges the irrationality of the disintegration because these groups of blacks share the common origin of Africa and some distant experiences rooted in a Spanish heritage.

The feud between Juan Moreno and John Brown is ironic because of their similar physical appearance and almost mirror image of each other. Indeed, despite their mutual hatred, their physical likeness astonishes both men: "Pero el día que Juan Moreno se encontró, cara a cara, con John Brown, como quien se espanta de su propia sombra (además del parecido físico y los mismos gestos y ademanes, ambos tenían pantalón remendado con parches de tela de diferentes colores y, curiosamente, del mismo estilo de costura), en un abrir y cerrar de ojos abandonó la" [But the day that Juan Moreno met face-to-face with John Brown, like someone who becomes frightened by their own shadow (other than the similar physical appearance and the same gestures and moves, both wore their pants patched with different color fabric and curiously with the same style of sewing), and in a split second he vanished] (Wilson, *Los nietos* 120–21). Upon their encounter, it is evident that there is not only a physical connection between the two but also a cultural one. The characters are obviously bonded by their common racial heritage. However, society has forced them to be rivals because John Brown is supposedly culturally incompatible with the Panamanian nation and does not reflect *hispanidad*.

These cultural differences have inspired feuds between the two families and have prevented romantic relationships. For example, a member of the Moreno family, Lesbiaquina Petrablanche de las Nieves de Monte Monarca Moreno, opposes the relationship between her niece Candelaria and the West Indian Guacayarima because it would be "una tremenda vergüenza para la familia Moreno" [a tremendous shame for the Brown family] (Wilson, *Los nietos* 171). Cubena utilizes metonymy to poke fun at the characters and to illustrate their prejudices. The name of the previously mentioned protagonist points not only to her sexuality but also to her obsession with whiteness. Her last name, Petrablanche de Las Nieves de Monte Monarca Moreno [Petrawhite of the Brown Monarch Mountain Snow], incites the reader to associate the character with whiteness and, most important, nonblackness.

The exaggerated length of the name reflects the ignorance of the character and the measures she takes to hide her blackness. Lesbiaquina echoes the beliefs of *Chombo*'s female characters Karafula and Fulabuta. In a conversation with her brother Aníbal Moreno, Lesbiaquina displays her prejudice against the West Indian community: "Nada de gente y mucho menos tan gente. Los chombos son brutos y estúpidos. Como son bembones no pueden leer bien ni pronunciar palabras castellanas y por eso celebran las nuevas leyes que los estúpidos no captan que son leyes para deportarlos. Sí, como tienen el pelo cuzcú y bien duro, la inteligencia no puede entrar en sus cabezas y por eso son brutos" [They aren't people and they are less than human. The *chombos* are unpolished and stupid. Since they are stupid they can neither read well nor pronounce Castilian words and therefore they celebrate the new laws that the stupid ones do not realize exist to deport them. Yes, because their hair is nappy and coarse, they are stupid and therefore unpolished] (Wilson, *Los nietos* 163). Lesbiaquina articulates all the national myths and prejudices of West Indians: their inability to speak fluent Spanish, their lack of intelligence, and their African features. When Aníbal pursues a job and writes on his application that he can speak English, Lesbiaquina is so concerned that others are going to think that he is a *chombo* that she cannot celebrate his accomplishment. She has adopted the national discourse, which designates West Indians and blacks as inferior. Lesbiaquina fails to see that she is denigrating herself when she makes these comments—she, too, is of African descent.

The West Indian population in *Los nietos* contrasts drastically with the color-conscious Afro-Hispanics. Nenén and Papá James are West Indian descendants from Jamaica and Barbados who have survived working on the Canal and confront racism in Panama. Wilson's favorable presentation of West Indians has sparked some criticism, as his texts most often present Afro-Hispanics as villains who help propagate the national anti–West Indian sentiment and racial oppression.[7] However, he seeks not disintegration but rather integration of these two opposing factions. Thus, the novel ends by rejecting the division among blacks in Panama and seeking integration within the black community.

Similar to the other novels of the trilogy, *La misión* aims to teach and realize black unity. It is populated with references to historical figures and events with the aim to reconstruct events of the past and incorporate blacks into history. Jackson was correct when he noted that with *Los nietos*, Cubena picks up where Manuel Zapata Olivella left off with *Changó, el gran putas* [Chango, Great Son of a Bitch] (1983), an Afro-American saga that originates in Africa, traverses Latin America and the Caribbean, and culminates in the United States. When Jackson uttered these comments, Cubena had not completed his trilogy; I would argue that he also continues this saga with *La misión* by incorporating the African Diaspora experience. The African worldview is central to the structure of the novel and the content. The novel vacillates between the past and the present, and between dreams and reality and myth and fiction, to narrate the unofficial story of Afro-descendants in the new world. Unlike the other two novels of the trilogy, *La misión* focuses more on Afro-American history and strays away from the Afro-Hispanic and West Indian polemic and the ills committed against West Indians in Panama. *La misión* revisits and reconstructs several major events in Afro-American history: the role of black conquistadors and black slaves during the Conquest, the Haitian Revolution, black participation in Cuba's struggle for independence, and the immigration of West Indians to Panama. In this respect, the narrative parallels *Changó, el gran putas*, which treats the Haitian Revolution under the leadership of Dutty Boukman and black participation in the nineteenth-century Spanish-American War, among other events. *La misión* encompasses the global and diasporic problem of displacement, disenfranchisement, and discrimination of African descendants. As a professor, Papimambí teaches Afro-Hispanic history, literature, and culture. Clearly, creating an Afrocentric philosophy is central to his pedagogy.

In *La misión*, Wilson incorporates the Garifuna, English-speaking blacks in Honduras who are descendants of African and Carib populations from the Antillean island of St. Vincent (Sieder 235).[8] Prior to their arrival in Honduras, the Garifuna were known as Black Caribs for their mixed African and Amerindian heritage, and they lived for generations as a free people in St. Vincent during the seventeenth and eighteenth centuries (Taylor, *Black Carib* 3–4). However, the 1763 Treaty of Paris, which awarded Britain the island, jeopardized their free status. After decades of struggle with the British, the remaining Black Caribs, roughly two thousand, were transported by British ships to the island of Roatán, off the Caribbean coast of Honduras, in 1797 (Taylor, *Black Carib* 7). The surviving population spread to other Central American regions, including Belize, Guatemala, and Nicaragua.

The population's diasporic and geographic connection to Panama is central to Wilson's message of Afro-diasporic unity. Wilson titles the chapters using numbers (*ában*, one; *biama*, two; *ürüwa*, three; *gádürü*, four; *seingü*, five; *sisi*, six; *sedü*, seven; *widü*, eight; *nefu*, nine; and *disi*, ten) in the Garifuna language and incorporates Garifuna words throughout, exhibiting a connection to other English-speaking Caribbean populations who are displaced in the Spanish-speaking Americas.

The Garifuna culture surfaces in *La misión* through the character of Ugundani Dangriga, one of Papimambí's students. Papimambí speaks to Ugundani in Garifuna, telling him about important events in black history and dispelling myths about Afro-descendants. Ugundani and Papimambí's embrace reflects "el inicio de la unión y la solidaridad de todos los caribeños y latinoamericanos de ascendencia africana: chombos, cocolos, cuculustes, juyungos, pichones, garífunas" [the beginning of the union and solidarity of all Caribbeans and Latin Americans of African descent: *chombos, cocolos, cuculustes, juyungos, pichones, garífunas*],[9] which forecasts the unity among displaced Afro-descendants (Wilson, *La misión* 137). The role of Professor Papimambí is to educate his students about Afro-Hispanic literature and culture, one of the central ways that the text includes historical omissions about Afro-descendants. Papimambí accomplishes this by teaching and mentoring, through a consciously racialized discourse and framework. His course on Latin American civilization not only integrates blacks into its pedagogical framework but also exclusively discusses blacks as agents of conquest. The course is arranged thematically, centering on the Conquest, maroons, the republic, literature, women, and heroes. His inclusion of women and maroons conveys his incorporation of minority voices, and his selection of historical figures conveys that this is not the typical Latin American studies course. When discussing the Conquest, he selects Juan Garrido, Estebanillo (Estebanico), Nuflo de Olano, and Juan Valiente—not Hernán Cortés, the Spanish conquistador of Mexico (Wilson, *La misión* 108). Much like the novel *La misión*, Papimambí's courses privilege the colonized over the colonizers. Thus, the novel is self-reflexive and functions as a metatext rewriting history. Cubena instructs us on how and what to teach. Thus, he de-centers the white Hispanic influence and discourse and re-centers the discussion on blacks.

When he is not teaching, Papimambí is in search of his ancestral ethnic memory. The black slaves and conquistadors Estebanico, Juan Valiente, Juan Garrido, and Nuflo de Olano form part of Papimambí's ancestral dreams. Cubena's incorporation of these figures suggests that "Africans were a ubiquitous and pivotal part of Spanish conquest campaigns in the Americas" (Restall 172). Restall notes that the roles played by people of African descent during the colonial period played out in three overlapping categories: (1) mass slaves shipped from Africa and the Iberian Peninsula and forced to work in labor gangs in the Americas; (2) unarmed auxiliary slaves or servants who served as personal dependents or agents of their Spanish masters; and (3) black conquistadors or armed auxiliary slaves (173–75). Valiente, Estebanico, Garrido, and Nuflo de Olano represent various degrees of these categories. It has been widely acknowledged that Juan Garrido was a black conquistador who participated in the siege of Tenochtitlán in Mexico along with Cortés, but he also participated in the conquests of Puerto Rico, Cuba, Guadeloupe, and Dominica, as well as the "discovery" of Florida (Restall 177). Wilson re-creates an encounter between Garrido and Cortés with humor and satire. On the island of Hispaniola—present-day Haiti and the Dominican Republic—Garrido and Cortés have the following exchange:

No comprendo. Tú no eres esclavo como el negro Estebanillo —comentó Hernán Cortés.
   Yo soy el único heredero del más poderoso reino a orillas del río Nilo y los alrededores del volcán Kilimanjaro —afirmó orgullosamente Juan Garrido.
   Claro. Y yo soy abuelo de los Reyes Católicos.
   Es la verdad. Yo soy el príncipe Obadelé . . .
   Claro. Yo soy tatarabuelo de Cid Campeador.
   Mi padre es . . .
   No entiendo. Tampoco eres negro ladino como Juan Valiente y Nuflo de Olano.
   Soy africano.

¿Qué haces aquí en Santo Domingo?

Además, debo agregar, con mucho orgullo, que soy descendiente del general africano Tarik.

Claro. Y yo soy Jesucristo.

Digo la verdad.

[I do not understand. You're not a black slave like Estebanillo, commented Hernán Cortés.

I am the sole heir of the most powerful kingdom on the banks of the Nile and around the Kilimanjaro volcano, said Juan Garrido proudly.

Sure. And I am the grandfather of the Catholic Kings.

It's true. I am the prince Obadelé . . .

Sure. And I am El Cid's great-grandfather.

My father is . . .

I do not understand. Nor are you a black Ladino like Juan Valiente and Nuflo of Olano.

I am an African.

What are you doing here in Santo Domingo?

And I must add, with great pride, I am a descendant of the African general Tarik.

Sure. And I am Jesus Christ.

I'm telling the truth.] (Wilson, *La misión* 53)

Wilson's use of humor pokes fun at Cortés's ignorance of blacks as agents of conquest. Cortés's astonishment over the presence of black conquistador Garrido reflects that of others who have been unaware of the presence of blacks in the Conquest of the Americas.

Both Juan Garrido and Juan Valiente were "auxiliary to Spaniards" and "agents of colonialism" (Restall 30). Valiente (1505–53) was a black conquistador who played a significant role in the conquest of Chile. Participating in battles against the Araucana Indians in Chile in 1546, Valiente was eventually rewarded for his efforts by the governor of Chile with an estate near the capital of Santiago (Rout 76). Estebanico (1500–39) historically accompanied Pánfilo de Narváez during an eight-year expedition from Florida to Mexico City (76). Nuflo de Olano was an enslaved black conquistador who accompanied Vasco Núñez de Balboa on his trip to Panama in 1513 (Restall 183). Wilson presents slaves not as passive or submissive but as agents of social change and conquest. Much like *Changó, el gran putas*, which captures the experience of slavery in the Americas and Africans' enslavement in Cartagena de Indias, *La misión* revises the literary and historical portrayal of slaves by presenting them as agents of colonialism and social change. In turn, Wilson rewrites and reinterprets the "official" story of the colonization of the Americas.

Each work of the trilogy shares a focus on black negation and denial; *mestizaje negativo*; the incorporation of historical figures, events, and names; the desire to eliminate intraethnic tensions among Afro-Panamanians; and racial improvement through education and not whitening. In effect, Wilson's trilogy "darkens" Panamanian history by focusing on lesser-known historical facts that pertain to those of African ancestry on the Isthmus of Panama. His decreased rage allows him to focus more widely on other Afro-diasporic groups in his trilogy. His last novel centers more on the diaspora experience than the Afro-Panamanian one, illustrating the possible union between Afro-Hispanics and West Indians. *La misión* concludes positively with black diasporic unity and prefigures many events and institutions in Panama that led to this successful integration: Día de la Etnia Negra, the George Washington Westerman Center, the Museo Afro-Antillano, and the Centro de Estudios Afro-Panamaneños. The institution of these cultural centers reflects the black movements that further resolved to forge Afro-Panamanian identity, unity, and diaspora. However, third- and fourth-generation Panamanian West Indian writers convey that the emphasis on Caribbean identity continues to muddle this union.

4

West Indian and Caribbean Consciousness in Works by Melva Lowe de Goodin, Gerardo Maloney, Carlos Guillermo Wilson, and Carlos E. Russell

I am a Panamanian West Indian, racially black, culturally mixed. Because I acknowledge the Caribbean influences, the European influences, the African, and the Latino influences because of living in Panama and the Spanish environment in which I am. Culturally, I know I'm mixed. Racially, I know I'm mixed as well. But I think I project more of an African racial image, so I identify racially as African. But culturally, I say I'm black, Latina . . . uh Caribbean, uh and that's how I . . . In Panama sometimes they call us *Panameños afro antillanos* which is Panamanians of Afro-Caribbean descent. The strongest influences in me are the racial ones. You know, my African past. African in the very broad sense including Africans in the Diaspora Caribbean. Since I spent so much time in the United States and among African Americans there, I identified pretty strongly with the African Americans when I was in the United States. The African dimension is very important in my life.

—Melva Lowe de Goodin, *Voices from Our America*

In Melva Lowe de Goodin's self-portrait, we witness the linguistic and cultural negotiation of identity that plays out in the speaker's mind.[1] In effect, it conveys that her identity formation is shaped simultaneously by ideologies of *mestizaje* and blackness. Her acknowledgment of racial (Africa) and cultural (Spanish) influences and the impact of U.S. racial ideology limit her complete identification as Afro-Panamanian. Moreover, being Afro-Panamanian incorporates all of these identities, ideologies, and influences. Her identification with others of the African Diaspora reflects the multiplicity and, above all, complexity that shapes the Panamanian West Indian community. Lowe de Goodin's racial politics recalls Hall's definition of cultural hybridity and "the process of becoming" (225). Of Panamanian West Indian ancestry, Melva Lowe de Goodin's alignment with the African Diaspora and the racial and political ideology of the United States echoes that of other members of her literary generation: West Indian writers born between 1934 and 1945.[2] It is clear that although these writers identify as Panamanian, their identity politics are rooted in the Caribbean Diaspora.

The writings of Lowe de Goodin, Gerardo Maloney, Carlos "Cubena" Wilson, and Carlos E. Russell exemplify that the Caribbean runs deep in Panama. Their works make clear that cultural hybridities of the Caribbean are plural and often indefinable, as Hall and Gilroy have proved. As writers of West Indian ancestry, their works problematize the British component of the Caribbean because it contests the national foundation of the nation. Moreover, their writings convey the complexities of identity in the West Indian community and in the Afro-Panamanian community at large.

My use of the term *Caribbean* in conjunction with *West Indian* reflects the changing space and place of the identity politics that (re)surface in these subjects' works. The term *Caribbean* possesses myriad interpretations and significations that have been discussed at length. For scholars of Latin America (e.g., Puri), the term *Caribbean* often excludes the Hispanic territories of the Dominican Republic, Puerto Rico, and Cuba. Others have noted how the designation excludes people of African descent (Puri; Tillis). The term *Caribbean* refers to the Anglophone, Francophone, and/or Hispanic archipelago and does not always reference someone of African ancestry, which is why I prefer *West Indian* when speaking of Caribbean descendants in Panama. I employ *West Indian* not only as a marker of black identity but also as an indicator of cultural hybridity and identity that is in the process of becoming, borrowing from Hall. However, West Indian writers in Panama also constitute the broader Caribbean. As Afro–Latin American writers of

Anglophone Caribbean ancestry, Lowe de Goodin, Wilson, Maloney, and Russell add layers to the already problematic racial identity in Panama. In turn, contemporary writers of British Caribbean ancestry challenge dominant discourses of homogeneity and whiteness in a Hispanic colony in favor of a black one that promotes a Caribbean heritage through a consciously racialized discourse. We witnessed this same identity politics in the novels of Wilson, in the previous chapter, who fought to incorporate Panamanian West Indian discourse into the national polity. I argued for Wilson's inclusion into the Panamanian literary canon because of his quest to rewrite Panamanian history and incorporate West Indians; in a separate study, I analyzed the effect of Panamanian *mestizaje* discourse on the black psyche in Wilson's fiction (Watson, "Are Panamanians"). This *mestizaje* discourse divided Afro-Hispanics from West Indians and contributed to intraethnic tensions between the two groups. Wilson's identity politics coincides with that of Lowe de Goodin, Maloney, and Russell in that he illustrates the importance of Panama's Caribbean heritage. Yet he is just as much concerned with educating his Afro-Hispanic brothers and sisters about their heritage and promoting a unified Afro-Panamanian identity. Maloney shares this belief and has participated in black movements in Panama that have helped forge Afro-Panamanian identity. He served as vice president of the first Black Panamanian Congress and president of the Second Congress of Black Cultures of the Americas, and he was creator and member of the Organizational Commission of the Afro-Panamanian Forum. As Smart has observed, Maloney is also a "Caribbean Man"—he served as the permanent representative of the Association of Caribbean States (2006–9) and as Panama's ambassador to Trinidad and Tobago (2005–9). Thus, his recognition as an Afro-Panamanian and his preference to use the term have not at all diminished his Caribbean ancestry, heritage, or pride. In this way, he differs from his contemporary Carlos Russell. While Russell professes a diaspora consciousness and an awareness of other Afro-descended populations, his writings are less concerned with Afro-Hispanic and West Indian unity. Similar to Lowe de Goodin and Wilson, he is a product of Panama and the United States. Thus, he professes a *Pana*-Caribbean consciousness, "meaning the superimposition of Caribbean culture on the Panamanian social matrix" (Russell, *Last Buffalo* 28). For Russell, there is no compromise when it comes to his Caribbean—that is, black—identity. The writings of members of this literary generation invite us to ask: What does it mean to be Caribbean/West Indian and Panamanian? And most important, what impact does Caribbean and West Indian identity have on the forging of Afro-Panamanian unity? Several black movements in Panama have aided in the process of forging Afro-Panamanian identity.

Black Movements in Panama

During the 1970s and 1980s, Panamanians of West Indian descent spearheaded organizations that aimed to resolve racial inequalities in Panama. Although they desired to analyze problems of all blacks and the possibility of the unity of Afro-descendants in Panama, a large number of the issues that arose centered on problems that inflicted the West Indian community. These organizations included Acción Reivindicadora del Negro Panameño [Redemptive Action for the Black Panamanian, or ARENEP], Unión Nacional del Negro Panameño [National Union for the Black Panamanian, or UNNEP], Asociación de Negros Profesionales [Association of Black Professionals, or APODAN], El Centro de Estudios Afro-Panameños [Center for Afro-Panamanian Studies, or CEDEAP], and Sociedad de Amigos del Museo Afroantillano de Panamá [Society of Friends of the West Indian Museum of Panama, or SAMAAP]. Much like U.S. civil rights organizations, these organizations were political in nature and aimed to unite the Afro-Panamanian community and to discuss concerns that affected the population, such as inequality, discrimination, and unemployment. Panamanian West Indians identified with the civil rights movement because of their marginalized situation in Panama, their ability to speak English, and because discrimination in the Canal Zone was based on a polarized racial system modeled after that of the United States. Many other West Indian leaders in Panama were inspired by the civil rights movement's quest for racial equality and its goal to integrate blacks into society. For example, ARENEP sought to eliminate racism in Panama (Maloney, "El movimiento" 151). Afro-Panamanians were not only concerned with national problems; they also participated in and organized forums to resolve issues that other diaspora populations faced. The Second Congress of Black Cultures of the Americas, which took place in Panama in 1980, was organized by CEDEAP. One year later, in 1981, Afro-Panamanians organized their own conference, the First Congress of the Black Panamanian, a forum devoted to studying black contributions to Panama, the black's role in sociopolitical struggles, Canal Zone worker problems, relations between Afro-Panamanians and Panamanians, and West Indian migration to the United States (Maloney, "El movimiento" 155).

Of the organizations previously mentioned, SAMAAP has had the most lasting effect on sustaining Panamanian West Indian culture and heritage. Founded in 1981 to preserve West Indian culture in Panama, SAMAAP secured maintenance and proper funding for the Panamanian West Indian Museum, which retains the history of black Panamanians. Also, SAMAAP sponsors annual celebrations to recognize ethnicity in Panama and the contributions of blacks on the isthmus. Both the museum and SAMAAP ensure that West Indian culture and heritage will be remembered and recognized not only by West Indians but also by non–West Indians in Panama and abroad. Similar to the National Association for the Advancement of Colored People, or NAACP, in the United States, the society also protests racial inequalities and discrimination in Panama, as the Lucy Molinar episode conveyed.[3]

Racial mobilization catapulted during the era of Omar Torrijos (1968–81), and several organizations mobilized to combat racism and discrimination against black Panamanians residing in Panama and abroad. Although his political platform continued to equate Spanish heritage with Panamanian nationality, thereby reinforcing the *mestizaje* rhetoric, the Torrijos regime attempted to attenuate discriminatory practices (Priestley and Barrow 232). Torrijos established the Partido Revolucionario Democrático [Democratic Revolutionary Party] in 1979 and initiated the signing of the Torrijos-Carter Treaty. Because Torrijos represented the masses and not the *rabiblancos*,[4] he excluded the traditional elites from political power and secured support from Panama's rural provinces. He "openly recruited political support among West Indian Panamanians and supported racially defined black mobilization" (Andrews 183). Torrijos's reforms and support for the masses coincided with those made in the Afro-Panamanian community.

His unexpected death in a mysterious plane crash in 1981 convinced his supporters that he was assassinated because of his progressive reforms for underrepresented sectors of the population. Many West Indians, including Maloney, believed that his death would negatively affect the black community, especially under the military dictatorship of Manuel Noriega, which led to the 1989 U.S. invasion of Panama. The invasion disproportionately affected the brown and black populations of El Chorrillo, Colón, and San Miguelito (Priestley and Barrow 232).

The changing platforms of black organizations and movements convey the various ways that organizations struggled to forge a unified Afro-Panamanian identity. The National Union of Panamanians, the Black Panamanian Recovery Action Group, the Association of Professional Workers, and the Twelve all held race-based agendas (Priestley and Barrow 231). By contrast, the Black Panamanian Queen Contest sought to incorporate all minority groups and decided against a strictly race-based agenda. The changing names of the contest best illustrate the problematic of naming and the inclusion of all blacks in Panama. Originally, the West Indian–Panamanian musical group the Exciters called the event the Miss Soul Queen Pageant, reflecting a more U.S.-style identification with blackness (Priestley, "Antillean-Panamanian" 61). The name of the pageant later changed from Miss Soul to Panameñísima Reina Negra [National Panamanian Black Queen] in 1978, which simultaneously embraced black heritage and Panamanian cultural identity. Clearly, there was opposition to the more inclusive label by West Indians abroad, who had adopted a more U.S.-style racial labeling that promoted blackness over cultural identity. West Indians residing in Panama were more willing to accept the label because of their cultural and national affiliation with the nation, whereas West Indians such as Russell rejected the term. This cultural and racial dynamic plays out incisively in the writings of both Maloney and Russell.

Black mobility resurged in 1999 and accomplished a number of gains (Priestley and Barrow 242). The Panamanian Committee Against Racism, under the leadership of attorney and author Alberto Barrow, emerged in 1999 as a pre-new-century organization advocating for civil rights for black Panamanians. Barrow emerged as a leader and spokesperson for the organization, engaging in national public speeches and debates about problems of race, race relations, and racial discrimination (Priestley and Barrow 237). One of the organization's platforms included the "restructuring of the nation-state to reflect the cultural, ethnic, religious, gender, and racial diversity of the nation" (237). The Panamanian Committee foreshadowed the establishment of future organizations in the new millennium, which were designed to bridge gaps among Afro-Hispanics and West Indians and to bring a collective voice of Afro-Panamanian identity to the national forefront.

President Mireya Moscoso approved Día de la Etnia Negra [Black Ethnicity Day] on May 30, 2000, the first time that blackness was recognized in Panama on a national level. Maloney memorializes this national celebration in his poem "Black Awareness Day" (*Street Smart* 102). Día de la Etnia Negra led to the establishment of the Comisión Coordinadora de la Conmemoración del Día de la Etnia Negra Nacional [Coordinating Commission for the Commemoration of National Black Ethnicity Day] (May 30, 2001) to "defend Black rights and challenge the existing racial paradigm" (Priestley, "Antillean-Panamanians" 5). Moscoso also passed the antidiscriminatory Law 16 on April 10, 2002, which "regulates the right of admission to public places," a small feat considering that she is the widow of racist president Arnulfo Arias, who passed several laws that vociferously discriminated against West Indians (Priestley and Barrow 234). The publication of Barrow's *No me pidas una foto: Develando el racismo en Panama* [Don't Request a Photo: Uncovering Racism in Panama] (2001) spearheaded a public debate about racism and centered on the lack of economic opportunities for people of color. One of the debates was fueled by the required photograph on job applications and the requirement that the applicant have "buena presencia" [a nice appearance], code for being white. The book led to a legislative bill requiring that job applications eliminate a photo requirement. Although the bill as written was not passed, in 2005 Law 11 "prohibited discrimination based on race, gender, class, religion or physical challenge" (Priestley and Barrow 243). Thus, the first decade of the new millennium was characterized by black mobilization and black unity, and various organizations (approximately twenty groups) were formed under the umbrella organization National Committee of Black Panamanian Organizations (242).

This committee was formed in 2004 and consisted of organizations from various black provinces and multiple diverse groups, including women and Rastafarians. The organization's primary goal was to weaken strained relations between West Indians and Afro-Hispanics, as well as divisions among the West Indian community abroad and in Panama. These political movements serve as a backdrop to the writings of Lowe de Goodin, Wilson, Maloney, and Russell: Not only do they shape their perspectives and ideologies, the writers themselves served as agents of black mobilization.

Melva Lowe de Goodin: A Female Perspective on West Indian Identity Politics

As one of Panama's few published West Indian female writers, Melva Lowe de Goodin (b. 1945) fills a void not only in the field of Afro-Panamanian literature but also in the field of literature written by Afro-Panamanian women. In *Afrodescendientes en el Istmo de Panamá, 1501–2012* [Afro-Descendants on the Isthmus of Panamá, 1501–2012], a biographical and historical compilation of Afro-descendants in Panama, Lowe de Goodin notes the dearth of information on the historical contributions of women of African descendant in the isthmus (67). However, Lowe de Goodin is not merely concerned with representing women of color in Panama; she explores the lives of all Panamanian West Indians in her work. In addition to her activism as a founding member of SAMAAP (1980) and as the organization's first president (1981), Lowe de Goodin is not only a writer, but she has also shaped much of the political activism in Panama during the latter part of the twentieth century. As the epigraph that precedes this chapter attests, the United States has shaped her identity politics just as much as her experiences living as black in a Hispanic nation. She received her bachelor of arts degree in English from Connecticut College, followed by a master of arts in English from the University of Wisconsin. She obtained both degrees during the late 1960s and early 1970s, decades marked by racial strife in the United States. Lowe de Goodin's experiences in the United States, coupled with her upbringing in the Canal Zone, have clearly shaped her racial identity politics as a black female West Indian in Panama.

Lowe de Goodin entered the literary sphere with the publication of her work *De/From Barbados a/to Panamá* (1999), a historical drama that reconstructs the migration of West Indian immigrants in 1909 to the isthmus during the construction of the Panama Canal. Lowe de Goodin resurrects the forgotten story of West Indian Canal workers that is absent from Panamanian national history. *De/From Barbados* is a relatively short drama, consisting of fifty-eight pages, seventeen scenes (including a prologue and an epilogue), and one act, yet it is filled with a lifetime of memories. Performed in 1985 and 1997 and published in 1999, this play promotes ethnic awareness and pride for a population once denigrated for its "incompatibility" with the Hispanic nation.

The scenes in *De/From Barbados* alternate between the present and the past, and between Spanish and English-based Creole. The drama begins in the present with Manuelita Martin, a secondary student descended from West Indians who is assigned to write an essay on the Panama Canal in celebration of its anniversary. She decides to write a report on the West Indian diggers, realizing that most of her peers will probably document the narratives of John Stevens or George Goethals, the engineers of the Canal. Her mother is elated and suggests that she write about Manuelita's paternal great-grandparents, Abuela Leah and Abuelo Samuel, whom her husband Jorge has invited to come spend the weekend with them. Through the memories of Abuelo Samuel and Abuela Leah, *De/From Barbados* relates the narrative of three friends, Samuel, James, and George, and their decision to leave their native home of Barbados for economic prosperity in Panama. James and George both die while working on the Canal, leaving Samuel and Leah, a Martinican washerwoman whom he marries, to pass their story down to Manuelita to be recorded in Panamanian national history.

The drama conveys the disjunction between third- and fourth-generation West Indians (the parents and grandparents) and the student Manuelita, who strive to communicate. The author utilizes oral history, Caribbean music, and flashback to re-create the immigrants' arrival to Panama. The play begins with the female protagonist, Manuelita, having a discussion with her mother, Violeta, about the West Indian contributions of the Canal. Manuelita's mother commences to tell her about the suffering that West Indians experienced and other unknown facts about West Indian Canal

Zone workers. The conversation between Manuelita and Violeta underlines the importance of women in the role of storytelling and the transmission of history. Often these stories remain outside of the historical archives that promote national narratives of heroism. The play is filled with reminders of Panamanian West Indian heritage that "speaks" to West Indians in Panama and abroad and educates non–West Indians about the nation's forgotten and untold story. In this way, Lowe de Goodin's historical drama reverberates many of the themes of Wilson's novels, which both authors incorporate to re-create black Panamanian history: West Indian exclusion, racial and linguistic discrimination, and black denial. Similar to Wilson, who "rewrote" Panamanian national history in his historical trilogy, Lowe de Goodin "attempts to rectify omissions of the contributions of West Indian workers to the canal and national identity within Panamanian history" (Zien 301).

De/From Barbados "rectifies omissions" by dispelling myths about West Indian Canal Zone workers and immigrants. One of the myths is that all West Indian workers were Jamaican. The drama dispels this national belief by citing the origin of arrival as Barbados instead of the commonly asserted Jamaica. Although more than 84,000 Jamaicans migrated to Panama to work on the French Canal, an additional 19,900 emigrated from Barbados to complete the Canal from 1904 to 1914.

The attitudes of the characters in the play mirror these national beliefs. After listening to Manuelita's story, her teacher observed, "Esta composición tuya me ha abierto los ojos a todos los sufrimientos del grupo afroantillano en la construcción del Canal. Pero tengo una inquietud. Yo pensé que casi todos habían venido de Jamaica porque como en Panamá le decimos 'jamaicanos' o 'jamaiquinos' a todos los afroantillanos" [Your composition has opened my eyes to all the sufferings of the Afro-Antillean group in the building of the Canal. But I have a concern. I thought most of them had come from Jamaica because in Panama we say 'Jamaicans' for all Afro-Antilleans] (Lowe de Goodin, *De/From Barbados* 27). Manuelita further dismisses this assumption by responding, "Para el Canal Francés, la mayoría vino de Jamaica, pero para el Canal Americano, la gran mayoría fueron contratados de Barbados" [For the French Canal, the majority came from Jamaica, but for the American Canal, the majority were contracted from Barbados] (Lowe de Goodin, *De/From Barbados* 27). Pupil Manuelita becomes the authority on the understudied minority population, thus reversing the role of teacher and student and further illuminating the lack of knowledge about West Indians in the nation. Manuelita's teacher clearly symbolizes other Panamanians who are ignorant of the West Indian population. Indeed, Manuelita "demonstrates a superior style of pedagogy" by educating her teacher and classmates (Zien 303).

A West Indian Caribbean consciousness permeates the entire drama through the integration of dialect, food, music, and ethnic memory. *De/From Barbados* incorporates West Indian music that embodies the Caribbean Basin: "West Indian Man" (Rubén Blades), "Colón Man" (author unknown), "Day-O (Banana Boat Song)" (Harry Belafonte), "Matilda" (Harry Belafonte), and "No Woman, No Cry" (Bob Marley). The songs function to create what Nwankwo calls "common memory" between the West Indian protagonists and the viewers and readers, who may or may not share the same experiences (3).[5]

Lowe de Goodin weaves the lyric "Colón Man" into the drama as the central protagonists Samuel and Leah recall memories of men returning to their native Barbados and Martinique with symbols of Panama Canal success: gold teeth, gold chains, and simply gold. Their recollection of these "Colón men" incites Leah to bellow out a portion of the song: "One, two, three, four / Colón man a come . . . With him gold chain" (Lowe de Goodin, *De/From Barbados* 10).

"Colón man" was the name "given to Caribbean laborers who travelled to work on Panama's railroad and Canal" (Frederick 13). The "Colón man" is a metaphor for the West Indian worker who migrated to Panama for economic prosperity. He entails the spirit behind the desire for the West Indian immigrant in search of gold and other emblems of success and wealth. It is no surprise then that the "Colón man" is a trope that runs throughout Anglophone Caribbean fiction, reflecting the migration and return of numerous West Indians to Panama and back.[6] Frederick observes, "The fictive Colón Man can be identified by his migration-forged masculinity, cocky attitude, material possessions, broadened worldview, and sometimes his work-related illnesses" (5). The protagonists Samuel, George, and James are also "Colón men" who migrated to Panama in search of good fortune. Underemployment, low wages, and overpopulation in the Caribbean motivated them to embark on the journey from the islands to Panama (Frederick 40). Although some "Colón men" returned home with emblems of their success and sent remittances to their loved ones, many others, such as the protagonists James and George, lost their lives to illness or injury in pursuit of prosperity.

Blades's "West Indian Man" (1992) narrates the travails of West Indian Canal Zone workers upon their arrival to Panama and paints a harsh portrait of the "Colón man." Blades dedicated the lyrics to Colón, Bocas del Toro, and Río Abajo in Panama, all areas that manifest a West Indian consciousness across the isthmus. "Came from the sea, to Panamá / to work in the jungle and build the canal / He got paid in silver, the white man in gold, / and the yellow fever took everyone's soul" (Blades). The song opens the historical drama and simultaneously informs the viewer and reader of the collective West Indian experience and the personal narrative of singer-songwriter Rubén Blades. Blades's paternal grandfather, of the same name, was an English-speaking native of St. Lucia who migrated to Panama.[7] Notwithstanding Blades's personal history, the lyrics inform the listener of West Indian hardship, discrimination, and identity formation. They convey that the West Indian experience is an integral part of the Panamanian one, impeding the separation of the two. The song references countries of the Anglophone and Francophone Caribbean, thereby connecting Panama to its Caribbean consciousness. By the end of the song, the West Indian man has become a symbol of the songwriter's personal history as well as an emblem of Panamanian nation building.

Harry Belafonte's popular song "Day-O" has national and international implications and reconstructs a Caribbean identity in the very North American Canal Zone. Widely known throughout the Western Hemisphere, the song reverberates West Indian, and by extension, Caribbean, identity. In the same fashion, his calypso "Matilda" (1953) is a metaphor of the economic hardship of the "Colón man." The song laments the story of a woman who took a man for all his pennies and echoes the trials and tribulations of the play's character George, who is duped by a prostitute (Matilda) who robs him of his earnings. "Matilda" is a marker "of cultural identity and belonging" and transports the reader and viewer to the West Indies (Rahim 285). In her study on calypsos, Rahim suggests that in narratives, calypsos "operate as an important indicator of identity and as a means of bridging the gap with home" (285). This applies to Lowe de Goodin's drama *De/From Barbados*. In the dramatized version of the play, the scene between Matilda and George closes with the prostitute dancing to the song, thus reinforcing that the earnings of the "Colón man" were often ephemeral. In this fashion, the calypso serves to re-create common memory, community, and a sense of belonging, and it bridges the cultural and geographical gap between Panama and the West Indies. The songs, coupled with the interplay of other reminders of West Indian culture, such as food (codfish with rice, coconut, and *guandu* beans) and moss drink (a nutritional drink also known as an aphrodisiac), re-create the Caribbean in the Canal Zone.

Lowe de Goodin's drama reveals the author's identity politics as black, female, West Indian, and Caribbean. The protagonists' journey represents the collective experience in Panama of West Indians who migrated to the isthmus for economic prosperity. Lowe de Goodin bridges a historical, linguistic, and cultural gap between the Caribbean and Panama through language and memory, conveying that the protagonists share a common ancestry.

Street Smart: Poems by Gerardo Maloney

Born in Panama City in 1945, Gerardo Maloney is a prominent Panamanian West Indian poet, essayist, filmmaker, and sociologist. Maloney earned his bachelor of arts degree from the prestigious Universidad Nacional Autónoma de México [National Autonomous University of Mexico] and his master of arts in sociology from the Facultad Latinoamericana de Ciencias Sociales [Latin American Department of Social Sciences] in Quito. He served as president of the second Congress of Black Cultures of the Americas, director of the Department of Sociology at the University of Panama in Panama City, and honorary president of the Black Panamanian Congress. From 1994 to 1999, he served as general director of Channel 11, Panama's educational radio and television station. He also documented West Indian experiences in the films *Los del Silver Roll* [Silver Roll People], *Calypso*, and *Tambo Jazz*. *Calypso*

(1991) documented Panamanian music and included a panel discussion on Afro-Panamanian music and literature; it became a major source for artists of the genre *reggae en español* [Spanish reggae] in Panama.[8] In addition, he has published numerous articles and essays about the problems faced by blacks in Panama, Ecuador, the United States, Costa Rica, and Brazil. Needless to say, Maloney is a scholar not only of Afro-Panama but also of the Americas. Like Wilson, Maloney possesses a diaspora consciousness and portrays the realities of Afro-Panama and the African Diaspora in general. Maloney examines these experiences of the diaspora incisively in his poetry, which includes *Juega vivo* [Get Hip] (1984), *Latidos: Los personajes y los hechos* [Heartbeats: The People and Their Deeds] (1991), and *En tiempo de crisis* [In a Time of Crisis] (1991). The poems of *Juega vivo* have been of much discussion (Smart, *Central American Writers*; Watson, "Are Panamanians"). Recently, Smart published a collection of Maloney's poetry that includes translated poems from *Juega vivo* and additional poems written since 2000. The title of the collection, *Street Smart* (2008), is an updated translation of the term *juega vivo*, which the author originally interpreted as "get hip." It encompasses poems written from the 1980s to the present (Smart, *Central American Writers*). *Street Smart* is composed of four sections—"Staggering Along," "Straightening Our Hair," "Towards Tomorrow," and "The New Century Perspective"—all of which are the focus of this chapter. "Staggering Along," "Straightening Our Hair," and "Towards Tomorrow" were originally published in *Juega vivo* in 1984. The last section, "The New Century Perspective," provides a new-millennium view of Maloney's West Indian consciousness with original poems written since 2000 and his relation to Africa, Panama, and the Caribbean.

Juega vivo was published originally in 1984, the same year as Blas Jiménez's poetry collection *Caribe africano en despertar* [Awakening the Caribbean African], and it possesses identical themes of displacement, dispersion, and disalienation. As Tillis notes, *Caribe africano* was a pivotal work on black Dominican identity, because it "challenges the notions of being Caribbean and African while culminating in the need for an awakening of this consciousness" ("Awakening" 17). In much the same way, Maloney's verses challenge blackness and Caribbeanness in Panama. "Staggering Along" recuperates popular figures from the Panamanian landscape and provides a quotidian view of their experiences. The personage of Aunt May "wept in silence for her homeland now more and more distant" and laments "[n]ow we know we come fi stay," realizing the impossibility of returning home (Maloney, *Street Smart* 27). Aunt May is a metaphor for African Diaspora figures who are dispersed throughout the Atlantic and who long to return home but find it difficult to go back for economic reasons. Aunt May is also a Caribbean figure, a symbol of the ancestral past rooted in the poet-speaker's ancestral ethnic memory. Similar to Miss Inés in the poem "Midday," she had been "eaten up by the years bearing two bitter burdens . . . never having been able to go back home" (Maloney, *Street Smart* 13). Pronounced "Miss Eyenez" in West Indian dialect, the poetic subject is "someone with a long unde-fined longing" (15). This longing for home is a metaphoric one that characterizes the situation of diasporic figures who desire to return to their ancestral territory. But it was also a real one for West Indian immigrants who retained the possibility of returning and were encouraged to repatriate by the Panamanian govern-ment. For Miss Inés, this may not be possible because "the end of her days is nigh" (15).

The poems of "Straightening Our Hair" deal with the loss of black identity, the realization of being black in a white world, and the reconciliation of a black consciousness. Much like the poems of "African," the second part of Jiménez's *Caribe africano*, this sec-tion deals with African identity loss in favor of a white, mestizo, or mulatto identity. When speaking of the poems that constitute "Af-rican," Tillis notes, "The selections that comprise this section attest to the complexities of affirming African ancestry in the Caribbean. Laced with the historical vilification and rejection of Blackness, these poems address the politics of identity construction. Addition-ally, certain poems expose a caste system of race stratification used to exonerate one from proclaiming Blackness" ("Awakening" 24). Tillis's acknowledgment of the loss of an Africanized identity in Jiménez's works is an appropriate evaluation of Maloney's poems in "Straightening Our Hair." This poetics of disalienation plays out in Maloney's poem of identity "Who?" The poet-speaker laments that blacks have whitened themselves and straightened their hair in the quest to assimilate (Maloney, *Street Smart* 89). The theme of *blanqueamiento*, or "whitening," is a trope that runs throughout Latin American literary discourse and prevails in African Diaspora literature, because whitening signifies a loss of African identity in favor of a colonial de-Africanized national identity (Piedra). The whitening was not only physical (hands and hair) but also resulted in an intellectual independence and silencing. In the quest to assimilate or fit in, the African Diaspora figure relinquished his autochthonous heritage. This poem recalls Blas Jiménez's piece "Identification," which conveys how straightening one's hair can lead to whiteness and Caribbean mulattoness. Jiménez notes, "Hair by being different shows personality traits evading Blackness on the road to change and Caribbean mulattoness" (139). In this respect, "straightening our hair" becomes a floating signifier for ethnic, racial, and cultural cleansing that played out in the new world as Caribbean mulattoness, *mestizaje*, and Creolization. Thus, straightening one's hair equates to identity loss and causes the poetic speaker to rhetorically ponder, "Who am I"?

In "Negros civilizados" [Civilized blacks], Maloney points to the fact that blacks, who are now "civilized," have exchanged "wisdom with egoism, virtue with cunning, generosity with smiles, camaraderie with boxed molasses, and bravery with simple-minded aphorisms" (Maloney, *Street Smart* 40). Ironically, whites say that blacks are now civilized because of colonization and slavery (40). Over time, blacks have lost the positive aspects of their culture and traded them for such trivial items as molasses and aphorisms. Through the use of irony and humor, Maloney demeans the colonizers for imposing their culture and value system on blacks and blames them for the African's subsequent loss of pride and self-worth. The title of the poem is both sarcastic and ironic because, according to the poet-speaker, blacks are anything but civilized if their behavior is measured by the present value system. In the end, the poet-speaker denounces European culture for having imposed its value system on blacks, a system that lacks civility for the poet-speaker Maloney.

The subject of "Leader" is astonished when he "got up one morning and discovered that he was black" (Maloney, *Street Smart* 43). The poet-speaker continues, "He went straight to the mirror to rub the sleep from his eyes. . . . He was startled; this was no dream" (43). The leader resembles *Curundú*'s Red Box and

Los cuatro espejos's Charles McForbes, who equally disapproved of their mirror image. While Beleño's Red Box never experienced complete reconciliation with his racial identity, like McForbes, the "leader" has an encounter with a mirror and realizes for the first time that he is black. The leader "experienced for the first time the irony of realizing that he was a Black who had been lost in the clouds of the fantasy of being white" (Maloney, *Street Smart* 43). Both McForbes and the leader embrace their blackness and abandon their disillusionment.

The third section of *Street Smart*, "Towards Tomorrow," provides a road map for the future of African Diaspora figures by recollecting past struggles and providing a collective voice to deal with the erasure of blackness. The poet-speaker incites blacks to act, engage, and invade their territory. The subjects take ownership of their present but do so by first remembering their past. "New Nomads" re-creates the horrific black experience of slavery and exile. Written in the 1970s, "New Nomads" posits the negative side of the Canal, which divided blacks according to color, class, and complexion. The Canal is viewed as a (neo)colonial enclave that contributed to even more racial division and oppression in Panama. Coupled with the inglorious legacy of slavery, the Canal only bolstered racial tensions. In "New Nomads," Maloney returns to Africa, the origin of all blacks, and describes the initial colonization of the Panamanian West Indian. With deception and greed, blacks were forced into slavery and transplanted to unknown regions, which commenced the nomadic experience of the African Diaspora figure. This nomadic experience is not one confined to the individual; the first part of the poem describes the collective African experience as a nomadic one, no doubt shaped by nostalgia, despair, and the effects of colonialism. As evidenced by the use of the first-person plural pronoun *we*, the shared experience of slavery categorizes all diaspora persons. From the common experience of slavery, Maloney moves to the particular experience of the Panamanian West Indian. The Panamanian West Indian experience is more complex, having undergone two stages of colonization: one in the West Indies and the other in Panama. West Indians migrated to Panama in search of more opportunities, only to find a new type of slavery and injustice where workers experienced

U.S. racial segregation and were distinguished by the gold roll and silver roll. Instead of freedom and economic prosperity, they encountered unfair treatment by "new owners" and "new masters" in "new lands." The repetition of *new* reinforces the feeling of exile, rootlessness, and displacement that black diaspora figures collectively endured. Similar to a nomad, the diaspora figure is in search of his or her home and identity. Thus, the poem's multiple references to the nomadic experience and to slavery make it a symbol not only of the Panamanian West Indian experience but also of the diaspora experience, universalizing the plight of the West Indian. Maloney's re-creation of the black experience of the African Diaspora aligns this poem with the novels of his contemporary Wilson, who re-creates the West Indian experience from slavery to New World racism.

"The New Century Perspective" shifts from the Panamanian landscape to the Caribbean one and alternates between the Caribbean Basin and the Isthmus of Panama. The shifting space is geographic and ancestral, and it reflects Maloney's residence in Trinidad as ambassador. Maloney returns to his British Caribbean roots in "The New Century Perspective" both literally and figuratively. In "T & T," an acronym for Trinidad and Tobago, the poet-speaker describes the Caribbean island as "a land flowering with ancestral wisdom . . . enormous creative energy . . . [and] cultural empowerment" (Maloney, *Street Smart* 108). Despite its geographic and cultural exploitation, the poet-speaker envisages Trinidad as an economic and cultural resource. Maloney's Trinidad is not one of Carnival but one of economic progress. The collection closes with "Gratitude," in which the poet-speaker expresses thanks to Panama's president Martín Torrijos (2004–9) for allowing him to return to the home of his ancestors and "for the chance to live out firsthand those sayings of my grandparents" (Maloney, *Street Smart* 118).[9] In "Gratitude," the poet-speaker is permitted an "unforgettable reconnection that our grandparents so longed for" (Maloney, *Street Smart* 117). The poet-speaker accomplished what so many diaspora figures are unable to do: return to the host country from which they were dispersed. "T & T" and "Gratitude" reflect the poet-speaker's connection to the Caribbean landscape and to his ancestors. Whereas the Caribbean subjects (Aunt

May) of *Juega vivo* (1984) realized an ancestral connection to the Caribbean via ethnic memory, the poetic subjects ("T & T" and "Gratitude") of *Street Smart*, written after 2000, connect physically, mentally, and ancestrally to the Caribbean Basin.

In "The New Century Perspective," the poet-speaker views the Canal less antagonistically than in "New Nomads" and is grateful for the legacy that it has bequeathed him and his Caribbean ancestors. The tone differs from that of "New Nomads," which criticizes the United States and Panama for implementing U.S.-style racism in the Canal Zone and for the creation of the segregated gold and silver rolls. In "Were It Not for the Canal," the poet-speaker pays homage to the Canal and acknowledges that his existence is tied to it. "Were it not for the Canal / I would never have given voice . . . I simply would not exist" (Maloney, *Street Smart* 113). The Canal is viewed as "Creator" and as an instrument of change that has forged Caribbean identity in the geographical space of Panama. Caribbean identity in Panama is tied to the Canal, which created multiple identities and diasporas. The Canal is essential to the poet-speaker's personal existence and references his West Indian ancestors Fitzgerald and Clara. Were it not for it, Panamanian West Indians would reside in another "Caribbean" geographical space (Maloney, *Street Smart* 113). The poet-speaker's use of *Caribbean* is important because it recognizes his rootedness in Trinidad and as a member of the broader Caribbean Diaspora.

Gerardo Maloney is a poet of Afro-Panama. His poetic repertoire simultaneously manifests a diasporic and Caribbean consciousness. Poems from "The New Century Perspective" enact a Caribbean poetics and convey that the Caribbean is a constitutive part of his ethnic memory and identity. But this does not signify a loss of his Panamanian heritage or identity. His poem "Black Ethnicity Day," which also is part of "The New Century Perspective," references the nation's struggle with black recognition and awareness and celebrates black pride. He applauds his nation for recognizing the accomplishments of its black ancestors. He illustrates that it is possible to be a Caribbean man and an Afro-Panamanian one without sacrificing this hybrid identity. In this way, he contrasts with his contemporaries Carlos Wilson and Carlos E. Russell, who both reside in the United States and exert a black nationalistic perspective.

Cubena's West Indian Rage

The previous chapter examined the importance of Carlos "Cubena" Guillermo Wilson's works and their lack of recognition in the Panamanian literary sphere. While Wilson's trilogy argues for Afro-diasporic unity by eliminating tensions between Afro-Hispanics and West Indians in Panama, his poems present a disgruntled poet-speaker, a result of Panama's denial of the nation's African heritage. The poems reveal that Panama's denial of blackness is not unique; in fact, it colors the entire African Diaspora experience. Furthermore, the poetry collection communicates a rage that is endemic to Wilson's works. In Wilson's poetry, he conveys a similar problematic of identity that also typifies the poetry of his contemporaries Maloney and Russell, that of a West Indian foreigner in a nation that has desired to obscure blackness. Wilson's sole poetry collection *Pensamientos del negro Cubena: Pensamiento afro-panameño* [Black Cubena's Thoughts: Afro-Panamanian Thought], originally published in 1977, was later reprinted as *Los mosquitos de orixá Changó (cuentos y poemas)* [The Mosquitoes of the Orisha Shango (Short Stories and Poems)] (1991) and *Raíces africanas: Los mosquitos de orixá Changó* [African Roots: The Mosquitoes of the Orisha Shango] (2005). Collectively, the poems in this work illustrate the problematic of Panamanian West Indian identity in the Panamanian nation-state and its denial of blackness. "Desarraigado" [Rootless] makes the protagonist's lack of African identity the central root of his identity conflict. The poet-speaker's rhetorical question to his African grandmother, "¿Abuelita africana, no me reconoces?" [African Grandmother, don't you recognize me?], which opens the poem, exhibits that the black diaspora figure is uprooted and dislocated from his or her African identity. Furthermore, language, religion, and culture complicate the poet-speaker's racial identification:

> Mi lengua es cervantina
> Mi letanía es cristiana
> Mi danza es flamenco
> Mi raza es mulata

> [My language is of Cervantes[10]
> My litany is Christian

My dance is flamenco[11]
My race is mulatto] (Wilson, *Los mosquitos* 111)

The poet-speaker's language (Spanish), religion (Catholicism), dance (flamenco), and race (mulatto) counter the displaced African's cultural, racial, and linguistic affiliation. In the case of West Indians, their language (English), religion (Protestantism), dance (calypso), and race (black) contrast and conflict with the Panamanian nation-state, marking them as culturally incompatible and incongruent with their compatriots. The poet-speaker's use of the term *mulatto* references the ideology of *mestizaje*, which weakens black racial identification with the hope of eliminating blackness from the national imaginary. Furthermore, the term *African*, which references his grandmother, exemplifies that this is a universal problematic that affects African Diaspora populations throughout the Americas.

In the same fashion, "In exilium" [In Exile] relates that blacks are in fact "exiled" from the continent of Africa once they have been transported to the Americas. Wilson employs exile as a metaphor of the poetic subject's displacement, dispersal, and dislocation. The poet-speaker's name, Carlos Guillermo Wilson, which he references in the poem, is incongruous with his African heritage:

¡Qué desgracia!
Ashanti soy
y me dicen
Carlos
¡Qué insulto!
Congo soy
y me llaman
Guillermo
¡Qué infamia!
Yoruba soy
y me apellidan
Wilson

[What a disgrace!
I am Ashanti
and they call me Carlos

What an insult!
I am Congo
and they call me Guillermo
What infamy!
I am Yoruba
and they name me Wilson] (Wilson, *Los mosquitos* 114)

Wilson's West Indian rage penetrates the poem, as he feels insulted by a name that negates his African identity. The poet-speaker's name reflects both British Caribbean (Wilson) and Latin American (Carlos Guillermo) colonization and conveys that the rootlessness commenced when his ancestors were enslaved first in the Caribbean and then migrated to Panama. "In exilium" recalls Nicolás Guillén's poem "Mi apellido" [My Last Name], which problematizes the poet-speaker's last name (Guillén) and its cultural and linguistic disassociation from Africa. Like Wilson, Guillén questions his identity after slavery imposed a new name on his ancestors. The language imposed on blacks after colonization created a dislocation from their ancestral heritage.

The problematic of identity and difference is inherent in the minority experience in the Americas. Wilson's poem "Las Américas" [The Americas] expresses solidarity with indigenous populations of Guatemala (Maya), Peru (Inca), and Mexico (Aztec). However, the poet-speaker distinguishes their suffering from that of blacks. He ends by noting that blacks have suffered the most beatings and insults. Thus, while the poet-speaker attempts to express solidarity with other displaced populations, his anger over the suffering of blacks in the New World compels him to elevate their afflictions over that of others. Despite this rage, "Mi raza" [My Race] presents ambivalence toward racial identification and attempts to resolve the problematic of racial identity; the poem concludes with the poet-speaker identifying himself simply as "human." Although the poem approximates a reconciliation of identity, the remaining stanzas complicate an idealistic identification because of geographic and cultural barriers. Although Wilson is a Panamanian West Indian, he has resided in the United States since the 1950s. In the United States, the poet-speaker recognizes that he is neither Panamanian nor North American (Wilson, *Los mosquitos* 115). This poem explicates the inner turmoil that black Latinos endure in the United States. Borrowing from W. E. B. DuBois's meta-phor of double consciousness, Jiménez Román and Flores define the black Latino's racial dilemma in the United States as a "triple consciousness" resulting from his or her Latino, black, and North American identity (15). Being both black and Latino in the United States proves problematic for the poetic subject and compels him to continue questioning his racial identity. Carlos Russell also re-sides in the United States and possesses much of the same identity conflict that Wilson's poetic verse conveys.

Carlos E. Russell and the Afro-Panamanian Brooklyn Diaspora

Afro-Panamanian literature extends beyond the borders of the Pan-amanian nation-state, as we witnessed with the works of Wilson. In Brooklyn, New York, a vibrant Panamanian community exists of approximately 30,000 Panamanian West Indians, who are now U.S. citizens. After the passing of the 1955 Remón-Eisenhower Treaty, thousands of non-U.S. citizens in the Canal Zone "lost their jobs, housing, and commissary-buying privileges, and were compelled to pay income taxes to the government of Panama" (Priestley 53). During this period, Panamanian West Indians suf-fered job losses in the private sector. The lack of economic ad-vancement and the changing racial and political dynamics of the Canal Zone led numerous West Indians to migrate to the United States, into the diaspora in Brooklyn. Many of these immigrants (approximately 8,168) migrated to the United States during the 1960s for education and economic advancement, but they main-tain cultural ties with the nation-state (Priestley 55). As Priestley notes, the West Indians who migrated to Brooklyn began to form a hybrid cultural and racial identity linking them racially with Afri-can Americans and culturally with other Latinos and West Indians, yet they strove to maintain a Panamanian national identity (53). Despite their residence abroad, many remained active in Panama-nian politics and were responsible for spearheading civil rights organizations, laws, and communities in Panama. Members of this Panamanian diasporic community spearheaded the National Conference of Panamanians in 1974, with the central goal of in-corporating West Indians, blacks, and indigenous persons into the

Panamanian nation-state (54). Carlos E. Russell (b. 1934) forms part of the diaspora in Brooklyn, having migrated there during the 1960s after a short stay in Chicago. His formation in Brooklyn in the 1960s during the height of the civil rights movement would shape his black intellectualism and awareness of African American literature and history (Pulido Ritter, "Carlos E. Russell" 14). Russell's roots in the African American civil rights movement have contributed to his insistence on maintaining Caribbean identity and, most important, blackness in Panama.

Russell is a poet and essayist who lives in the United States and represents many other Panamanian nationals who migrated there during the second half of the twentieth century for economic advancement. He is professor emeritus of the City University of New York–Brooklyn College; he has taught classes on Latin American and African culture and politics, as well as African American literature; and he has served as dean of the School of Contemporary Studies of Brooklyn College, a program that he designed and established. Russell has also served as acting director of the Division of International and Urban Affairs at Medgar Evers College, the City University of New York, and has been associate editor at the *Amsterdam News* and *Liberator* magazine. Russell has dedicated his life to the preservation of Panamanian West Indian culture, language, and heritage through his literature and activism, and he writes primarily in English to represent Anglophone Caribbean culture in Panama. His formation in the United States is just as important as his upbringing in Panama. Russell was educated at one of Panama's most prestigious schools, the National Institute, which has educated future dignitaries, military personnel, and the like. At the institute, he was instructed on how to be Panamanian and not black. Stereotypes abounded in the institute, where a racist teacher acknowledged how surprised she was that a black West Indian could write so well in Spanish. This stifled Russell's literary creation in Spanish because the teacher told him bluntly, "Tú no pudiste saber escrito este cuento . . . porque tú eres jamaiquino" [You could not have written this short story . . . because you are Jamaican] (Watson, "Entrevista con Carlos"). The effects were devastating. Russell acknowledged the impact of the teacher's statements: "Yo nunca más podía escribir ningún artículo o cuento literario en español porque yo no puedo según ella"

[I never was able to write another article or literary short story in Spanish because I couldn't according to her] (Watson, "Entrevista con Carlos"). Although Russell writes today in Spanish and English, he writes most of his works in English to challenge the official discourse of anti–West Indian sentiment that this teacher and others espoused. Russell's fears as a young boy of racism, discrimination, and oppression were so profound that he acknowledged that he did not dare to ask a Panamanian girl out on a date because he was black. His background in Panamanian schools contrasted with that at home, where his stepfather exposed him to the literary works of Montesquieu and Rousseau. Furthermore, it was in the intellectual and political environment of New York where he became entrenched in the civil rights movement that gave rise to his defense and promotion of Caribbean culture in Panama. He became the editor of the New York newspaper the *Liberator*, a pan-Africanist, socialist, and diasporic pamphlet that promoted the Black Panther movement (Pulido Ritter, "Introducción" 2). Russell acknowledges the influence of the United States and these movements on his black intellectualism, consciousness, and formation in the following recollection: "Saliendo de Panamá, madurándome acá. Yo me defino como africano cuyos parientes nacieron en el Caribe pero quien se hizo hombre en las calles de Brooklyn y en las calles de Chicago" [Leaving Panama, maturing here. I define myself as an African whose relatives were born in the Caribbean but who became a man in the streets of Brooklyn and the streets of Chicago] (Watson, "Entrevista con Carlos"). It is no surprise that Russell's poetry and prose deal with the question of identity and the reconciliation of the Panamanian West Indian's cultural, linguistic, and ethnic ties to Africa, the Caribbean, and Panama. His collections of poetry include *Miss Anna's Son Remembers* (1976), *An Old Woman Remembers* (1995), and *Remembranzas y lágrimas* [Memories and Tears] (2001). *Remembranzas* is a compilation of poems in Spanish and English, many of them reproduced from his 1976 collection *Miss Anna's Son*. Both *Miss Anna's Son* and *Remembranzas* are bilingual tributes to Panamanian West Indian immigrants who paved the way for present generations to succeed. While his poems recall his West Indian ancestry, Russell's essays, published separately, delve into the problematic of being Caribbean and Panamanian.

The poems "Silenciosamente" [Silently] and "¿Quién soy?" [Who am I?] echo that of Maloney's "Who?" and the problematic of identity of the African Diaspora figure in the Panamanian nation-state. In "Silenciosamente," Russell alludes to the Panamanian West Indian's threefold ethnicity and to the complexity of the Caribbean Panamanian experience:

> En silencio
> Y no tan silenciosos
> Nosotros . . . expatriados
>> tras una miríada de risas
>> escondemos nuestras penas. . . .
> ¿Quiénes somos?
> . . . .
> Cantamos
> Lloramos . . . en silencio
> Nos escondemos tras una máscara
>> pero no tan silenciosos.

> [Silently
> and not so silently
> We . . . expatriates
>> behind a myriad of laughter
>> hide our pain. . . .
> Who are we?
> . . . .
> We sing
> We cry . . . silently
> We hide behind a mask
>> but not so silently] (Russell, "Cuatro poetas" 110)

"Silenciosamente" demonstrates that identity is elusive and often indefinable. This is especially true when dealing with the West Indian community, a population forced to articulate this identity utilizing the national paradigm, which characterizes everyone as Hispanic and devoid of an African heritage. In Russell's case, the articulation of this identity is even more complex because he resides in the United States and because he is black, West Indian, and Panamanian. In addition, he is an *expatriado*, an expatriate removed from his native Panama. Although Russell's poem reminds us that the diaspora experience is one of silence, isolation, and loneliness, the last verses of the poem point to the West Indian's resiliency and ability to challenge the national paradigm.

While "Silenciosamente" focuses on the collective identity of the diaspora, "¿Quién soy?" reflects an individual's search for identity. Published originally in *Miss Anna's Son* in 1976 and republished in *Remembranzas* in 2001, the poem remains pertinent to the reader and the author today for its unresolved issues of identity:

> Chombo
> Mestizo
> Latino
> > o Criollo.
> ¿Quién soy?
>
> [Who am I?
> Chombo
> Mixed-raced
> Latin
> > or Creole.
> Who am I?] (Russell, *Remembranzas* 8)

The terms *chombo*, *mestizo*, *latino*, and *criollo* reflect the poet-speaker's hybrid identity. Needless to say, none of these terms adequately describes the Panamanian West Indian. Each term further illuminates the plurality and multiplicity of the poet-speaker's identity. Moreover, they possess multiple meanings and reflect the difficulty of articulating a single identity. For example, while *chombo* is a derogative word that refers to West Indians in Panama, it can also be used in a positive way. Furthermore, the term can refer to West Indians from the Francophone or Anglophone Caribbean. Although the term has been identified with blackness, it does not reflect the diversity among the West Indian population. The other terms reflect the same dilemma. While *mestizo*, *latino*, and *criollo* refer to the poet-speaker's hybrid cultural identity as a Hispanic, they do not necessarily define him as a Panamanian of African descent. *Mestizo* in itself is problematic because, as Puri has pointed out, in Latin America "discourses of hybridity have been implicated in managing racial politics—either by promoting cultural over racial hybridity or by producing racial mixes acceptable to the elite" (45). The term *mestizo* reflects national projects of race mixing to exclude and elide populations of color. A term utilized in the United States to identify populations of Latin American descent, *latino* possesses the same problems for many U.S. Latinos of African descent because it fails to incorporate their African heritage, thus leaving many to adopt a more U.S.-based binary racial codification by opting for black (Flores and Jiménez Román 323). Individually, these terms do not adequately describe the poet-speaker's multiplicity. In effect, the poet-speaker is all of these things, but he has difficulty reconciling this multiplicity because the national rhetoric has not allowed him to celebrate his Africanness along with his *panameñidad*. In effect, none of the terms effectively describes his "tri-ethnicity," which leaves the poet-speaker at the end pondering the same rhetorical question.

Russell's work represents a black Panamanian West Indian nationalism and not an Afro-Panamanian one. The reimagining of the Panamanian nation-state is one that would incorporate West Indians and not Afro-Hispanics into the national polity. Clearly, his black West Indian nationalism stems from a rage that he and others like Wilson feel toward the nation-state for not embracing the immigrant turned citizen population after the construction of the Panama Railroad and the Canal. While Wilson has resolved many of these issues, as evidenced by the unity professed in his most recent novels, Russell disapproves of the nation-state. In "I can dance the 'tamborito,'"[12] the poet-speaker reflects:

> We ain't no real Panamanian
> In the true-true sense of the word
> At all at all man.
> My people have never gotten the chance
> To strut them stuff and even them arrogance,
> nor get, like anybody else
> Them rightful place in the universe . . .
> Not at all, not at all, man.
> I am still despised as a "negro"
> . . . .
> But as an African and Caribbean man
> Where truth is bright as the sun

> In this country where as a child I ran
> My people have never been equal
> At all, at all man. (Russell, *The Last Buffalo* 79–81)

As the last verses of the poem suggest, Russell is speaking of his experience as an African and a Caribbean. Although it is implied that the nation has despised all "negros," it is clear, from the language that the text is written in (English) and the West Indian slang and dialect, that Russell is "speaking" to his West Indian brothers and sisters who have been denied acceptance in Panama. Clearly, the hesitation to become (Afro-)Panamanian stems from decades of racial intolerance, national anti–West Indian sentiment, and a profound love for his Anglophone Caribbean ancestry. It remains difficult to renounce his Caribbean heritage for his Panamanian one.

Russell's Caribbean heritage and blackness are in opposition to the Panamanian nation-state and remain outside of its cultural, racial, and political boundaries. The tone of his literary repertoire reminds us of U.S. black national radicals in the 1960s and 1970s who professed a proud black heritage. "Lamentations of an Ex-Slave" (2008) points to this anger and black exclusion that persists in the present:

> You see, your language,
> The one you drummed into me,
> Speaks only of your virtues
> And exalts only you.
> Because of you
> And what you have done to me
> I cannot speak to you
> In sounds and images
> That speak well of me.
> In your language I exist
> Only as an appendage,
> A metaphor,
> An after-thought,
> A creation of yours! (Russell, "Lamentations" 329)

As a postcolonial poem, Russell accuses the colonizer of the denial of language, religion, and above all African identity. The loss of language signifies a loss of culture, identity, and ethnic memory. Although the poet-speaker feels wronged, he is no longer a victim and self-identifies as an ex-slave, one no longer "shackled" by the colonizer. It is unclear whether Russell is lambasting his Anglophone colonizer or the (neo)colonization his ancestors experienced in Panama, having to replace their native English with Spanish. However, as Russell shared with me in an interview, the location of colonization is unimportant. Whether it occurred in the Anglophone Caribbean or in Panama is insignificant because "ambos son idiomas de aquellos que oprimieron y que siguen oprimiendo al africano. El africano nunca hablaba portugués, no hablaba inglés, no hablaba español, tenía su propio idioma. Pero en el momento que fueron subyugados o eclipsados, tuvieron que aprender el idioma del opresor y al aprender el idioma del opresor lo que pasó con aquellos también incluyeron que se convirtieron en pseudo ingleses, pseudo norteamericanos, pseudo españoles, pseudo portugueses" [both (English and Spanish) are languages of those who oppressed and continue oppressing the African. The African never spoke Portuguese, did not speak English, spoke no Spanish, had his own language. But in the moment that they were subjugated or eclipsed, they had to learn the language of the oppressor, and after learning the oppressor's language, what happened to them resulted in them converting into false Englishmen, false North Americans, false Spaniards, false Portuguese] (Watson, "Entrevista con Carlos"). The problematic of language expressed in "Lamentations of an Ex-Slave" echoes that of his book-length essay *The Last Buffalo: "Are Panamanians of Caribbean Ancestry an Endangered Species?"* which laments the disappearance of English use among Panamanian West Indians. The language loss for the West Indian was enacted twice in two different geographical spaces: the Anglophone Caribbean and Panama. Russell recuperates the metaphor of language, which was used against West Indians to deny them citizenship. The poet-speaker was forced to learn Spanish, and this angers him because it was viewed as superior to English. Russell professes anger toward the colonial system that has forced whiteness and language upon its citizens and imposed a colonial order that reinforces linguistic, cultural, and racial differences.

In "Caliban's Contemporary Caribbean Dilemma" (2005), Russell continues the same interrogation of identity that plagued him

in his 1970s poems "¿Quién soy?" and "Silenciosamente." Similar
to *The Last Buffalo*, Russell discusses the plight of the displaced
African figure who is unable to identify with the homeland of his
colonizers. He recalls his experiences in Cuba while helping to cut
sugarcane along with black activists Angela Davis and Kendra
Alexander. Russell, Alexander, and Davis all travelled to Cuba as
part of the "Venceremos Brigade" [We Shall Overcome Brigade] in
1969 to harvest ten million tons of sugarcane.[13] The situation of
Cuba provides the essayist with a metaphor of displacement that
he experiences as someone of African Anglophone ancestry born
in a Spanish colonized territory. However, this feeling of displacement is not one endured exclusively by Panamanian West Indians
but by all African Diaspora figures, because "they too were struggling with the question of their identity and commitment to the
nation in which they were born" as Russell notes ("Caliban's Contemporary" 88). Russell appropriates the metaphor of Caliban as
a signifier of the displaced African Caribbean figure who is unable
to identify with his colonizer but longs to be like him.

Caliban has been a long-standing metaphor of Latin America's
indigenous heritage since the turn of the twentieth century. A figure from Shakespeare's comedy *The Tempest* (1623), Caliban is
the son of the witch Sycorax and is a deformed African slave (half
monster and half man) who inhabits Prospero's island. In Shakespeare's version, Prospero attempts to "civilize" his slave Caliban
through religion and moral education. Caliban reappears at the
turn of the twentieth century in José Enrique Rodó's seminal essay *Ariel* (1900). In *Ariel*, Caliban represents barbarity, sensuality,
and sexuality and is a product of "utilitarian democracy." Clearly,
Rodó wanted to fend off North American imperialism but did not
want to do so at the expense of the ruling "criollo" elite. Rodó's
essay was extremely important because it led to decades of Spanish
American *arielismo*, which promoted Latin American youth and
promise through spirituality, something that the United States did
not possess because of its greed and focus on materialism. In light
of the Spanish-American War of 1898, which gave Spain, Puerto
Rico, Guam, and the Philippines to the United States, Latin America
sought to distance itself from the imperial hegemony. While North
America thrived materially, it did so at the cost of its spirituality, a

tenet that the figure Ariel embodied and that was embraced for decades by so-called *arielistas*. Ariel represented spirituality, promise, and most important, Latin America's "criollo" elite. By contrast, Caliban symbolized "sensuality and stupidity," qualities that Rodó wanted Latin America to overcome. Caliban not only represented the utilitarianism from which Rodó wanted to escape; he was also a sign of backwardness as opposed to progress and elitism. Decades later, Latin Americanists would redefine Caliban as a symbol of Spanish America. Recuperated in *Calibán* (1971), Roberto Fernández Retamar posited that the promise of Latin America lied not with Ariel, as Rodó believed, but with Caliban, a symbol of Latin America's autochthonous roots. A communist and staunch supporter of the Fidel Castro regime, Fernández Retamar wrote from the perspective of the Cuban Revolution and presented Latin America's autochthonous heritage, newly symbolized by Caliban. Thus, his text presented Caliban as a symbol and the future of Latin American and Caribbean promise. As Fernández Retamar suggests in his intertextual dialogue with Rodó, "Our symbol then is not Ariel, as Rodó thought, but rather Caliban" (14). Unlike Rodó, Fernández Retamar embraced Latin America's supposed "barbarity" and its indigenous "mestizo" roots and heritage. Thus, Russell's appropriation of the metaphor of Caliban situates his work and this discussion into other debates on *latinoamericanidad* in the field of Caribbean and Latin American studies.

In "Caliban's Contemporary," Russell revisits the Caliban debate and reinscribes the figure into the national debate about Caribbean and West Indian heritage in Panama as those Caribbeans who are displaced, dispersed, and dislocated. While Fernández Retamar wrote on the heels of Castro's 1959 revolution, Russell wrote from a black nationalist's perspective that promoted blackness over *panameñidad*. Caliban symbolizes more than the diasporic Africans who have been denied an autochthonous heritage as a result of (neo)colonialism. Written in a stream of consciousness, the essay vacillates between the essayist's dreams and his reality, which is plagued by both doubt and despair over the current situation of displaced Caribbeans. The essay commences metaphorically with a dream located in an "undefined Caribbean," where the people he "saw were undefined, and without any existing counterpart outside of [his] unconscious world . . . [and] were struggling with the question of their identity and commitment to the nation in which they were born" (Russell, "Caliban's Contemporary" 87–88). The "dream" allows him to further contemplate issues in his present-day reality that plague him and hinder the articulation of his plural identity. He notes that the dilemma of double consciousness espoused by DuBois continues to plague diaspora figures in the present. Thus, the double consciousness that conflicted the Afro-Panamanians Hernández, Escobar, and *Gamboa Road Gang*'s Atá during the last century remains a vibrant viable conflict in the present. This experience of the African Diaspora figure is one of all Calibans as the title of his piece notes, that is, natives who have been literally and metaphorically displaced from their homelands. It is this displacement that causes a dual identity and compels all Calibans to ask, "Who am I?" (Russell, "Caliban's Contemporary" 95). As Russell notes, "It is this twoness, ever present in his soul, that creates the confusion that denies Caliban the emergence of his true self"(95). "Caliban's Contemporary" recognizes that "there may be no immutable or permanent solution or answer to that problem/question" of identity (89).

Russell's Caliban is a metaphor of the displacement of Caribbeans and other African descendants throughout the diaspora who are in search of their identities. Russell is concerned with the Caribbean heritage in Panama and recognizes the possible loss of his heritage and own recognition in his native Panama. In a conversation that I had with Russell in 2010, it was clear that he remains equally concerned with the loss of Caribbean heritage and identity in Panama. He lamented, "Creo yo que la realidad del panameño de ascendencia antillana está en peligro porque existe en Panamá a mi juicio un proceso de asimilación en la cual aquellos que no hablan español podrían perder su base cultural y para mi ese momento sería el momento de extinción de la comunidad antillana y lo digo porque creo yo que la realidad de nuestra nación Panamá es una en que ha existido siempre de una manera sistémica (sistemática) el racismo y una antipatía y un prejuicio real en cuanto al africano . . . el panameño de ascendencia antillana" [I think that the reality of the Panamanian of West Indian descent is in danger because there is in Panama, in my estimation, a process of assimilation in which those who do not speak Spanish could lose their cultural base, and for me that moment would be the moment of extinction of the Antillean community, and I say this because I think that the reality of our Panamanian country is one in which systematically there have always existed racism, antipathy, and prejudice about the African . . . the Panamanian West Indian descendant] (Watson, "Entrevista con Carlos"). Russell's assertions that the West Indian community will become extinct are real, not metaphorical. Unfortunately, these strong beliefs, shared by some members of the West Indian community and which result from the nation's overt discrimination against the group, have impeded the forging of an Afro-Panamanian identity.

Afro-Panamanian identity remains in opposition to Panamanian national identity politics. Wilson and Russell exude a "West Indian rage" in their efforts to describe the West Indian influence in the Panamanian nation-state. Maloney and Russell write from opposite sides of the spectrum. Maloney's connection with his Caribbean heritage allows him to embrace his West Indian heritage and is not viewed as in conflict with his Panamanian identity. Meanwhile, Russell evokes anger at the nation's lack of inclusion. Lowe de Goodin strives to incorporate the Caribbean into Panama through the preservation of memory. Russell's works further develop the problematic of identity of the Panamanian West Indian, which the author likens to other displaced ethnic populations in Latin America and the Caribbean. His refusal to cede his West Indian heritage to an authentic Panamanian one explicates the anger that is evident in the tone of his poems and essays. The texts analyzed in this chapter convey that the Caribbean constitutes an integral part of Panamanian culture and identity and contributes to its ethnic hybridity and heterogeneity. Lowe de Goodin, Wilson, and Maloney integrate the Caribbean into the Panamanian national polity. By contrast, Russell's texts superimpose one identity over the other. His view of the Caribbean counters the national foundation of the nation. These contrasting views of Caribbean cultural identity and hybridity play out in the forging of a unified Afro-Panamanian identity in the new millennium and beyond.

5

Beyond Blackness?

New-Generation Afro-Panamanian Writers Melanie Taylor and Carlos Oriel Wynter Melo

When I first met Melanie Taylor Herrera (1972) in 2003, she had recently published her first collection of short stories, *Tiempos acuáticos* [Aquatic Seasons] (2000), and it was clear that she was an emerging author in the field of Panamanian fiction. During our hour-long interview, I engaged Taylor on myriad topics, ranging from her experiences in the United States to the inspiration for her fiction. One of the questions that I posed to Taylor was about her racial identity. She noted, "Primero, me considero un ser humano" [First of all, I consider myself a human being] (Watson, "Entrevista a Melanie" 2003). In a more recent interview, Taylor summarized her identity politics as follows: "Soy una mujer urbana, hija de los logros del feminismo del siglo XX, afro y consciente de serlo pero no circunscribo mi escritura a temas afros ni a temas de denuncia social ni siquiera a temas exclusivamente panameños" [I am an urban woman, daughter of the achievements of twentieth-century feminism, black and aware of it, but I do not restrict my writing to black themes or themes of social criticism or even exclusively Panamanian topics] (Watson, "Entrevista a Melanie" 2013). Much like her literary contemporary Carlos Oriel Wynter Melo (1971), Taylor represents a new generation of black writers in Panama: race is omnipresent and a part of their identity but does not restrict or limit the topics that they engage in their literary works. Unlike third- and fourth-generation Panamanian West Indian writers, Taylor and Wynter Melo are "rooted in" but not "restricted by" race or racial identity (Dyson xiii). As Panamanians with West Indian ancestry, they represent a new generation of writers born in the 1970s who appropriate blackness; yet this appropriation does not necessarily manifest in their literary works.[1] Clearly, it is premature to discuss postblackness or postracial identity in Latin America or Panama, where so many African descendants have just begun to discover their blackness. However, Taylor and Wynter Melo's appropriation of blackness recalls Hall's notion of cultural identity and diaspora and the "process of becoming" (225). Regarding cultural identity and difference, Hall reminds us, "We cannot speak for very long, with any exactness, about 'one experience, one identity,' without acknowledging its other side—the ruptures and discontinuities which constitute, precisely, the Caribbean's 'uniqueness.' Cultural identity, in this second sense, is a matter of 'becoming' as well as of 'being.' It belongs to the future as much as to the past" (225). Hall further elaborates, "This second sense of difference challenges the fixed binaries which stabilise meaning and representation and show how meaning is never finished or completed, but keeps on moving to encompass other, additional or supplementary meanings" (229). This notion of identity and difference is precisely what one encounters in the literary repertoire of Taylor and Wynter Melo, whose works expand notions of blackness and racial identity and exemplify that there are a multiplicity of ways of being black and Panamanian. Clearly, it is imperative to recognize the differences in the articulation of blackness among Afro-descendants in Panama. Taylor and Wynter Melo problematize black identity politics in twenty-first-century Panamanian literary discourse. Moreover, the writings of Taylor and Wynter Melo convey the complexity and hybridity of diaspora identities, "which are constantly producing and reproducing themselves anew, through transformation and difference" (Hall 235). Hall's notion of cultural identity and difference signals not only the importance of recognizing diaspora populations but also the cultural and racial distinctions within these very same populations. Thus, not only do differences exist between black Panamanians and other diasporic African populations; there is also diversity among black populations within the Panamanian nation-state, as the literary trajectory of Afro-Panamanian authors conveys. Unlike the nineteenth-century Afro-Hispanic poets Hernández and

Escobar, who problematized their black identity and felt conflicted because of it, the writings of Taylor and Wynter Melo do not convey this problematic; yet both writers manifest a hybrid black and Panamanian identity.

The Panamanian Short Story

Taylor and Wynter Melo have distinguished themselves as short-story writers in Panama. Salomón Ponce Aguilera (1868–1945) merits distinction as Panama's first short-story writer, having published a variety of *cuentos* in newspapers and literary journals during the last decade of the nineteenth century (Jaramillo Levi, *Panamá cuenta* 14). Although the Panamanian *cuento* dates back to the late nineteenth century, the twentieth century ushered in some of the isthmus's most recognized short-story writers.[2] Of these writers, Rogelio Sinán (1902–94) has garnered national and international fame. Sinán's short stories are colored by racial phobias, popular belief in superstitions, and biblical myths, among other themes (Jaramillo Levi, *Panamá cuenta* 16). The Panamanian short-story writer and critic Enrique Jaramillo Levi has molded much of the discourse centered on the contemporary Panamanian *cuento*. With regard to Taylor and Wynter Melo, Jaramillo Levi has helped shape their literary careers by anthologizing them in his collections of Panamanian short stories. Selected works of both writers appear in his anthologies *Panamá cuenta: Cuentistas del centenario (1851–2003)* [Panama Tells Short Stories: Centennial Short-Story Writers, 1851–2003] and *La minificción en Panamá: Breve antología del cuento* [Mini-Fiction in Panama: Brief Anthology of the Short Story] (2004), among others.

Feminist Discourse in Short Stories by Melanie Taylor

Melanie Taylor is both a Panamanian author and a professional musician. She holds a bachelor's degree in psychology and a master's in music therapy. Although she writes both poetry and prose, Taylor is recognized nationally and internationally as a short-story writer in Panama, Central America, and Europe. In 2009, she was awarded the Central American Rafaela Contreras Prize for women writing short fiction, and she has received several recognitions for her poetry and short stories. Her works include *Tiempos acuáticos* [Aquatic Seasons] (2000), *Amables predicciones* [Friendly Predictions] (2005), *Microcosmos* [Microcosm] (2008), *Camino a Mariato* [Walk to Mariato] (2009), and *Atrapasueños* [Dreamcatcher] (2010). A common thread that unites her literary repertoire includes female protagonists who struggle with contemporary themes that plague the twenty-first century: identity, suicide, silence, and solitude. Similar to other Latin American women writers, Taylor utilizes interior monologue to portray women who are alienated from their families and society, and most important, from themselves. This female alienation often results from passivity, ignorance, and a lack of self-knowledge (Johnson 43).

Tiempos acuáticos (2000) comprises six short stories, the first of which is "Torrejitas de maíz" [Corn Fritters]. "Torrejitas de maíz" is what Jaramillo Levi considers a *minicuento*, that is, "un cuento en chiquito" [a little short story] or "una historia contada mediante cierta secuencia narrativa y determinados recursos estéticos afines" [a story told through certain narrative sequence and determined related aesthetic resources] (*La minificción* 15). "Torrejitas" treats an unnamed female protagonist who copes with the abandonment of her former lover (Manuel) through food. The protagonist's grandmother and aunt remain perplexed by her apparent indifference to Manuel's abandonment and betrayal. Clearly, her family members do not comprehend her silence and assume that it signifies indifference or passivity. However, she spends an entire week discretely collecting thorns from her Aunt Enilda's rosebushes for the preparation of her exquisite dish. Unbeknownst to them, she secretly plans revenge by cooking Manuel his favorite dish, *torrejitas de maíz*. The reader gains insight into this plot through the interior monologues of the protagonist, who has not expressed an interest in cooking. After preparing the meal, the protagonist gets dressed up, paints her lips with red lipstick, and pays Manuel a personal visit to request his forgiveness for her supposed bad behavior, even though he was the culprit. The dish is offered as a form of reconciliation to show him that she has learned her lesson. The last line of the narrative informs the reader of the protagonist's secret revenge: "Y mientras mastique el dolor le transfigurará el rostro e hilillos de sangre saldrán por sus labios, y yo estaré allí sentada frente a él, serena y risueña, viéndolo sufrir" [And while he chews, the pain will transform his face and blood will trickle from his lips, and I'll be sitting there in front of him, serene and smiling, watching him suffer] (Taylor, *Tiempos acuáticos* 10).

Cooking is a literary trope that permeates Latin American women's fiction. Thus, Taylor's appropriation of the culinary trope aligns her discourse with that of other Latin American female writers who "appropriate food to express gender and social concerns" (Scott 123). The central protagonist of *Como agua para chocolate* [Like Water for Chocolate] (1989), Tita de la Garza, is the most salient example, as she utilizes food to cope with her assigned role as caretaker of her mother (Doña Elena). In *Como agua*, food serves as a reminder of the protagonist's unjust suffering and broken heart. Upholding a long-standing family tradition, Tita is destined to serve as caretaker of her mother as the youngest daughter, and consequently, she cannot marry her soul mate, Pedro. Collectively, *Como agua* and "Torrejitas" convey that the domestic sphere serves as the woman's only space to be voiced and to take control of her life. In "Torrejitas," the female protagonist avenges her ex-lover ironically by appropriating the traditional role of woman as cook, servant, and subservient. The protagonist utilizes this ascribed role to take back the dignity that her lover pilfered. Similar to Rosario Ferré's "La muñeca menor" [The Youngest Doll], Taylor's "Torrejitas de maíz" vindicates the female protagonist by allowing her to avenge herself and triumph in the end.[3]

"Tiempos acuáticos" treats the difficult topics of silence and suicide. The central female protagonist, Tokio, confronts lifelong issues relating to silence, solitude, and suicide that stem from her own mother's apparent suicide when Tokio was merely two years old. Spiraling into a deep depression and despair, Tokio confesses early on through interior monologue that not even death desires her. This prepares the reader for the subsequent interior monologue that chronicles Tokio's quest to terminate her existence.

Tokio attempts to commit suicide by igniting the gas oven and placing her head inside, only to be discouraged by the fact that her head is too big for the task. Tokio's grandmother enters the kitchen during the precise moment when she attempts to end her life. Her grandmother handles this event the same way she grappled with her daughter's (Tokio's mother) own apparent suicide: avoidance and denial. The grandmother feigns ignorance and rewrites the narrative by surmising that the smell of gas stemmed from Tokio's unsuccessful attempt to bake a cake.

Upset that she cannot even complete the "simple" task of suicide, Tokio continues her quest by cutting her left wrist with a razor blade. Once again, her suicide efforts are thwarted when a stranger, Lucas Passat, comes to the door looking for her older brother, who has just left to pursue studies in Mexico. Like her grandmother, the stranger reacts with apparent indifference but saves Tokio by bandaging her wrists. Tokio is immediately attracted to the dark character and agrees to meet Lucas at his apartment; she then loses her virginity. After engaging in uneventful sex, she requests that Lucas take her to the beach. To his surprise, she does not want him to stay and urges him to leave, signifying that she no longer needs him. In a clear role reversal, Tokio employs Lucas for her own needs to free herself from depression, loneliness, and solitude. Clearly, she has manipulated him for her own self-gratification.

The narrative culminates with the female protagonist's mental liberation through the metaphor of water, which references the title and symbolizes her liberation from her own depression. As she informs the reader, "Con cada brazada mi deseo de vivir aumenta" [with every stroke my desire to live increases] (Taylor, *Tiempos acuáticos* 43). Every stroke signifies Tokio's struggle to become liberated from a cycle of depression and silence that has inhibited her from realizing her true, complete self. Water is both liberating and liberator, and it signifies the birth of her new existence and active participation in life.

Camino a Mariato's (2009) "La sombra" intertwines the triumvirate of gender, identity, and ethnicity.[4] Specifically, it deals with the female protagonist María del Pilar, who is so obsessed with her appearance that she goes to great lengths to conceal her identity and past life. The insurmountable measures—perfectly dyed hair, breast implants, and nose job—that she has taken to achieve perfection attest not only to the importance of *el que dirán* in Latin American society but also to her own insecurities, which manifest as the narrative transpires. Upon leaving a department store, María glances at a mirror that reflects her immaculate image.

"El alma le volvió al cuerpo cuando se vio a sí misma como siempre, su cabello rojo nítidamente en su lugar, ni un rizo rebelde, todo lacio; sus anteojos de la marca apropiada enmarcando sus ojos verdes; su nariz recta y aguileña; su piel tersa; su cuerpo que, aunque no de modelo de pasarela, para sus treinta y ocho años estaba más que bien y bien vestido con las marcas adecuadas y ni que decir de sus uñas bien pintadas" [Her soul returned to her body when it saw itself as always, her red hair neatly in place, not a stray curl, all straight; her designer glasses framing her green eyes; her nose straight and aquiline, her skin smooth; her body, although it could not pass for a runway model, for her thirty-eight years her body looked better than good and she was well dressed with appropriate name brands and not to mention her well-manicured fingernails] (Taylor, *Camino a Mariato* 30). During this first encounter with the mirror, María not only views the image that depicts her as a woman of society but also sees a shadow that reveals itself as an image of her former life. Perplexed by the apparition of the shadow, María initially dismisses it as "una tontería" [foolishness] or "juego de su mente" [mind game] (Taylor, *Camino a Mariato* 30). When the shadow reveals itself a second time, it recalls María before her enigmatic transformation: "Era ella con su cabello negro y rebelde, con la nariz 'chatita'" [It was her with her black and rebellious hair, with her flat nose] (30). This second apparition perplexes her more, yet she chooses to ignore it. The third time María sees her shadow, it possesses a more complete image of her former self: "Estaba en el espejo de baño . . . con el cabello rebelde y oscuro, la nariz sin operar y esos senos microscópicos que María odiase" [It (her shadow) was in the bathroom mirror . . . with her wild and dark hair, her presurgery nose and those microscopic breasts that María hated] (32). This image not only exposes her more African or ethnic features (flat nose and dark rebellious hair) but also her minute breast size. This third apparition sends María into a spiraling decay, which compels her housekeeper to call an ambulance. Ultimately, María is admitted to a hospital for her apparent *locura*, or "craziness." Not understanding her identity crisis, her husband, Jorge, believes that new breast implants will resolve María's current state of mind because her decade-old implants are imbalanced. Upon arriving from the hospital with new implants, María is haunted a fourth time by her shadow, which recollects her old neighborhood, childhood, and humble origins. Witnessing the protagonist dialogue with herself, María's housekeeper and personal manicurist certainly think she has gone cuckoo, so to speak. Clearly, the shadow represents María's subconscious and fear that someone will discover her true identity and hidden past.

María's *sombra* is personified, and it serves as a reminder of the female protagonist's ethnic identity and obscured past. She attempts to climb the social ladder by looking more European. Her nose job, breast implants, and dyed hair enhance her femininity and make her appear less ethnic and more appealing to her husband and society. After a month has transpired, the fifth and final apparition of the *sombra* no longer haunts María, and she has found a way to cope simultaneously with her present and past.

Taylor forms part of a tradition of Latin American writers who employ the mirror to open a lens to the problematic of racial identity and convey how society's image of beauty impairs female protagonists' self-images.[5] María's initial encounter with the mirror and her shadow is analogous to the identity crisis of the central protagonist Charles McForbes of *Los cuatro espejos*. McForbes encounters his image on four separate occasions in the mirror, as the title suggests. With each encounter he comes closer to reconciling his identity as an Afro–Costa Rican.[6] Although María is not black, it is clear that she has African features that she desires to suppress. Much like McForbes, who views his image on four separate occasions before his complete identity reconciliation, María comes closer to grappling with her hidden past after each encounter with the mirror and her shadow. María's *sombra* is more complex because it not only obscures her ethnic identity but also reflects her struggle with society's image of beauty. When she initially views her shadow in the department store mirror, it is a fragment of her complete image. As Scott notes, "The mirror that shows only a fragment of what is visible—a partial view—symbolizes the impact of society's notions of ideal beauty. It reduces women to just exteriority, preventing them from seeing who they really are" (53). The subsequent revelations of the shadow divulge more complete images of María to foment identity reconciliation. Thus, by the completion of the narrative, the *sombra* no longer haunts her inner soul.

While a majority of Taylor's short stories deal with contemporary issues relating to female subjects, "El viaje" [The Voyage] transports the reader to the colonial period and deals with the topics of slavery, rebellion, and female solidarity. The title "El viaje" references the Middle Passage, or the transport of millions of African slaves from Africa to the New World. The opening lines of "El viaje" describe the experience of this tragic event: "el olor nauseabundo de las defecaciones, los orines, la sangre y la comida podrida; los gritos desgarradores de aquellos que morían sufriendo los más terribles dolores atados a sus grilletes; el llanto de los niños y de los infantes, a veces aún tratando de succionar el seno de una madre ya muerta; las conversaciones a gritos de un lugar a otro del barco entre aquellos que podían entenderse" [the nauseating odor of excrement, urine, blood, and rotten food; the piercing screams of those who died suffering the most terrible pain attached to their shackles; children's and infants' cries, sometimes even trying to suck a dead mother's breast; the conversations screaming from one location to another on the boat between those who could understand] (Taylor, *Camino a Mariato* 73). The author references the death, decadence, and decay of the transport of Africans before their arrival to the plantations and the experience of horror and inhumane treatment. The opening lines of "El viaje" recall Nancy Morejón's "Mujer negra" [Black Woman] (1975), which commences with the transatlantic voyage of the black woman from Africa to Cuba. The female protagonist of "Mujer negra," like those of "El viaje," represents the collective black experience of forced migration and displacement.

"El viaje" takes place in colonial Panama during the late seventeenth century and describes the lives of six black women who work as servants in a convent: Mercedes, María la Flaca [Skinny Mary], María la Gorda [Fat Mary], María Piedad [Mary the Merciful], Teresa, and Caimana. These women's lives are plagued by slavery and servitude and the ensuing arrival of pirates, spearheaded by Henry Morgan, the buccaneer who invaded colonial Panama in 1671.[7] The takeover of Panama by Morgan inspires a fear among not only the slaves and servants but also the masters and mistresses.

"El viaje" takes place during the background of this historical event and deals with the ways that it affects the lives of domestic slaves residing in a convent. María la Gorda is sent to labor at San Juan de Dios hospital. Other domestics opt to escape, feeling that in doing so they would improve their odds of survival. Caimana and María Piedad flee before Morgan arrives. Caimana escapes to a neighboring *palenque*, a refuge for runaway slaves. During Caimana's escape, she recalls her treacherous journey from Africa to Panama and her separation from her husband and children. This first separation has stripped Caimana of both fear and faith in a superior being. Aided by two *cimarrones*, or runaway slaves, Caimana's escape appears to be a breeze, considering the suffering that she had previously endured. María Piedad decides to flee the convent before Morgan's arrival as well. She escapes with the help of her lover, Juan, who resides on a neighboring plantation. Her escape with Juan to the neighboring town of Pacora, a place where blacks can live as a free people, symbolizes her newfound freedom and that of their unborn baby.

The pirates arrive and begin their incendiary destruction of Panama. The remaining servants, María la Flaca, Teresa, and Mercedes, decide to stay behind at the convent and await their fate. Fearing the torture, rape, and takeover by pirates, the women enclose themselves in the smoke-filled convent and perish by asphyxiation. Once inside the convent, a pirate discovers Mercedes. He grabs her by the waist, they struggle, and she catches hold of his saber, which she buries deep into her body. Surprised by the women's desire to take their own lives, the pirate surmises, "¿Tal era el odio a la esclavitud que preferían morir de esa manera?" [Such was the hatred of slavery that they preferred to die this way?] (Taylor, *Camino a Mariato* 82). Clearly, these women preferred death to life than to be subjugated to further inhumane treatment at the hands of the pirates. Collectively, the six female protagonists serve as agents of change to dismantle the social structures of colonial slavery.

"El viaje" fills a historical void and counters the masculine adventures of Henry Morgan. The pirate assures the reader that his encounter with the black slaves in the convent will never make the historical archives: "Escribiría, luego de muchas tribulaciones para regresar a su Europa natal, un libro denominado *Los bucaneros de América*. Omitiría el detalle del convento, prefirió dejarlo como un recuerdo personal" [He would then write about many tribulations to return to his native Europe, a book named *The Buccaneers of*

America. He would omit the detail about the convent, he preferred to keep it as a personal memory] (Taylor, *Camino a Mariato* 83).[8] The narrative conveys that this historical anecdote is not one that you would find in the historical archives, as the intertextual reference to *The Buccaneers of America* (1678) indicates. "El viaje" conveys the hardships of colonial blacks who were forced into subservience and servitude at the hand of a foreign master. This colonial narrative complements and counters Carlos Wilson's *La misión secreta,* which primarily centers on the heroism and adventures of black *conquistadores* and *cimarrones* who served as agents of social change. While the protagonists of *La misión* also counter the official story, as men, they reinforce national narratives of male heroism. Taylor's "El viaje" provides an emendation and illustrates "herstory," one that resides in enclosed spaces outside masculine narratives of heroism and nation building.

Carlos Oriel Wynter Melo's Postmodernist Fiction

In 2007, Carlos Oriel Wynter Melo was selected by the Hay Festival of Literature and the Arts, UNESCO, and the Bogotá Cultural Secretariat as one of thirty-nine writers younger than thirty-nine who were most representative of "new" literary tendencies in Latin America. His first published work, *El escapista* [The Escapist] (1999), won Panama's national José María Sánchez short-story prize, thus establishing him as a promising writer in the literary sphere. An industrial engineer by trade and professor at the Universidad Interamericana de Panama, Wynter Melo has spent much of his literary career cultivating the field. He has served as editor of the journal *Letras de fuego* and as vice president of the Association of Panamanian Writers. He is also founder and director of Fuga Editorial and president of Fundación para la Gestión del Arte [Foundation for Art Administration]. His short-story collections include *El escapista* (1999), *Desnudo y otros cuentos* [Nude and Other Short Stories] (2001), *El escapista y demás fugas* [The Escapist and Other Escapes] (2003), *Invisible* (2005), *El niño que tocó la luna: Leyendas, cuentos y narraciones* [The Child Who Touched the Moon: Legends, Short Stories, and Narrations] (2006), *El escapista y otras reapariciones* [The Escapist and Other Reappearances] (2007), *Cuentos con salsa* [Short Stories with Salsa] (2008), and *Vivir donde América se hace cruz* [Living Where America Makes a Cross] (2010).[9]

"Nicanor da la vuelta" [Nicanor Turns Around], from *El escapista y otras reapariciones*, grapples with death and the monotony of life. Nicanor's life is plagued by the same daily routine. Every day he takes care of his parents, by serving them breakfast and retrieving the daily newspaper for his father. He performs these tasks out of familial loyalty and obligation. His parents often remind him that he does this "porque era lo que tenía" (because it was what he had to do), "porque [es] el buen hijo" [because he is a good son] (Wynter Melo, *El escapista* 41). Nicanor's only refuge is reading. Reading provides him pleasure because the fictitious protagonists are "dream like," "limitless," and not restricted by the confines of ordinary life. One day he discovers what appears to be an intriguing narrative: the novel *Nicanor da la vuelta*. Nicanor seeks refuge in the novel, desiring an escape from his monotonous existence, only to discover that the metafictive narrative mirrors his own mundane reality. Realizing that his life and that of the protagonist are intertwined, he comes to the conclusion that nothing will liberate him from his boring existence except death. Moreover, he realizes that his life will most likely become like that of his own parents, with little hope for spontaneity.

"Nicanor da la vuelta" situates Wynter Melo's literary work with other postmodern and postboom fiction. The self-referentiality and metafictive aspects of the narrative are the most salient characteristics that align his fiction with other tenets of postmodernity: reflexivity, irony, subversion, and parody. Hutcheon defines *postmodernism* as "a period label generally given to cultural forms since the 1960s that display certain characteristics such as reflexivity, irony and a mixing of popular and high art forms" (612). Williams establishes the link between postmodernism and Latin American fiction by noting that much of the fiction published by boom writers after 1968 can be considered postmodern (*Modern* 118).[10] Wynter Melo's fiction is postmodern in that it "works to subvert dominant discourses" and to establish truth claims (Williams 118). *Nicanor da la vuelta* references the same lines of the narrative "Nicanor da la vuelta." Thus, it subverts and challenges the authority of the narrative by simultaneously blurring the line between fiction and reality and calling into question its veracity. Are we reading fiction or reality? Is Nicanor mimicking the life of the protagonist of the novel or vice versa? In turn, it challenges the authority of the author, the narrator-protagonist, and the text. At the conclusion of the short story "Nicanor," the protagonist realizes that he is reading about his own life. In turn, Nicanor the protagonist "reads" his own narrative, structured by author Wynter Melo. Clearly, it is ironic that the novel he is reading parallels that of his own life. Not only is Nicanor's existence pathetic, it is also humorous.

Similar to the postmodern novel *La forma del silencio* [The Form of Silence] (1987), by María Luisa Puga, "Nicanor da la vuelta" suggests that reality constructs the narrative and that narrative constructs reality (Williams, *Modern* 148). The novel *Nicanor da la vuelta* echoes passages from the narrative and life of the protagonist Nicanor: "porque era lo que tenía," "porque si la mamá y el papá" [because he had to do it, because if Mom and Dad] (Wynter Melo, *El escapista* 44). Thus, the lives of the protagonists from both works of fiction merge and are a product of each other. They each call into question the boundaries between fiction and reality and the actual construct of both narratives.

Various short stories in Wynter Melo's canon treat the theme of nudity: "Apariciones" [Apparitions], "Desnudez metafísica" [Metaphysical Nudity], and "Hombre y mujer" [Man and Woman], to name a few. In Wynter Melo's narratives, nudity serves as metaphor for identity crisis and the revelation of one's true self. "Hombre y mujer" deals with Verónica and Agustín, a sculptor and art dealer, respectively. Unmarried Agustín and Verónica have a child together, which does not prevent Agustín from having sexual relationships with other women. Verónica senses that he is sleeping around. Feeling vulnerable and betrayed, she cries, "Agustín . . . tú no sabes lo que es ser mujer; me siento usada, no sé si me quieres realmente o sólo soy la que esculpe y la que coge" [Agustín . . . you do not know what it is to be a woman; I feel used, I don't know if you really love me or if I am only the one you make over and have sex with] (Wynter Melo, *El escapista* 77). Not too long after her revelation and the birth of their child, Agustín acquires Verónica's gestures, customs, and habits. His inner spirit becomes so intertwined with Verónica's that he grows a single breast and even possesses the ability to breast-feed their son when Verónica's milk dries up. A mutual friend who is a painter insists that Agustín participate in an artistic show as a living sculpture, displaying publically his sole breast. Intrigued by Agustín's breast, the participants touch, kiss, and grope him. By the end, Agustín feels used, abused, and violated, sentiments that Verónica and women experience on a regular basis as a result of being objectified by men. In a clear role reversal, man experiences the objectification that women constantly endure. In turn, Wynter Melo reverses the ascribed roles of women and men to criticize the sexist treatment of women that persists in modern society. In postmodern fashion, "Hombre y mujer" parodies the culture of machismo and subverts this culture through the humorous portrayal of a single-breasted man. Wynter Melo initially portrays Verónica as a submissive woman haunted by her partner's infidelities, a familiar cultural and literary trope. The author challenges this very same trope by inverting and subverting society's misogynistic treatment of women through the parody of man. As a participant in the parody, Verónica sympathizes with Agustín, yet admonishes him not to shed tears over the inhumane treatment, because "men don't cry." Thus, she reminds him of the coded behaviors that society has ascribed to man and woman. Up until now, it appears that Verónica is an innocent, insecure, naive woman who finds it difficult to deal with Agustín's infidelities. However, her subtle reproach conveys her gratification regarding Agustín's objectification by society.

Wynter Melo recuperates the theme of nudity and established gender roles in "Desnudez metafísica" [Metaphysical Nudity], which centers on a male narrator-protagonist who feels insecure with his body image. The narrative deals with the corporeal insecurity of the protagonist and his hypermasculine antithesis Toti. Accompanied by their female companions, Toti rips off his shirt in display of his masculinity. Intimidated by his friend, the male protagonist laments, "Tengo un lunar velludo sobre mi tetilla izquierda, sobre donde posiblemente está mi corazón. Ahora mostrarlo me resulta difícil. Sobre todo porque Lore y Natasha miran y cuchichean. Me pregunto si piensan que estoy gordo. Desde donde Lore se sienta, pudieran notarse los rollos de mi abdomen. Me inquieta la posibilidad porque Toti es muy delgado y la comparación podría darse" [I have a hairy mole on my left breast, where my heart possibly lies. Now showing it is difficult for me. Especially because Lore and Natasha are looking and whispering. I wonder if they think I'm fat. From where Lore is sitting, they could notice the rolls of my abdomen. I am concerned because Toti is very slim and the similarities [between us] would be evident] (Wynter Melo, *Cuentos con salsa* 37–38). Like Taylor's female protagonist María de Pilar in "La sombra," the narrator-protagonist struggles with body image. The male protagonist's negative self-image is coupled with an insecurity that stems from his friend's hypermasculinity, which is viewed as standard male behavior. Feeling pressured by Toti's overt demonstration of masculinity, Toti bears his chest as well. Sensing his insecurities, the narrator-protagonist's female companion Natasha muses that there are three types of persons: the weak, the strong, and the weak who pretend to be strong. Ultimately, she explains that appearing weak can also be a sign of strength, which references the narrator-protagonist's nonmasculine behavior. Natasha validates the narrator-protagonist and invalidates Toti's hypermasculinity. Clearly, Toti represents men who feign strength to obscure their own insecurities. The narrative offers a fresh perspective on body image and shows the vulnerabilities of men; moreover, it provides an alternative to Latin American machismo.

Similar to "Desnudez metafísica," "Un día con los Pérez Olsen" [One Day with the Pérez Olsen Family] treats the problematic of female obesity and society's image of women. The Pérez Olsens invite the narrator-protagonist, whom they identify as "la gorda" [the fat woman], to spend the day with them at their local pool's clubhouse. The female protagonist fears swimming and wearing a bathing suit in public. The Pérez Olsens identify the narrator-protagonist simply as "la gorda," thus dehumanizing her and negatively codifying her body. While in the pool, the couple's son is infatuated with the female protagonist's large breasts and caresses them under water. Instead of telling him to stop, she allows him to continue because "en el agua soy otra mujer" [in the water I am another woman] (Taylor, *Cuentos con salsa* 49). When the couple returns to the pool, they interpret the scene as the female protagonist lusting after their young son because he would never be attracted to "una gorda." Ironically, the Pérez Olsens are overweight and ugly, but the wife feels superior to the narrator-protagonist.

Ultimately, the narrator-protagonist leaves the Pérez Olsens' home feeling unashamed, because she recognizes their dysfunctional behavior. Ironically, they not only are in denial of their own weight issues but also have a dysfunctional marriage: the husband abuses his wife verbally and physically. Wynter Melo's "Un día" forms part of a host of Latin American narratives that treat the problematic of women and obesity.[11] However, many of these works are from the vantage point of Latin American women writers. Wynter Melo's short stories convey that similar to women, men grapple with issues of body image ("Desnudez metafísica") and are victims of society's obsession with the corpus, whether male or female ("Hombre y mujer"). Furthermore, Wynter Melo's treatment of these issues, through satire or parody, conveys a desire to dismantle societal norms regarding men and women.

Contemporary issues of the human experience in the current age unite Taylor's and Wynter Melo's narratives. The unnamed central protagonists that populate many of their narratives convey that they represent other figures that experience the same issues in a complex modern society. However, they are not *tipos*, or types, but multifaceted characters who demonstrate the complexities of living in modern society and who struggle with identity conflicts. As new-generation Afro-Panamanian writers, the fiction of Taylor and Wynter Melo conveys the intricacies of the black experience that are rooted in the African Diaspora but not restrained by it.

Conclusion
Forging Afro–Panamanian Identity?

I am black. Proud to be black. Love to be black. Would not
want to be anything else. Am of West Indian descent. And I'm
a Panamanian. Proud to be Panamanian too. I'm a black, West
Indian Panamanian. Cien por ciento Panamanian [100 percent Panamanian]. And my Spanish is better than my English.
—Grace Maynard Clark, *Voices from Our America*

The forging of Afro-Panamanian identity continues to be com-
plicated by perceptions of cultural, racial, and national identity
that are shaped by ideologies of *mestizaje* and blackness. Literature prior to 1960 in Panama is primarily that of Afro-Hispanics,
while after 1960, West Indians voice their concerns and react to
the racist nation-building rhetoric directed at them. The split in
Afro-Panamanian literature illustrates the cultural and racial
fragmentation and the ideological shift from *mestizaje* oriented
to black. However, recent literature by writers born after 1970
conveys a hybrid (black) Panamanian identity that speaks to the
process of becoming (Afro-)Panamanian.

The first black writers of the Panamanian nation-state wrestled
with the literary declaration of their blackness and negotiated a
space in the nation-state. Similar to other Afro-Hispanics across
the diaspora, they suppressed racial difference during this period. Escobar and Hernández displayed different styles of racial
awareness and identification, but race plagued the consciousness
of both poets. Racial codification countered the official discourse
of the nation, which promoted a unified Panamanian nationality.
Escobar's "Chispas" conveys his frustration with the nation-state
and the situation of blacks at large who lack a voice. Hernández
echoes Escobar's frustration, as evidenced by his dichotomous self-

portrait that ends in negating his black identity. Their expression of blackness countered the official discourse of *mestizaje*. Thirty years would pass between their writings and those of the next Afro-Hispanic writer to leave behind published works.

The burgeoning anti–West Indian sentiment gave way to racial identification among Afro-Hispanics. Beleño downplayed racial awareness to demean West Indians and, most important, the United States. Beleño speaks as a "Panamanian" echoing a unified national sentiment against imperialism. His identity as a black writer is not questioned, problematized, or enacted; he is Panamanian, and therefore he possesses the right to question the legitimacy of the other "dark" brothers and sisters on the isthmus who are racially, culturally, and linguistically codified as outsiders.

Panamanian West Indian discourse challenged the early twentieth-century anti–West Indian sentiment and fought to incorporate the Caribbean into the national paradigm. Third- and fourth-generation Panamanian West Indians attempted to forge a unified Afro-Panamanian identity. Much like third-generation West Indian Costa Rican writers, such as Eulalia Bernard and Quince Duncan, they "reveal a continuous play of tensions between an affinity for West Indian culture and their national allegiance" to Panama, as Mosby pointed out (235). Lowe de Goodin, Wilson, Maloney, and Russell all display various degrees of these tensions, but Russell is the most determined, refusing to relinquish his Caribbean heritage for his Panamanian one. Much like the protagonists in the novel who shape his trilogy, Wilson makes it his mission to forge Afro-Panamanian and Afro-diasporic unity, but a majority of his writings display an anti-Afro-Hispanic sentiment, which attenuates over time. Maloney's writings are clearly rooted in the diaspora and display Caribbean and Panamanian consciousness, yet they are not viewed in conflict. Lowe de Goodin's drama exudes this same identity politics. Russell's rage is less with his Afro-Hispanic brothers and sisters and more with the Panamanian nation-state that educated its citizens to be racist and anti–West Indian. Thus, he refuses to renounce his black nationalism.

Literature by new-generation black Panamanian writers conveys that their identity politics is rooted in but not restricted by a racialized identity. Born after 1970, their identity politics is not shaped by the racist anti–West Indian sentiment that informed the identity politics of third- and fourth-generation West Indian writers. Yet they are very much aware of racial issues, problems, and discrimination. As such, the writings of Melanie Taylor and Carlos Oriel Wynter Melo for the most part do not possess racial themes, yet blackness clearly constitutes their identity. For example, in the May 2013 special addition of *Palenque*, a magazine that centers on Afro-descendants in Panama and abroad, Taylor was featured as one of the journal's writers.[1] She also was part of a photo mirage on the cover of the magazine, as one of many Afro-descendants in the nation. Perhaps this generation of writers comes closest to an approximation of a unified Afro-Panamanian identity.

Becoming Afro-Panamanian necessitates a negotiation of Caribbean identity. This negotiation is characteristic of other dispersed Anglophone Caribbean populations in the Spanish-speaking Americas. West Indian populations in Costa Rica enact a similar struggle with identity. As Mosby noted, "The literature written by blacks of West Indian descent demonstrates that cultural identity transforms over time and 'is a matter of becoming' as well as 'being' and that it belongs to the future as much as the past" (235). The West Indian Grace Maynard Clark conveys this in her proclamation of identity.[2] Maynard Clark's assertion of her Afro-Panamanian identity conveys a cultural and racial discourse rooted in Africa, the Caribbean, and Panama. Of Panamanian West Indian ancestry, Maynard Clark's reconciliation of her Anglophone black Caribbean heritage with her Panamanian one illustrates the process of generations of West Indians becoming Afro-Panamanian.

Forging Afro-Panamanian identity involves the manifold processes of racial and cultural identity formation: (1) attenuating tensions between Afro-Hispanics and West Indians, (2) Afro-Hispanic black awareness, and (3) West Indian negotiation of Panamanian heritage. In the new millennium, organizations were spearheaded to forge Afro-Hispanic and West Indian relations and to reduce intraethnic tensions. Black movements have helped forge a unified Afro-Panamanian identity and mobilize racial awareness. During the decades between 1980 and 2000, several historical buildings and tributes to Afro-Panamanian culture were realized. The establishment of the West Indian museum; the Pueblito Afro-Antillano, or Afro-Antillean Town; and the Centro George Westerman, or George Westerman Center, in 1980, 1998, and 2000, respectively, all convey an interest in preserving West Indian culture, heritage, and memory. Día de la Etnia Negra, or Black Ethnicity Day, established in 2000, celebrates a collective Afro-Panamanian history and culture. The enactment of a national antidiscrimination law (2002) and the creation of a municipal anti-discrimination office in Panama City (2001) also demonstrate the nation's acknowledgment of past ills against blacks (Andrews 186). Although black movements have aided in forging Afro-Panamanian identity and relations, tensions remain, impeding a unified Afro-Panamanian identity. Integration among Afro-Hispanics and West Indians remains stifled because the former identify with national paradigms of race while the latter do not. The previously mentioned Día de la Etnia Negra and the creation of the cultural journal *Palenque* foment cultural and racial awareness of all Panamanians of African descent.

Further studies might determine how present-generation Afro-Panamanians identify beyond the new millennium. Additional studies could also examine the role of performance (*congos*,[3] *reggae en español*) on the impact of forging Afro-Panamanian identity. This process of becoming plays out not only in the literary sphere but also in cultural productions and performances. Studies by Craft Alexander and Zien reveal the importance of performing *afro-panameñidad* in both literature and cultural productions. Cultural performances convey traces of African identity rooted in the nation's colonial African past as evidenced by the *congo* performances in Portobelo.

Becoming Afro-Panamanian requires that the nation and its inhabitants resolve age-old issues of identity and diaspora. If we view identity as one that is "in process," as Hall suggests, and in "constant transformation," then the unresolved issues of Afro-Panamanian unity, identity, and diaspora are understood. Becoming Afro-Panamanian is just as difficult for Afro-Hispanics as it is for West Indians, because they both require a reconciliation of a fragmented hybrid identity. This process of becoming is not only of the past but also of the future. The 2010 census perhaps sheds some light on racial self-awareness in Panama; for the first time the census requested that Panamanians of African descent identify as black, colonial black (Afro-Hispanic), or West Indian.[4] Despite reported deficiencies in the 2010 census process, 9 percent of the total population identified as black, although the Panamanian DNA project found that 33 percent of Panamanians are of known African descent.[5] Of the 313,289 who acknowledged African ancestry, 142,003 identified as *negro*, 65,113 identified as *negro antillano*, and 77,908 identified as *negro colonial*. Do these statistics illustrate a forging of a unified black identity? If we substitute *negro* for *Afro-Panamanian*, which conveys a sense of black identity, then perhaps yes. Roughly half of the participants opted for black instead of the ethnic categories (Afro-Hispanics and West Indians) that divide Afro-Panamanians. The 2010 census advances the concept of a forged Afro-Panamanian identity, and that—as Carlos "Cubena" Wilson says—means the future will be better.

Notes

Introduction

1. I utilize the term *Afro-Hispanic* to refer to blacks in Panama who are direct descendants of enslaved Africans. It is worth noting that in Panama the common term used to refer to this group of blacks is *negro colonial*, or "colonial black." In this study, I prefer *Afro-Hispanic* to compare the group to other black populations throughout Latin America, and this is the common term used in Afro-Hispanic studies.

2. Criollos are European-descended Panamanians.

3. "El Orejano" is an essay in which Belisario Porras describes the customs and physical characteristics of the province Los Santos, where he was born.

4. The following works by Westerman address these issues: *Un grupo minoritario en Panamá* [A Minority Group in Panama] (1950), *The West Indian Worker on the Canal Zone* (1951), and *Urban Housing in Panama and Some of Its Problems* (1955).

5. This information was provided by the Contraloría General de la República de Panamá [General Comptroller of the Republic of Panama], which conducts the national Panamanian census. This information can be located at the website http://www.contraloria.gob.pa.

6. The Congress ceased after 1988 during the postinvasion decade, primarily because the U.S. invasion of Panama and the subsequent overthrow of military dictator Manuel Noriega hampered black mobilization and popular organizing (Priestley and Barrow 234). The killing of leaders, the incarceration of members, and the devastation of minority communities all affected the ability of these organizations to continuously mobilize (234).

Chapter 1. National Rhetoric and Suppression of Black Consciousness in Poems by Federico Escobar and Gaspar Octavio Hernández

1. Sosa and Mendoza both served in the Black Liberal Party and held a variety of positions in the Panamanian government. In 1908, Mendoza became second in command under President José de Obaldía and served as president of the Republic of Panama from March 1910 to September 1910 after Obaldía's death. As Andrews notes, the United States refused to recognize his leadership because of his blackness and encouraged his resignation.

2. The Partido Independiente de Color was founded in 1908 by Evaristo Estenoz and Pedro Ivonet and was established in response to the lack of recognition by the Cuban government in their participation in Cuba's wars of independence (1868–78 and 1895–98), which led to José Martí's untimely death in 1895. After Cuba obtained its independence in 1898, many Afro-Cubans believed that the Cuban government would formally recognize them for their participation in the independence wars. But the fact that the party's membership had reached between ten thousand and twenty thousand by 1910 disturbed many outsiders, who saw it as anathema to Cuba's perceived racial democracy (Helg, "Race and Black Mobilization" 60). As a result, the party was declared illegal in 1910 under the Morúa law. In 1912 members of the party, along with outside supporters, revolted in the province of Oriente against the dismissal. Reaction to the revolt by Cuban military opposition led to the massacre of thousands of party members, although officials reported that only dozens died in Cuba's little-known race war (Fuente 207; Helg, "Race and Black Mobilization" 63).

3. Prescott (*Candelario Obeso*), Jackson (*Black Image*), and Branche all have noted that Obeso is a precursor to *negrista* literature.

4. Prescott points out in his poignant study "'Negro nací': Authorship and Verses Attributed to Candelario Obeso" that the poem that for many years was believed to be written by Obeso was authored by the Mexican poet Joaquín Villalobos and that the four verses form part of Villalobos's poem "Amor de negro" [A Black Man's Love]. Prescott also determined that Villalobos most likely was not of African descent (6, 7). However, for the purposes of this study, the poem "Negro nací" is examined in the context of Escobar's poem "Nieblas." At the time, Escobar believed that Obeso was the author.

5. According to Duke, the Afro-Cuban periodical *La igualdad* [Equality] became the "mouthpiece" of the Central Directorate of Societies of Color, a black Cuban organization spearheaded by Juan Gualberto Gómez y Ferrer (1854–1933) (96–97). Thus, it provided an opportunity for blacks to voice their concerns and opposition.

6. In Panama the *negrista* movement spearheaded by Víctor Franceschi and Demetrio Korsi possessed an anti–West Indian sentiment and portrayed black West Indians as foreigners and the quintessential other. For information on the Panamanian *negrista* movement and national anti–West Indian sentiment, see Watson's "Poetic Negrism and the National Sentiment of Anti–West Indianism and Anti-Imperialism in Panamanian Literature."

7. A barcarole is a folk song sung by Venetian gondoliers or a piece of music composed in that style.

8. In "Literary Whiteness and the Afro-Hispanic Difference," Piedra noted that writers of African descent, such as Spain's Juan Latino (1518–96), constantly equivocated between "writing white" to avoid racial identification and writing for their country of origin. Expressing racial awareness in their works was extremely problematic because "[n]onwhites could write as long as they did not address the issue of difference" (312). Thus, many Afro-Hispanic writers chose a national affiliation by avoiding racial identification in their works. However, while many avoided issues of racial identity or prejudice, others indirectly contested the system of rhetorical whiteness by employing parody or satire to exhibit their frustration with the dominant culture.

9. A *pollera* is a traditional Spanish dress.

10. Writers of the literary generation of the republic returned to the patriotic themes that characterized Latin American romanticism. These writers of the first generation of the Panamanian republic and the last generation of *modernista* writers, such as Ricardo Miró (1883–1940), Enrique Geenzier (1887–1943), and Gaspar Octavio Hernández (1893–1918), idealized Panama's past; praised its colonial buildings; and celebrated Panama's independence from Colombia, which it gained in 1903 (Szok 104).

Chapter 2. Anti–West Indianism and Anti-Imperialism in Joaquín Beleño's Canal Zone Trilogy

1. In *Crisol* (1936), José Isaac Fábrega (1900–86) described Panama as a *crisol de razas* comprising a native African, European, and indigenous population as well as immigrants from the United States and the Caribbean. Notwithstanding the title of Fábrega's text, which suggested a *crisol de razas* in which various races coexist harmoniously, he argued that it was precisely this diversity that threatened Panama's autochthonous roots. Furthermore, he argued that Panama's national foundation was rooted in the Spanish language.

2. *50 millas de heroicidad* (1941) chronicles the construction of the Canal (Miró, *La literatura panameña* 54). Renato Ozores's (1910) *Puente del mundo* (1951) examines four generations of the Lander family, who witness the construction of the Panamanian Railroad (1850–55), the French Canal (1880–1903), and the Panama Canal (1904–14). As the title suggests, the novel explores the effects of Panama's geographic position and subsequent exploitation of it (García, *Historia* 167). *Pueblos perdidos* (1963) reveals the destruction of towns located in areas that were exploited economically to meet the needs of the Canal (Martínez Ortega, *Diccionario* 138). Yolanda Camarano de Sucre's *La doña del paz* (1967) focuses on historical aspects of the years prior to the construction of the Canal (Pérez-Venero 17). It should be remembered that writers outside of the isthmus also focused on problems of the Canal Zone. The Ecuadoran writer Demetrio Aguilera Malta's (1900–81) *Canal Zone* (1935) condemned U.S. imperialism and racial discrimination in chronicling a youth's (Pedro Coorsi) struggle to find his place

during the U.S. occupation of Panama. Colombia's José Manuel Restrepo's (1781–1863) *Dinero para los peces* [Money for the Fish, 1945] described the effect of U.S. domination in Panama during the early twentieth century (Pérez-Venero 11). In effect, the Canal Zone not only attracted national attention but also concerned writers from all over Latin America who condemned and protested against U.S. imperialism in general.

3. In *The Canal Builders*, Greene details how the Panama Canal led to North American empire and wealth and how "it was seen as a display of America's *domestic* strengths in a world setting" (9).

4. In the United States, historically, if you had one drop of African blood, you were considered black. As Davis suggests, "This definition reflects the long experience with slavery and later with Jim Crow segregation" (5).

5. Jim Crow laws separated blacks from whites in all areas of society and became a metaphor for racial segregation and inequality in the U.S. South.

6. I use the term *colored* here to designate all nonwhite Panamanians including *mestizos*, *mulatos*, and blacks.

7. *Curundú* refers to the U.S. military base in the Canal Zone.

8. *Flor de banana* deviates from the Canal Zone theme and describes the exploitation of the native populations in Chiriquí, a region located in Panama's interior.

9. In his seminal work *Central American Writers of West Indian Origin*, Smart considers Beleño to be a non–West Indian precursor to Panamanian West Indian literature, but he does not mention Beleño's race.

10. The Filós-Hines Treaty was negotiated to prolong U.S. possession of the military bases. The treaty was signed and announced on December 10, 1947. However, it was reversed two weeks later (León Jiménez 15).

11. The traditional bildungsroman chronicles a youth's hardships and usually ends in some positive way in which the youth overcomes these struggles to assume his or her place in society. The anti-bildungsroman defies this tradition and ends with the youth's destruction or inability to overcome adversity and to become a productive worker of the adult world. Although Perús does not characterize the text as an anti-bildungsroman, she notes that it does not share the same characteristics of the traditional one (35).

12. A latifundio is a feudal agrarian land system in Latin America that dates back to the colonial period and is based on the exploitation of workers. This system gave rise to race- and class-based social and economic stratification. In Beleño's novels, the *latifundio zoneíta* is a metaphor for social injustice and racial discrimination in the Canal Zone.

13. One should bear in mind that in 1902, the overall population of Panama was eighty thousand, and by 1940, thirteen thousand West Indians remained in the Canal Zone and twenty thousand in the rest of the republic (Duncan and Powell 61). Therefore, by the early twentieth century, the West Indian population almost doubled that of the overall Panamanian population. This explains the protagonist's fear of the West Indian population taking over.

14. *Huasipungo*, *Doña Bárbara*, and *Don Segundo Sombra* are social protest novels that deal with issues of landownership and ethnic discrimina-

tion. The term *huasipungo* is a Quechua word that refers to a plot of land that belongs to indigenous persons. The novel was famous for illustrating the exploitation of Ecuador's indigenous peoples by the nation's elite. *Doña Bárbara* is a regionalist novel that treats the confrontation between civilization and the "barbaric" aspects of rural Venezuela. The central protagonist of *Don Segundo Sombra* is the gaucho, or Argentine cowboy, and the novel deals with the unromantic aspects of gaucho life and views him as a *sombra*, or "shadow," on the Argentine plains.

15. *La vorágine* [The Vortex] treats the harsh conditions of Colombia's rubber factories and the travails of a young couple through the personified Colombian jungle, which becomes a metaphor for abuse. *Los de abajo* [The Underdogs] is considered the quintessential novel of the Mexican Revolution (1910–20) and chronicles the participation of Demetrio Macías. *La trepadora* [The Climber] by Rómulo Gallegos deals with Victoria, daughter of Hilario Guanipa, who abandons the country to move to the city and marry to improve her social status, and deals with issues of power and race mixing. *Jubiabá* is a Brazilian novel that deals with the friendship between the candomblé magician Jubiabá and a poor black boy named Balduino who works in a tobacco plantation and is accused of violence toward a young woman. The Brazilian realist novel *Cacao* relates the life of José Cordero, who becomes destitute after the death of his wealthy father because his uncle takes control of the money, leaving José to work first in his uncle's factory and then on a cocoa bean plantation.

16. The terms *English-based Creole* and *English* are used interchangeably to identify the language spoken by the West Indian population. However, it is important to recognize that the English referred to is an English-based Creole. Brereton acknowledges that "the language spoken by the Caribbean people who immigrated to Panama, their descendants, and by others who have learned it from them is an English-based Creole. Creoles are languages with multi-lingual roots and are primarily lexified by one language but show influences of one or more other languages in their lexicon, syntax and phonology. Throughout the city of Panama the language of Antillean Panamanians is commonly known as English" (v–vi).

17. This quote was translated by Inés V. Sealy. Unless otherwise stated, all translations are my own.

18. During the Jim Crow era, blacks in the United States had to address whites using the word *Sir* to demonstrate the proper respect due to a white man because of the latter's superiority to the black.

19. The *indigenista* movement in Latin America arose during the second decade of the twentieth century and responded to injustices against indigenous peoples primarily in the Andean countries of Ecuador, Bolivia, and Peru. The genre dealt with issues of landownership, displacement, and the economic and social disenfranchisement of indigenous peoples of the Andes. José Carlos Mariátegui is one of the premier writers of this movement; his *Seven Essays on the Interpretation of the Peruvian Reality* (1928) discusses ways to correct injustices against Peruvian indigenous peoples.

20. *Chombo* is a derogatory term used against West Indians in Panama. I use it here not to offend but to echo the anti–West Indian sentiment in Beleño's works. Furthermore, Wilson used the word as a way to express his rage over Beleño's portrayal of West Indian women, who the former identifies as *chombas*.

21. Calypso is a style of Afro-Caribbean music that originated in Trinidad and Tobago.

22. This quote was translated by Inés V. Sealy. Unless otherwise stated, all translations are my own.

23. This quote was translated by Inés V. Sealy. Unless otherwise stated, all translations are my own.

Chapter 3. Revising the Canon

1. *Mestizaje negativo* literally means "negative race mixing," as opposed to *mestizaje positivo*, or "positive race mixing." *Mestizaje positivo* involves a "blending of cultures in which there is equal respect for both," whereas *mestizaje negativo* "means that a minority culture is absorbed as an inferior culture" (Jackson, *Black Writers in Latin America* 14).

2. Mosby noted that Duncan's novels *Hombres curtidos* [Hardened Men] (1971), *Los cuatro espejos* [The Four Mirrors] (1973), *La paz del pueblo* [The Peace of the Town] (1976), and *Final de Calle* [End of the Street] (1979) "question realism and the construction of myths of national identity by moving his protagonists to an experimental plane of a multiperspectival and temporally altered world" (121).

3. *Afro-realism* is a term coined by the Afro–Costa Rican writer Quince Duncan to describe the realities of Afro–Latin America from an insider's perspective, and it has its roots in the African and Caribbean griot of oral tradition.

4. Richard L. Jackson's *The Black Image in Latin American Literature*, published three years earlier in 1976, treats black themes and the black as subject in Latin American literature but does not focus on literature produced by blacks. Jackson's second publication, *Black Writers in Latin America*, examines what he identifies as the "authentic black experience," or literature written by black writers. Furthermore, it is worth noting that DeCosta's pioneering work *Blacks in Hispanic Literature: Critical Essays* (1977) also utilizes an Afrocentric model to discuss black writing. However, this edited collection deals with the black image in Spanish and Latin American literature as well as black writing.

5. *Castilian* refers to Spanish from Spain and is considered to be proper or "correct" Spanish.

6. Wilson employs the literary technique of *tremendismo negrista* to denounce racism and discrimination. *Tremendismo* is a literary current that was prevalent in Spanish literature during the aftermath of the Spanish Civil War (1936–39). It employs the use of the grotesque and exaggeration to describe the harsh living conditions and environment during the aftermath of the war by writers such as Camilo José Cela. Cela's *La familia de Pascual*

Duarte [The Family of Pascual Duarte] (1942) is a prime example of this literary trend. A term coined by Adalberto Ortiz and elaborated by Ian Smart, *tremendismo negrista* points to this same exaggeration and the use of the grotesque with the aim to combat discrimination and racism.

7. In "At What Price Solidarity? Homophobia and Cubena's Anti-Racist Program," Gallers argues that Cubena's use of homosexuality in his literary canon to convey Panama's racism is homophobic and misogynistic (54). An example of this is the case of racist Afro-Hispanic Lesbiaquina, whose name alludes to her being a lesbian.

8. According to McForbes, three competing theories exist regarding Garifuna ethnogenesis. The first and most widely asserted theory posits that in 1635 or 1675, a slave ship bound for the New World sank close to the coast of St. Vincent island. Upon their arrival, the native population killed the European slave masters and welcomed the blacks. The black population mixed with the native Indians, creating a new ethnic group, the Black Caribs or the Garifuna. The sparse historical evidence regarding shipwrecks near the Island of St. Vincent puts into doubt this theory for some historians. An alternative explanation of Garifuna ethnogenesis "argues that sea-faring African royalty made their foray in the Caribbean almost two centuries prior to the first European contact. It is believed by some that contact between the African princes and the native population produced the first Garifuna" (McForbes 51). A third theory contends that escaped or abducted Africans from European settlements were enslaved a second time on the island of St. Vincent by the native population. This theory refutes that natives and Africans coexisted harmoniously and that the black population was victimized and raped.

9. *Cuculustes* is a Nahuatl word for curly hair used on the Costa Chica of Oaxaca, Mexico; *juyungo* is a pejorative used against blacks in Ecuador and was brought to the forefront with Adalberto Ortiz's seminal text *Juyungo*, published in 1941. *Pichón* is a racial epithet used in Cuba to refer to blacks of West Indian or Haitian ancestry. The *cocolos* emigrated from the Anglophone Caribbean islands of St. Kitts, Nevis, and Anguilla to the Dominican Republic to work on the sugar plantations from the 1880s to the 1920s. Similar to the situation of the West Indian population in Panama, Dominicans despised *cocolos* because they were culturally and linguistically different from the dominant population (Stinchcomb 64; Howard 24).

Chapter 4. West Indian and Caribbean Consciousness in Works by Melva Lowe de Goodin, Gerardo Maloney, Carlos Guillermo Wilson, and Carlos E. Russell

1. The epigraph was taken from the website Voices from Our America (http://voicesamerica.library.vanderbilt.edu/home.php), an interdisciplinary project that collects, preserves, and disseminates forgotten, hidden, and neglected narratives of American experience.

2. The term *generation* refers to those writers of Caribbean ancestry in Panama born between 1934 and 1945. Thus, it refers to the literary

generation, not to the years that the writer's ancestors resided on the isthmus. Members of this literary generation include Gerardo Maloney (b. 1945), Carlos Russell (b. 1934), Carlos Wilson (b. 1941), and Melva Lowe de Goodin (b. 1945).

3. As I stated in the introduction, on June 9, 2009, *Parecen noticias* [Looks Like News], a popular weekly program in Panama that satirizes politics, parodied Panama's recently nominated minister of education Lucy Molinar in a segment called "Yo quiero a Lucy" [I Love Lucy]. The program created a caricature of Molinar using the stereotypical image of a gorilla. The association of Molinar with a gorilla is offensive because she is black.

4. *Rabiblancos* were the white minority of elites whom the government represented prior to Torrijos's assuming power.

5. Nwankwo defines "common memory" as "the possession of knowledge of an event, feeling, or experience by individuals who may or may not share a group identity" (3). Furthermore, "if a group of people, heretofore unknown to each other, go through an experience together they can be said to have common memory" (3).

6. Frederick's *"Colón Man a Come": Mythographies of Panama Canal Migration* examines the recurrent figure of the Panama Canal worker in Caribbean literature, song, and memoir. Specifically, it traces the literary trope of the Colón Man in Anglophone-Caribbean fiction and epistolary narratives: *The Harder They Come, In the Castle of My Skin, Banana Bottom,* "Window," *Tropic Death,* and *Tree of Life.*

7. According to Cruz, Blades's grandfather Reuben Blades was from St. Lucia and was an accountant drawn to Panama by the building of the railroad and the Canal (16–17).

8. Often confused with the commercialized genre reggaeton for its similar sound and origins, *reggae en español* [Spanish reggae] is a hybrid musical dance form that blends elements of Jamaican dancehall and reggae with Spanish lyrics. Panama gave birth to *reggae en español* in the late 1970s in the urban West Indian *barrios* of Río Abajo and Parque Lefevre in the capital city of Panama. Needless to say, *reggae en español* is just as much a product of West Indian migration and the Anglophone Caribbean (Jamaica and Barbados) as it is of Central America.

9. Martín Torrijos is the son of former president General Omar Torrijos Herrera (1929–81).

10. Miguel de Cervantes is the author of the seminal Spanish novel *Don Quixote: Man of La Mancha* (part 1, 1605; part 2, 1615). The novel and the author are associated with Spanish national heritage, language, and culture.

11. Flamenco is a style of music, song, and dance from Andalusia, Spain. Wilson uses it here as a metaphor for Spanish heritage and identity.

12. The *tamborito* is the national song of Panama and is a romantic couple's dance that dates back to the seventeenth century.

13. According to the website Venceremos Brigade (http://www.vencer emosbrigade.net): "In 1969, a coalition of young people formed the Venceremos [We Shall Overcome] Brigade, as a means of showing solidarity with

the Cuban Revolution by working side by side with Cuban workers and challenging U.S. policies towards Cuba, including the economic blockade and our government's ban on travel to the island. The first Brigades participated in sugar harvests and subsequent Brigades have done agricultural and construction work in many parts of the island."

Chapter 5. Beyond Blackness?

1. Taylor's father's family came from Jamaica and Barbados during the nineteenth century, whereas her mother's family is racially mixed with black, *cholo* [of pure or mixed indigenous heritage], and white. Likewise, Wynter Melo's paternal grandparents emigrated from Jamaica to Panama during the construction of the Canal, and his maternal grandparents were native Panamanians.

2. In his short-story anthology *Panamá cuenta: Cuentistas del centenario (1851–2003)* Enrique Jaramillo Levi introduces three categories: (1) writers who focus on rural areas—Moisés Castillo (1899–1974), Ignacio de J. Valdés Jr. (1902–59), José E. Huerta (1899–1983), Lucas Bárcena (1906–92), Gil Blas Tejeira (1901–75), César A. Candenado (1906–93); José María Núñez Quintero (1894–1990), José María Sánchez (1918–73), Eustorgio Chong Ruiz (b. 1931); José Guillermo Ros-Zanet (b. 1930), Mario Augusto Rodríguez (1917–2009), and Carlos Francisco Changmarín (1922–2012); (2) writers who began publishing in the 1970s—Griselda López (b. 1938), Pedro Rivera (b. 1939), Benjamín Ramón (b. 1939), Gloria Guardia (b. 1940), Bertalicia Peralta (b. 1940), Moravia Ochoa López (b. 1941), Dimas Lidio Pitty (b. 1941), Roberto Luzcando (b. 1939), Enrique Chuez (b. 1934), Bessy Reina (b. 1941), Enrique Jaramillo Levi (b. 1944), Julia del C. Regales (b. 1953), and Héctor Rodríguez C. (b. 1955); and (3) contemporary women writers—Rosa María Britton (b. 1936), Beatriz Valdés (b. 1940), Isis Tejeira (b. 1936), Giovanna Benedetti (b. 1949), Consuelo Tomás (b. 1957), Katia Malo (b. 1961), Aida Judith González Castrellón (b. 1962), Yolanda J. Hackshaw M. (b. 1958), Melanie Taylor (b. 1972); Digna R. Valderrama (b. 1965); Amparo Márquez (b. 1948), and Marisín Villalaz de Arias (b. 1930) (16–19).

3. "La muñeca menor" [The Smallest Doll] deals with a young girl who is bitten by a *chágara* bug that is never removed from her leg because of a greedy physician who wants to profit from her injury. The girl never marries, but instead devotes her life to her nieces and celebrates their birthdates by making a doll in their likeness. The physician's son, who is aware of his father's misdeeds, marries the youngest daughter. The last doll that the aunt makes for her youngest niece is made of porcelain, honey, and diamond earrings for her eyes. Out of greed, the son sells one of the diamond eyes. Over time, he becomes worried because he notices that his wife (the youngest niece) is not aging. One day he wakes up, and her eyes bleed *chágaras*, the same insect that his father refused to remove from the aunt out of greed.

4. Mariato, or Mariato Point, is situated in the southern part of the Veraguas Province in central Panama.

5. As Renée Scott explains in *What Is Eating Latin American Women Writers?* (2009), "Other writers utilize the mirror to explore the theme of self-contemplation" (125). Rosario Castellano's *Mujer que sabe latín* [Woman Schooled in Latin] rejects the false images that mirrors present to women. Andrea Blanque's "Inmensamente Eunice" [Immensely Eunice] employs the mirror to characterize Eunice's conflicts with her obese body, which encourages constant scrutiny in front of the mirror (Scott 67). Rosa Nissán's *Los viajes de mi cuerpo* [My Body's Journeys] (2003) is about a forty-year-old divorced overweight woman who desires to escape her own image upon viewing it in the mirror (75).

6. In "Invisibility, Double Consciousness and the Crisis of Identity in *Los cuatro espejos*" Martin-Ogunsola notes that Charles McForbes encounters his mirror image on four separate occasions: after a talk on race relations in Costa Rica, during a consultation with his psychiatrist, in a mirror that he buys from a street vendor, and in a mirror at his bathroom. With each sighting of his mirror image, Charles comes closer to a reconciliation of his identity as a black Costa Rican.

7. Henry Morgan was a Welshman who came to Jamaica to form part of an expedition led by Christopher Myngs in the mid-seventeenth century (Latimer 135–36). Since the seventeenth century, *buccaneer* and *pirate* have become synonymous, as the narrative "El viaje" illustrates (Latimer 4; Lane 96). Simply put, buccaneers sought silver and other goods from Spanish colonies through plunder. The rise of the buccaneers of the Caribbean coincided with the rise of Britain and the decline of Spain as a dominant player in European and Mediterranean politics (Latimer 5). Morgan is infamous for the sacking of Portobelo (Panama) in 1668 and the burning of Panama City in 1671 (Lane 14). Years later in 1671, Morgan set about planning a massive attack on Panama City, which geographically was more difficult to reach. Led by 1,800 men, Morgan arrived in Panama at the mouth of the Chagres River in December 1670. Panama had already begun evacuating the city, as citizens had learned of their impending arrival. Panama was important to Spain and the buccaneers because it was involved in the trans-shipment of Peruvian silver from the Pacific to the Atlantic, where it was exchanged for goods and African slaves. According to Esquemeling's *The Buccaneers of America*, Morgan and his followers set the city on fire, although other accounts declared that Spanish homeowners and their servants emblazoned the city (Lane 120). However, legend has it that Morgan burned Panama.

8. John Esquemeling's *The Buccaneers of America* (1678) is a true account of the most remarkable assaults committed of late years upon the coasts of the West Indies by the buccaneers of Jamaica and Tortuga. Specifically, it contains the exploits of Sir Henry Morgan and the burning of Panama.

9. The 2007 publication of *El escapista y otras reapariciones* unites the original narratives of *El escapista* (1999), *El escapista y demás fugas* (2003), and *Desnudo y otros cuentos* (2001) as well as new short stories published between 1999 and 2007.

10. Williams cites Manuel Puig and Severo Sarduy as examples.

11. See Scott's *What Is Eating Latin American Women Writers?*

Conclusion

1. *Palenque* (http://www.revistapalenque.com) is the first Afrocentric magazine in Panama focusing on human rights, culture, music, and history of African descent in Latin America and the Caribbean.

2. Grace Maynard Clark was born in Río Abajo (in the Canal Zone) in 1946. This excerpt was taken from the website Voices from Our America, an interdisciplinary project that collects, preserves, and disseminates forgotten, hidden, and neglected narratives of American experience.

3. The *congos* are a black performance tradition in the Portobelo region and date back to colonial Panama. They represent Afro-Hispanic or Afro-colonial tradition. As Craft Alexander notes, "Congo cultural nationalism celebrates 16th century Cimarrón resistance to racial domination in Panamá" (130).

4. These statistics were provided by the website of the Contraloría General de la República de Panamá (http://www.contraloria.gob.pa), which conducts the census.

5. In *La variable étnica en el marco legal de Panamá* [The Ethnicity Variable in the Legal Framework in Panama] (2012), Attorney Barrow notes that the 2010 census possessed numerous deficiencies and inaccuracies. First and foremost, 700,000 people were not questioned by census takers. Panama has a total population of approximately 3,408,813 persons. For every ten people who were questioned, six were not asked the following question about race: "¿En este hogar hay alguien que se considera negro(a) o afrodescendiente?" [In this home is there anyone who considers him- or herself to be black or an Afro-descendant?] (52).

Bibliography

Alfaro, Olmedo. *El peligro antillano en la América Central*. Panama City: Imprenta Nacional, 1924. Print.

Andino, Mario Daniel. "Identidad, conflicto y resistencia en Curundú." *Diaspora* 13 (2003): 81–89. Print.

Andrews, George Reid. *Afro-Latin America: 1800–2000*. Oxford: Oxford University Press, 2004. Print.

Arroyo, Justo. "Racial Theory and Practice in Panama." *African Presence in the Americas*. Ed. Carlos Moore. Trenton, NJ: Africa World Press, 1995. 155–62. Print.

Asante, Molefi. *The Afrocentric Idea*. Philadelphia: Temple University Press, 1987. Print.

———. *Afrocentricity: The Theory of Social Change*. Trenton, NJ: Africa World Press, 1992. Print.

Barraza Arriola, Marco Antonio. *Antología de escritores del istmo centroamericano*. San Tecla, El Salvador: Clásicos Roxsil, 1999. Print.

Barrow, Alberto. *La variable étnica en el marco legal de Panamá*. Panama City: Editorial Fuga, 2012. Print.

———. *No me pidas una foto: Develando el racismo en Panamá*. Panama City: Universal Books, 2001. Print.

Barton, Charles L. *Towards the Development of Panama: The Afro-Panamanian Contributions*. New York: Carlton Press, 1976. Print.

Beleño Cedeño, Joaquín. "Autobiografía." *Revista lotería* 373 (1988): 18–19. Print.

———. *Curundú Lane*. Panama City: Ministerio de Educación, 1963. Print.

———. *Gamboa Road Gang / Los forzados de Gamboa*. Panama City: Ediciones Cultural Panameña, 1960. Print.

———. *Luna verde*. Panama City: Imprenta Articsa, 1951. Print.

———. "Una crónica periodística: Temas áridos ante los hechos de ayer." *Revista lotería* 373 (1988): 52–53. Print.

Biesanz, John. "Cultural and Economic Factors in Panamanian Race Relations." *American Sociological Review* (1948): 772–79. Print.

Birmingham-Pokorny, Elba. "The Afro-Hispanic Woman's Role in the Re-Writing of Her History in Carlos Guillermo Wilson's *Cuentos del negro Cubena* and *Chombo*." *Denouncement and Reaffirmation of the Afro-Hispanic Identity in Carlos Guillermo Wilson's Works*. Ed. Elba Birmingham-Pokorny. Miami: Ediciones Universal, 1993. 119–28. Print.

———. *An English Anthology of Afro-Hispanic Writers of the Twentieth Century*. Miami: Ediciones Universal, 1995. Print.

———. "Interview with Dr. Carlos Guillermo Wilson." *Denouncement and Reaffirmation of the Afro-Hispanic Identity in Carlos Guillermo Wilson's Works*. Ed. Elba Birmingham-Pokorny. Miami: Ediciones Universal, 1993. 15–26. Print.

Blades, Rubén. *Amor y control*. Sony U.S. Latin, 1992. CD.

Branche, Jerome. *Colonialism and Race in Luso-Hispanic Literature*. Columbia: University of Missouri Press, 2006. Print.

Brereton, Leticia C. Thomas. *Dictionary of Panamanian English*. Panama City: Librería Universitaria, 2001. Print.

Brown, Joan L. *Confronting Our Canons: Spanish and Latin American Studies in the 21st Century*. Lewisburg, PA: Bucknell University Press, 2010. Print.

Cartey, Wilfred G. *Black Images*. New York: Teachers College Press, 1970. Print.

Castro, Juan de. *Mestizo Nations: Culture, Race and Conformity in Latin American Literature*. Tucson: University of Arizona Press, 2002. Print.

Chacón Gutiérrez, Albino, and Carlos Cañas Dinarte, eds. *Diccionario de la literatura centroamericana*. San José, Costa Rica: Editorial Costa Rica, 2007. Print.

Clifford, James. "Diasporas." *Cultural Anthropology* (1994): 303–38. Print.

Conniff, Michael L. *Black Labor on a White Canal: 1904–1981*. Pittsburgh, PA: University of Pittsburgh Press, 1985. Print.

Craft Alexander, Renée. "'Una raza, dos etnias': The Politics of Be(com)ing/Performing 'Afropanameño.'" *Latin American and Caribbean Ethnic Studies* (2008): 123–47. Print.

Cruz, Barbara. *Rubén Blades: Salsa Singer and Social Activist*. Springfield, NJ: Enslow Publishers, 1997. Print.

Davis, F. J. *Who Is Black? One Nation's Definition*. Philadelphia: Pennsylvania State University Press, 2005. Print.

DeCosta-Willis, Miriam, ed. *Blacks in Hispanic Literature: Critical Essays*. Port Washington, NY: Kennikat Press, 1977. Print.

Délano, Poli. *Cuentos centroamericanos*. Barcelona: Editorial Andrés Bello. 2000. Print.

Derby, Lauren. "Race, National Identity and the Idea of Value." *Blacks, Coloureds and National Identity in Nineteenth-Century Latin America*.

Ed. Nancy Priscilla Naro. London: Institute of Latin American Studies, 2003. 5–37. Print.

DuBois, W. E. B. *The Souls of Black Folk*. 1903. New York: Penguin Books, 1989. Print.

Duke, Dawn. *Literary Passion, Ideological Commitment: Toward a Legacy of Afro-Cuban and Afro-Brazilian Women Writers*. Lewisburg, PA: Bucknell University Press, 2008. Print.

Duncan, Quince. *Los cuatro espejos*. San José, Costa Rica: Editorial Costa Rica, 1973. Print.

Duncan, Quince, and Lorein Powell. *Teoría y práctica del racismo*. San José, Costa Rica: Editorial Departamento Ecuménico de Investigaciones, 1988. Print.

Dyson, Michael Eric. "Tour(é)ing Blackness." Foreword. *Who's Afraid of Post-Blackness? What It Means to Be Black Now*. Touré. New York: Free Press, 2011. xiii–xx. Print.

Edison, Thomas Wayne. "The Afro-Caribbean Novels of Resistance of Alejo Carpentier, Quince Duncan, Carlos Guillermo Wilson, and Manuel Zapata Olivella." PhD diss. University of Kentucky, 2002. Print.

Escobar, Federico. *Patrióticas*. Panama City: Tipografía Moderna, 1923. Print.

———. "Chispas." *La igualdad* 27 (1893). Print.

Fábrega, José Isaac. *Crisol*. Panama City: Star and Herald, 1936. Print.

Fanon, Frantz. *Black Skin, White Masks*. New York: Grove Press, 1967. Print.

Fernández Retamar, Roberto. *Caliban and Other Essays*. Translated by Edward Baker. Minneapolis: University of Minnesota Press, 1989. Print.

Figueroa Navarro, Alfredo. *Dominio y sociedad en el Panamá colombiana, 1821–1903*. Panama City: Editorial Universitaria, 1982. Print.

Flores, Juan, and Miriam Jiménez Román. "Triple-Consciousness? Approaches to Afro-Latino Culture in the United States." *Latin American and Caribbean Ethnic Studies* (2009): 319–28. Print.

Fortune, Armando. *Obras selectas*. Ed. Gerardo Maloney. Panama City: Instituto Nacional de Cultura, 1994. Print.

Franceschi, Victor. "El hombre blanco en la poesía negra." *Revista lotería* 4 (1959): 134–39. Print.

Frederick, Rhonda. *"Colón Man a Come": Mythographies of Panama Canal Migration*. Lanham, MD: Lexington Books, 2005. Print.

Fuente, Alejandro de la. "Looking into the Nation's Heart: Gloria Rolando's Approximation to 1912." *Caribbean Studies* (2008): 207–10. Print.

Gallers, Anita. "At What Price Solidarity? Homophobia and Cubena's Anti-Racist Program." *Secolas Annals* 35 (2003): 54–60. Print.

García S., Ismael. *Historia de la literatura panameña*. Mexico City: Universidad Nacional Autónoma de México, 1964. Print.

———. *Medio siglo de poesía panameña*. Mexico City: Talleres Gráficos de Impresas Modernas, 1956. Print.

Geggus, David. "The Influence of the Haitian Revolution in Blacks in Latin America and the Caribbean." *Blacks, Coloureds and National Identity in Nineteenth-Century Latin America*. Ed. Nancy Priscilla Naro. London: Institute of Latin American Studies, 2003. 38–59. Print.

Gellner, Ernest. *Nationalism*. New York: New York University Press, 1997. Print.

Gilroy, Paul. *Small Acts: Thoughts on the Politics of Black Cultures*. London: Serpent's Tail, 1993. Print.

Gólcher, Ileana, ed. *Este país, un canal: Encuentro de culturas*. Panama City: Proyecto Ética Cívica y Cultura Democrática, 1999. Print.

Greene, Julie. *The Canal Builders: Making America's Empire at the Panama Canal*. New York: Penguin Press, 2009. Print.

Hall, Stuart. "Cultural Identity and Diaspora." *Framework* 36: 222–37. Print.

Helg, Aline. "A Fragmented Majority: Free 'of All Colors,' Indians, and Slaves in Caribbean Colombia during the Haitian Revolution." *The Impact of the Haitian Revolution in the Atlantic World*. Ed. David Geggus. Columbia: University of South Carolina Press, 2001. 157–75. Print.

———. "Race and Black Mobilization in Colonial and Early Independent Cuba: A Comparative Perspective." *Ethnohistory* (1997): 53–74. Print.

Hernández, Gaspar Octavio. *La copa de amatista*. Panama City: Imprenta Nacional, 1923. Print.

———. *Iconografía*. Panama City: Imprenta "Esto y Aquello," 1916. Print.

———. *Obras selectas*. Panama City: Ministerio de Educación, Dirección Nacional de Cultural, 1966. Print.

Herzfeld, Anita. "The Creoles of Costa Rica and Panama." *Central American English*. Ed. John Holm. Heidelberg, Germany: Groos, 1983. 131–55. Print.

Howard, David. *Coloring the Nation: Race and Ethnicity in the Dominican Republic*. Oxford, UK: Signal Books, 2001. Print.

Howell, Luisa. "Popular Speech and Culture in *Los nietos de Felicidad Dolores*." *Diasporas* 13 (2004): 40–44. Print.

Hutcheon, Linda. "Postmodernism." *Encyclopedia of Contemporary Literary Theory: Approaches, Scholars, Terms*. Ed. Irena R. Makaryk. Toronto: University of Toronto Press, 1993. 612–13. Print.

Jackson, Richard L. *The Black Image in Latin American Literature*. Albuquerque: University of New Mexico Press, 1976. Print.

———. *Black Literature and Humanism in Latin America*. Athens: University of Georgia Press, 1988. Print.

———. "Black Phobia and the White Aesthetic in Spanish American Literature." *Hispania* 58 (1975): 467–80. Print.

———. *Black Writers and the Hispanic Canon*. New York: Twayne Publishers, 1997. Print.

———. *Black Writers and Latin America: Cross-Cultural Affinities*. Washington, DC: Howard University Press, 1998. Print.

———. *Black Writers in Latin America*. Albuquerque: University of New Mexico Press, 1979. Print.

Jaramillo Levi, Enrique. *Panamá cuenta: Cuentistas del centenario, 1851–2003*. Panama City: Grupo Editorial Norma, 2003. Print.

———. *Poesía panameña contemporánea (1929–1979)*. Mexico City: Liberta-Sumaria, 1980. Print.

———. *Sueños compartidos: Compilación histórica de cuentistas panameños, 1892–2004*. Panama City: Universal Books, 2005. Print.

Jiménez, Blas. *Caribe africano en despertar*. Translated by Antonio D. Tillis. London: Mango Publishing, 2010. Print.

Jiménez Román, Miriam, and Juan Flores, eds. "Introduction." *The Afro-Latin@ Reader: History and Culture in the United States*. Durham, NC: Duke University Press, 2010. 1–15. Print.

Johnson, Lygia. "Enfoques temáticos y estilísticos sobre *Detrás de la reja.*" *Detrás de la reja*. Eds. Celia Correa de Zapata and Lygia Johnson. Caracas: Editorial Arte, 1980. 30–44. Print.

Kymlicka, Will. *Politics in the Vernacular: Nationalism, Multiculturalism and Citizenship*. Oxford: Oxford University Press, 2000. Print.

Lane, Kris E. *Pillaging the Empire: Piracy in the Americas (1500–1750)*. London: M. E. Sharpe, 1998. Print.

Latimer, Jon. *Buccaneers of the Caribbean: How Piracy Forged an Empire*. Cambridge, MA: Harvard University Press, 2009. Print.

Laurenza, Roque Javier. *Los poetas de la generación republicana*. Panama City: Editorial La Moderna, 1933. Print.

León Jiménez, Elda Maúd. *Omar Torrijos: Un camino por recorrer*. Panama City: Fundación Omar Torrijos, 1996. Print.

Lowe de Goodin, Melva. *Afrodescendientes en el Istmo de Panamá, 1501–2012*. Panama City: Editora Sibauste, 2012. Print.

———. *De Barbados a Panamá / From Barbados to Panama*. Panama City: Editoras Géminis, 1999. Print.

Maloney, Gerardo. *Juega vivo!* Panama City: Ediciones Formato Dieciseis, 1984. Print.

———. "El movimiento negro en Panamá." *Revista panameña de sociología* 5 (1988): 145–58. Print.

———. *Street Smart*. Translated by Ian Smart. Washington, DC: Original World Press, 2008. Print.

Martin-Ogunsola, Dellita. "Invisibility, Double Consciousness and the Crisis of Identity in *Los cuatro espejos*." *Afro-Hispanic Review* 2 (1987): 9–15. Print.

Martínez Ortega, Aristides. *Las generaciones de poetas panameños*. Panama City: Tareas, 1992. Print.

———. "La identidad nacional en la poesía panameña." *Tareas* 113 (2003): 137–44. Print.

Martínez Ortega, Aristides, Franz García de Paredes, and Ricardo Segura Jiménez, eds. *Diccionario de la literatura panameña*. Panama City: Universidad de Panamá, 2002. Print.

McCollough, David. *The Path between the Seas: The Creation of the Panama Canal, 1870–1914*. New York: Simon and Schuster, 1977. Print.

McForbes, Michelle. "Proto-Garifuna: The Language of the Kalipona on the Eve of the Africans' Arrival in St. Vincent." *PALARA* 15 (2011): 51–65. Print.

McGuinness, Aims. *Path of Empire: Panama and the California Gold Rush.* Ithaca, NY: Cornell University Press, 2008. Print.

———. "Searching for 'Latin America': Race and Sovereignty in the 1850s." *Race and Nation in Modern Latin America.* Eds. Nancy P. Appelbaum, Anne S. Macpherson, and Karin Alejandra Rosemblatt. Chapel Hill: University of North Carolina Press, 2003. 87–107. Print.

Miró, Rodrigo. *Cien años de poesía en Panamá (1858–1952).* Panama City: Librería Avance, 1966. Print.

———. *La literatura panameña (origen y proceso).* San José, Costa Rica: Imprenta Trejos Hermanos, 1970. Print.

Mosby, Dorothy. *Place, Language and Identity in Afro–Costan Rican Literature.* Columbia: University of Missouri Press, 2003. Print.

Mujica, Bárbara. "Teaching Literature: Canon, Controversy, and the Literary Anthology." *Hispania* 80 (1997): 203–15. Print.

Nwankwo, Ifeoma C. K. "The Art of Memory in Panamanian West Indian Discourse: Melva Lowe de Goodin's *De/From Barbados a/to Panama.*" *PALARA* 6 (2002): 3–17. Print.

Ojeda, Martha. "Nicomedes Santa Cruz frente al canon literario peruano: Argumentos para su inclusión." *PALARA* 8 (2004): 5–19. Print.

Olliz Boyd, Antonio. "The Concept of Black Awareness as a Thematic Approach in Latin American Literature." *Blacks in Hispanic Literature: Critical Essays.* Ed. Miriam DeCosta. New York: Kennikat Press, 1977. 65–73. Print.

Omi, Michael, and Howard Winant. *Racial Formation in the United States: From the 1960s to the 1990s.* New York: Routledge, 1994. Print.

Padrón, Francisco Morales. "El caso del canal de Panama." *Revista cultural lotería* 336–37 (1984): 5–25. Print.

Peña, Concha. *Gaspar Octavio Hernández: Poeta del pueblo.* Panama City: Publicación del Departamento de Bellas Artes del Ministerio de Educación, 1953. Print.

Pérez-Venero, Mirna Miriam. "Raza, color y prejuicios en la novelística panameña contemporánea de tema canalero." MA thesis. Louisiana State University, 1973. Print.

Perús, Francoise. "Crisis, identidad y diálogo en *Luna verde* de Joaquín Beleño." *Revista cultural de Excelsior* 19 (1989): 28–37. Print.

Piedra, José. "Literary Whiteness and the Afro-Hispanic Difference." *New Literary History* 18 (1987): 303–32. Print.

Prescott, Laurence E. *Candelario Obeso y la iniciación de la poesía negra en Colombia.* Bogotá: Publicaciones del Instituto Caro y Cuervo, 1985. Print.

———. "'Negro nací': Authorship and Voice in Verses Attributed to Candelario Obeso." *Afro Hispanic Review* (1993): 3–15. Print.

Priestley, George. "Antillean-Panamanians or Afro-Panamanians? Political Participation and the Politics of Identity during the Carter-Torrijos Treaty Negotiations." *Transforming Anthropology* (2004): 50–67. Print.

Priestley, George, and Alberto Barrow. "The Black Movement in Panamá: A Historical and Political Interpretation, 1994–2004." *Souls* (2008): 227–55. Print.

Pulido Ritter, Luis. "Carlos E. Russell: Memoria diaspórica nacional y crítica de la nación panameña." *Istmo: Revista virtual de estudios literarios y culturales centroamericanos* (2009). Web. http://istmo.denison.edu/n18/articulos/pulido.html.

———. *Filosofía de la nación romántica.* Panama City: Colección Ricardo Miró, 2007. Print.

———. "Introducción: Entrevista con Carlos E. Russell." *Istmo: Revista virtual de estudios literarios y culturales centroamericanos* (2010): 1–3. Web. http://istmo.denison.edu/n21/articulos/2-watson_sonja_form.pdf.

Puri, Shalini. *The Caribbean Postcolonial: Social Equality, Post-Nationalism, and Cultural Hybridity.* New York: Palgrave Macmillan, 2004. Print.

Rahim, Jennifer. "(Not) Knowing the Difference: Calypso Overseas and the Sound of Belonging in Selected Narratives of Migration." *Music, Memory, Resistance, Calypso and the Caribbean Literary Imagination.* Eds. Sandra Pouchet Paquet and Patricia Joan Saunders. Miami: Ian Randle Publishers, 2007. 283–306. Print.

Ramírez C., Luis E. *Panamá y su historia: Una visión diferente de la historia nacional.* Panama City: Imprenta Artística, 2002. Print.

Restall, Matthew. "Black Conquistadors: Armed Africans in Early Spanish America." *Americas* (2000): 171–205. Print.

Rout, Leslie B. *The African Experience in Spanish America.* Princeton, NJ: Markus Wiener Publishers, 2003. Print.

Ruiloba C., Rafael. "Joaquín Beleño: El poder sagrado de la dignidad y la verdad en la trilogía del canal." *Revista lotería* 412 (1997): 78–95. Print.

Russell, Carlos E. "Caliban's Contemporary Caribbean Dilemma." *Wadabagei: A Journal of the Caribbean and Its Diaspora* (2005): 86–99. Print.

———. "Cuatro poetas o nueve poemas." *Revista nacional de cultura* 5 (1976): 97–111. Print.

———. "Lamentations of an Ex Slave." *Latin American and Caribbean Ethnic Studies* (2009): 329–30. Print.

———. *The Last Buffalo: "Are Panamanians of Caribbean Ancestry an Endangered Species?* Charlotte, NC: Conquering Books, 2003. Print.

———. "Panama's Caribbean People and the New Century." *Black Diaspora* (2000): 37–38, 62–63. Print.

———. *Remembranzas y lágrimas.* Panama City: n.p., 2001. Print.

Scott, Renée S. *What Is Eating Latin American Women Writers? Food, Weight and Eating Disorders.* New York: Cambria Press, 2009. Print.

Seales Soley, La Verne Marie. "Entrevista con Carlos Guillermo Cubena Wilson." *Afro Hispanic Review* (1998): 67–69. Print.

Sepúlveda, Melida Ruth. *El tema del canal en la novelística panameña.* Caracas: Universidad Católica Andrés Bello, 1975. Print.

Shaw, Donald. *Nueva narrativa hispanoamericana: Boom, posboom, posmodernismo.* Madrid: Cátedra, 1999. Print.

Sieder, Rachel. "Honduras." *No Longer Invisible: Afro-Latin Americans Today.* Ed. Minority Rights Group. London: Minority Rights Publications, 1995. 235–42. Print.

Smart, Ian. *Amazing Connections: Kemet to Hispanophone Africana Literature.* Washington, DC: Original World Press, 1996. Print.

———. *Central American Writers of West Indian Origin: A New Hispanic Literature.* Washington, DC: Three Continents Press, 1984. Print.

Stinchcomb, Dawn F. *The Development of Literary Blackness in the Dominican Republic.* Gainesville: University Press of Florida, 2004. Print.

Strom, Diana L. "The Novels of Joaquín Beleño C.: A Critical Appraisal of *Curundú, Luna verde, Gamboa Road Gang* and *Flor de banana.*" MA thesis. University of Wisconsin, 1980. Print.

Szok, Peter A. *"La última gaviota": Liberalism and Nostalgia in Early Twentieth-Century Panamá.* Westport, CT: Greenwood Press, 2001. Print.

Taylor, Christopher. *The Black Carib Wars: Freedom, Survival, and the Making of the Garifuna.* Jackson: University Press of Mississippi, 2012. Print.

Taylor, Melanie. *Camino a Mariato.* Managua: Editorial Amerrisque, 2009. Print.

———. *Tiempos acuáticos.* Panama City: Universidad Tecnológica de Panamá y Cuadernos Marginales, 2000. Print.

Tillis, Antonio. "Awakening the Caribbean African: The Socio-Political Poetics of Blas Jiménez." *Caribe africano en despertar.* London: Mango Publishing, 2010. 13–32. Print.

———. *Manuel Zapata Olivella and the "Darkening" of Latin American Literature.* Columbia: University of Missouri Press, 2005. Print.

Wade, Peter. *Blackness and Race Mixture: The Dynamics of Racial Identity in Colombia.* Baltimore: Johns Hopkins University Press, 1993. Print.

Watkins, Patricia. "Los aspectos socio-políticos en la trilogía canalera de Joaquín Beleño." PhD diss. Florida State University, 1996. Print.

Watson, Sonja Stephenson. "'Are Panamanians of Caribbean Ancestry an Endangered Species'? Critical Literary Debates on Panamanian Blackness in the Works of Carlos Wilson, Gerardo Maloney, and Carlos Russell." *Latin American and Caribbean Ethnic Studies* (2009): 231–54. Print.

———. "*Changó, el gran putas:* Contemporary Afro-Hispanic Historical Novel." *Afro-Hispanic Review* (2006): 67–86. Print.

———. "Entrevista a Melanie Taylor." Unpublished interview. August 1, 2003. Panama City, Panama.

———. "Entrevista a Melanie Taylor." Unpublished interview. June 24, 2013. Email.

———. "Entrevista con Carlos Russell." *Istmo: Revista virtual de estudios literarios y culturales centroamericanos* (2010). Web. http://collaborations .denison.edu/istmo/n21/articulos/media/carlos_russell.mp4.

———. "*The Grandchildren of Felicidad Dolores* and the Contemporary Afro-Hispanic Historical Novel: A New Reading." Ed. Antonio D. Tillis. *Critical Perspectives on Contemporary Afro-Hispanic Literature.* New York: Routledge Press, 2012. 30–50. Print.

———. "Poetic Negrism and the National Sentiment of Anti–West Indianism and Anti-Imperialism in Panamanian Literature." *Callaloo 35* (2012): 459–74. Print.

Watson Miller, Ingrid. *Afro-Hispanic Literature: An Anthology of Hispanic Writers of African Ancestry.* Miami: Ediciones Universal, 1991. Print.

Webster, Johnny. *En un golpe de tos sintió volar la vida—Gaspar Octavio Hernández: Obras escogidas.* Lanham, MD: University Press of America, 2003. Print.

Westerman, George. *Cincuenta años (1903–1953) de negociaciones de un tratado entre los EEUU de Norte América y la República de Panamá.* Panama City: Imprenta de la Academia, 1953. Print.

———. *Los inmigrantes antillanos en Panamá.* Panama City: Impresora de la Nación, 1980. Print.

———. *Un grupo minoritario en Panamá.* Panama City: Liga Cívica Nacional. 1950. Print.

———. *Urban Housing in Panama and Some of Its Problems.* Panama City: Institute for Economic Development, 1955. Print.

Williams, Claudette M. *Charcoal and Cinnamon: The Politics of Color in Spanish Caribbean Literature.* Gainesville: University Press of Florida, 2000. Print.

Williams, Raymond Leslie. *The Modern Latin-American Novel.* London: Prentice Hall International, 1998. Print.

Wilson, Carlos Guillermo. *Chombo.* Miami: Universal Editions, 1981. Print.

———. "The Image of the Chombitas in Joaquín Beleño's *Gamboa Road Gang.*" *Proceedings of the Black Image in Latin American Literature.* Slippery Rock, PA: Department of Modern Languages and Culture, Slippery Rock University, 1989. 75–85. Print.

———. *La misión secreta.* Alexandria, VA: Alexander Street Press, 2005. Print.

———. *Los mosquitos de orixá Chango: Cuentos y poemas.* Eatontown, NJ: Ediciones Nuevo Espacio, 2000. Print.

———. *Los nietos de Felicidad Dolores.* Miami: Universal Editions, 1991. Print.

———. "Sinopsis de la poesía afro-panameña." *Afro-Hispanic Review* (1987): 14–16. Print.

Wynter Melo, Carlos Oriel. *Cuentos con salsa: Narraciones del Panamá urbano.* Panama City: Grupo Editorial Norma, 2008. Print.

———. *El escapista y otras reapariciones.* Bogotá: Panamericana Editorial, 2007. Print.

Zien, Katherine. "Toward a Pedagogy of Redress: Staging West Indian Panamanian History in *De/From Barbados a/to Panamá*." *Latin American and Caribbean Ethnic Studies* (2009): 293–317. Print.

Zoggyie, Haakayoo. *In Search of the Fathers: The Poetics of Disalienation in the Narrative of Two Contemporary Afro-Hispanic Writers*. New Orleans: University Press of the South, 2003. Print.

———. "Subversive Tales, Transgressive Laughs: Reading Carlos Guillermo Wilson's *Chombo* as Satire." *College Language Association* 2 (2003): 193–211. Print.

Index

Abuela Leah (in *De/From Barbados*), 102, 104

Abuelo Samuel (in *De/From Barbados*), 102, 104

Acción Reivindicadora del Negro Panameño (ARENEP), 97

African Diaspora, 147–48; Black Caribs, 89–90; black conquistadors, 89, 91–92; Caliban as metaphor for, 124–26; constructing an African identity, 78–80; Cubena addressing, 70, 76–77, 113–14; in Cubena's trilogy, 78–86; and denial of blackness, 113; and "diaspora consciousness," 24; Escobar addressing, 27–29; Hall on, 129; in *La misión secreta*, 82; Lowe de Goodin's alignment with, 94–95, 145; Maloney and, 107–12, 145; and national discourse of homogeneity, 4; nomadic experience of, 110–11; in Olivella's *Changó*, 89; and perception of death, 85; and recognition of shared experience, 6; Russell and, 96, 116–20, 124, 126; as shared heritage for Afro-Hispanics and West Indians, 86, 89–91

"African Routes, Caribbean Roots, Latino Lives" (*LACES*), 3

Afrocentric Idea (Asante), 78

Afrocentricism, 78–79

Afrocentricity (Asante), 78

Afro-Cubans, 150n2

Afrodescendientes en el Istmo de Panamá (Lowe de Goodin), 101

Afro-Hispanic Literature (Watson Miller), 73

Afro-Hispanics, 5, 149n1; denying African roots, 88; historical novels by/about, 77–78; history of, 2; identity formation of, 6; and literature scholarship, 73–78, 144; as *moreno* or *negro*, 12; and national anti-West Indian sentiment, 13–16; perceived as fully integrated and assimilated, 14, 18, 32, 47; tensions with West Indians, 3–13, 86–93, 100–101, 113, 146–48; "writing white," 35

Afro-Panamanian(s): Afro-Panamanian Forum, 96; comprising multiple diasporas, 3, 5; forging a unified identity for, 99–100, 127, 144–48; Lowe de Goodin and identification,

Afro-Panamanian(s) (*continued*)
95; Maloney's preference for term,
96; shared experience of, 6; use of
term, 5, 8, 15–16, 96
Afro-realism, 154n3
Aguilera, Rodolfo Jr., 43
Aguilera Malta, Demetrio, 151–52n2
Agustín (in "Hombre y mujer"), 140–41
Alexander, Kendra, 124
Alfaro, Olmedo, 13
Amables predicciones (Taylor), 131
Amazing Connections (Smart), 79
"Las Américas" (Wilson), 115
Andino, Mario Daniel, 54
Andrews, George Reid, 13, 147
Anguilla, 155n9
Annabelle Rodney (in *Gamboa*), 49,
60–61, 63, 65–67
anti-bildungsroman, 152n11
anti-imperialism, 124
antillanidad, 51
antillanos, use of term, 12–13, 15–16,
94, 148
Antología de escritores del istmo cen-
troamericano, 71
Antón Mandinga (in *La misión*
secreta), 82
APODAN (Asociación de Negros
Profesionales), 97
Aquileo J. Echevarría Prize, 76
ARENEP (Acción Reivindicadora del
Negro Panameño), 97
Argentina, 153n14
Ariel (Rodó), 124
arielismo, 124–25
Arosemena, Justo, 10
Arroyo, Justo, 46, 59
Asante, Molefi, 60, 78
Ashanti naming customs, 79
Asociación de Negros Profesionales
(APODAN), 97
assimilation: and age, 2; lamenting,
108–9, 126–27; promotion by West
Indians, 13–14; Westerman on, 15,
80; West Indians accused of resist-
ing, 11, 13–15, 56

Association of Caribbean States, 96
Association of Panamanian Writers,
138
Association of Professional Workers,
99
Atá (in *Gamboa Road Gang*): committing suicide in prison, 63, 65;
double consciousness of, 66, 126;
as new Panamanian, 63; refusing
to self-identify as black, 63–66;
relationship with a white woman,
60–61, 63–65; struggling to find
place in society, 47, 58; wrongly
accused of rape, 49, 60–61
Atrapasueños (Taylor), 131
"At What Price Solidarity?" (Gallers),
155n7

Balboa, Vasco Núñez de, 11, 84, 92
Ballagas, Emilio, 19
Barbados, 103–4
barcaroles, 34, 151n7
Barrow, Alberto, 98–100
Bayano (in *La misión secreta*), 82
Belafonte, Harry, 104, 105
Beleño, Joaquín: on Canal Zone as
U.S. plantation, 43–44; Canal Zone
trilogy, 41, 42, 46–56; disagreements with Cubena, 86; early
life of, 46; internalizing racism,
67; marginalizing of West Indian
characters, 67; and *mestizaje,* 60;
questioning legitimacy of other
blacks, 145; racial background of,
46–47; Smart on, 152n9; on West
Indians as by-product of Canal, 42,
67; working in Canal Zone, 46
Belize, 90
Bernard, Eulalia, 145
Biesanz, John, 14–15
bildungsroman and anti-bildungsroman,
152n11
binaries, challenging of, 129
"biological visibility" of West Indians,
14
Birmingham-Pokorny, Elba, 3, 85

"Black Awareness Day" (Maloney), 100
"Black Bard." *See* Escobar, Federico
Black Caribs, 155n8
black conquistadors, 89, 91–92
Black Cultures of the Americas, 96, 98, 106
"Black Ethnicity Day" (Maloney), 112
"black internationalism," 6
Black Liberal Party (Partido Liberal de Negros), 18, 150n1
black movements in Panama, 15, 97–101, 146
blackness: associated with sensuality/ sexuality, 60; black women as doubly marginalized, 62; consciousness of, 39, 109–10; denial of (Canal Zone trilogy), 57–58; explaining attraction to, 60–61; gorilla caricatures, 1; Panamanian fear of "black nation" label, 42; preventing writers from gaining acceptance, 76; seen as corruption, deformity, 50–51; seen as negation, 6, 36–39; as theme by Escobar, 24–28; and use of U.S. race code in Zone, 44–45, 58, 67, 97. *See also* chombo(s)
Black Panamanian Congress/Conference (Congreso del Negro Panameño), 16, 96, 98, 106
Black Panamanian Queen Contest, 99
Black Panamanian Recovery Action Group, 99
"Black Swan." *See* Hernández, Gaspar Octavio
Black Writers and the Hispanic Canon (Jackson), 73
Black Writers in Latin America (Jackson), 73, 78
Blades, Rubén, 104, 105, 156n7
Blanque, Andrea, 158n5
blanqueamiento/"whitening," 63, 109
Bocas del Toro, Panama, 105
body image, 140–43; in "Desnudez metafísica," 141–42; in "Inmensamente Eunice," 158n5; in "La sombra,"

133–35; in "Un día con los Pérez Olsen," 142–43. *See also* mirrors; self-image
Bolívar, Simón, 9
Bolivia, 153n19
"El bombero" (Wilson), 72
boom novels, 75, 78
Boukman, Dutty, 89
Brereton, Leticia C. Thomas, 153n16
Britain and the Caribbean, 95–96, 158n7
Brooklyn, New York, 116–18
Brown, Joan L., 74–77
Brown, John (in *Los nietos*), 86–87
Brown, Salvador (in *Curundú*), 53–55
Buccaneers of America (Esquemeling), 137–38, 158n8
"buena presencia," 100

Cacao, 52, 153n15
Caimana (in "El viaje"), 136–37
Calibán (Retamar), 125
"Caliban's Contemporary Caribbean Dilemma" (Russell), 123–27
La Calle 10 (Zapata Olivella), 75
Calypso (Maloney), 106–7
Camarano de Sucre, Yolanda, 43, 151n2
Camino a Mariato (Taylor), 131, 133–38, 157n4
Canal Builders (Greene), 152n3
Canal/Canal Zone: acknowledging West Indian "Colón man," 103–6; Beleño portraying sexual violence in, 61–62; construction of, 11, 22, 151–52n2; as "Creator," 112; exacerbating existing racial conflict, 67; gold and silver rolls, 44, 112; Jim Crow and one-drop rule in, 44–45, 58, 152nn4–5; migrant workers on, 2, 103–4; perceived as foreign, 12; as place of international transit, 10; representing both promise and imperialism, 43; U.S. occupation and Canal construction, 7
Canal Zone (Aguilera Malta), 151–52n2

Canal Zone novels, 43
canon of Panamanian literature, 2,
    70–72; inclusion of *Gamboa Road
    Gang* in, 86; omission of Cubena's
    trilogy from, 73–78, 96; themes of
    blackness and whiteness in, 24–28
"Cantares de Castilla de Oro"
    (Hernández), 35–36
Caribbean/Caribbean Diaspora, 95–
    96, 112
Caribe africano en despertar (Jimé-
    nez), 107–9
"Carta a un amigo" (Porras), 9
Cartey, Wilfred G., 19
Castellano, Rosario, 158n5
Castilian Spanish, 154n5
Castro, Fidel, 125
Castro, Juan de, 12
CEDEAP (El Centro de Estudios Afro-
    Panameños), 97–98
Cela, Camilo José, 154–55n6
census, self-identity terms on, 15–16,
    147–48
*Central American Writers of West
    Indian Origin* (Smart), 3, 66
Central Directorate of Societies of
    Color, 150n5
Centro de Estudios Afro-Panameños
    (CEDEAP), 97–98
Centro George Westerman, 146
Cervantes, Miguel de, 11, 113,
    156n10
Chambacú, corral de negros (Zapata
    Olivella), 75
Changó, el gran putas (Zapata Oliv-
    ella), 89, 93
Charles (in *Los cuatro espejos*), 57–58,
    110
Chile, 92
Chiriquí people, 152n8
Chombo (Wilson), 70, 76, 80–81, 83–
    84
chombo(s), 65–66, 80; Atá as (in
    Gamboa Road Gang), 63–66;
    Beleño's portrayal of, 60, 67; *chom-
    bas*, 60, 154n20; *chombo-gringo*,

64; distinguished by language, race,
    culture, 14–15; many meanings of,
    120; Red Box as (in *Curundú*), 58,
    66
Cien años de poesía en Panamá
    (Miró), 23–26
civil rights movement, U.S., 1, 85, 97
Clark, Grace Maynard, 144, 146,
    159n2
"Claroscuro" (Hernández), 35–39
cocolos, 90, 155n9
"Coincidencia" (Hernández), 35–36
Colombia, 9, 153n15
Colón, Panama, 9, 43, 48, 105
"Colón Man," 104–6
"Colón Man a Come" (Frederick),
    156n6
colored, use of term, 152n6
color spectrum and racial identity, 12
"common memory," 104, 156n5
Como agua para chocolate, 132
Confronting Our Canons (Brown),
    74–75
congos, 147, 159n3
Congreso del Negro Panameño (Black
    Panamanian Conference), 16, 96,
    98, 106
conquistadors, black, 89, 91–92
Cortés, Hernán, 90–92
Craft Alexander, Renée, 5–6, 147,
    159n3
Creole (language), 56, 102, 153n16.
    See also criollos/creoles
Creolization, 109
criollos/creoles, 9, 32, 120, 124–25,
    149n2
Crisol (Fábrega), 43, 151n1
crisol de razas, 151n1
Los cuatro espejos (Duncan), 57–58,
    110
Cuba, 124–25, 150n2
"Cubena." *See* Wilson, Carlos Guill-
    ermo "Cubena"
cuculustes, 90, 155n9
Cuentos del negro Cubena (Wilson),
    69

cuentos/short stories, 130
"El culto del idoma" (Hernández),
  31, 42
cultural identity: as basic social bond,
  4; as becoming, 129, 146; and difference, 129; and hybridity, 5–6,
  112, 116, 120–21, 127, 130, 144;
  process of forming, 146; promoting
  blackness over, 99; "similarity" and
  "difference" in forming, 5–6
Curundú (Beleño): language in,
  55–56; meaning of *curundú*, 152n7;
  plot of, 48–49, 53–54; portraying U.S. imperialism, 46–47; racial
  prejudice in, 53–54, 60–61; Red
  Box, 49, 57–58, 66, 109; religious
  prejudice in, 54–55; views of
  women in, 60–62

Dangriga, Ugundani (in *La misión*), 90
Davis, Angela, 124
Davis, F. J., 4, 152n4
"Day-O (Banana Boat Song)" (Bela-
  fonte), 104, 105
De/From Barbados a/to Panamá
  (Lowe de Goodin), 102
del Cabral, Manuel, 19
democracy, U.S. ideal vs. U.S. actions,
  49
*Denouncement and Reaffirmation
  of the Afro-Hispanic Identity . . .*
  (Birmingham-Pokorny), 3
"Desarraigado" (Wilson), 113–14
"Desnudez metafísica" (Wynter
  Melo), 141–42
Día de la Etnia Negra/Black Ethnicity
  Day, 100, 147
"diaspora consciousness," 24
*Diccionario de la literatura cen-
  troamericana*, 71
Diccionario de la literatura panameña,
  71
Dinero para los peces (Restrepo),
  152n2
Dominican Republic, 9, 10, 107, 155n9
Doña Bárbara, 52, 152–53nn14

Don Segundo Sombra, 52, 152–53nn14
double consciousness, 66, 116, 126,
  158n6
DuBois, W. E. B., 66, 116, 126
Duke, Dawn, 150n5
Duncan, Quince: and Afrocentrism,
  79; and *Afro-realism*, 154n3; and
  boom novels, 75; *Los cuatro espejos*, 57–58, 110; as third-generation
  West Indian writer, 145; as West
  Indian writing in Spanish, 73;
  winning contest with anonymous
  submission, 76

Ecuador, 153nn14, 19
Edison, Thomas Wayne, 46–47, 74
"Ego sum" (Hernández), 37–39, 41
En Chimá nace un santo (Zapata
  Olivella), 75
*English Anthology of Afro-Hispanic
  Writers of the Twentieth Century,
  An*, 73
English-based Creole, 153n16
English-speaking Caribbeans, 3
Enriquillo: Leyenda dominicana, 10
En tiempo de crisis (Maloney), 107
En un golpe de tos sintió volar la vida
  (Webster), 4
escapism, 20, 34, 40
El escapista (Wynter Melo), 138–40
Escobar, Federico, 21; as "Black
  Bard," 20; "Chispas," 27–29, 144;
  early life of, 20; espousing *mestizaje*
  rhetoric, 27; exhibiting racial pride,
  7; idealistic claims of, 23; in literary
  canon, 70; and *negrista* move-
  ment, 19–20; "Nieblas," 23–29;
  on Panama as melting pot, 22; and
  panameñidad, 17, 22; *Patrióticas*,
  21–23; and themes of blackness and
  whiteness, 24–28, 130
"Escudo Cubena" shield, 79–80
Esquemeling, John, 158n8
Estebanillo (Estebanico), 82, 90–92
Estenoz, Evaristo, 150n2
ethnic cleansing/*mestizaje negativo*, 70

Exciters musical group, 99
expatriados, experiences of, 119–20

Fábrega, José Isaac, 43, 151n1
La familia de Pascual Duarte (Cela),
  154–55n6
Fanon, Frantz, 57, 58
Felicidad Dolores, Los nietos de (Wil-
  son), 70, 81, 84–89
Felipillo (in *La misión secreta*), 82
feminist discourse, 130–38. *See also*
  women
Fernández Retamar, Roberto, 125
Ferré, Rosario, 132
50 millas de heroicidad (Aguilera), 43,
  151n2
Filós-Hines Treaty, 48, 152n10
Filosofía de la nación romántica
  (Ritter), 9
flamenco, 113–14, 156n11
Flor de banana (Beleño), 46, 152n8
Flores, Juan, 116, 121
La forma del silencio (Puga), 140
Fortune, Armando, 17
"Fragmented Majority, A" (Helg), 9
France, 11, 22, 23
Franceschi, Víctor, 32, 150n6
Frederick, Rhonda, 104–5, 156n6
Fuentes, Carlos, 75

Gallegos, Rómulo, 52, 153n15
Gallers, Anita, 155n7
Galván, Rubén (in *Curundú*), 47, 53–
  54
*Gamboa Road Gang/Los forzados de
  Gamboa* (Beleño), 46, 47; decrying
  racism but reinforcing stereotypes,
  59–60; double consciousness in, 66,
  126; required reading in Panama-
  nian schools, 86. *See also* Atá (in
  Gamboa Road Gang)
García, Ismael, 39, 42
García Márquez, Gabriel, 75
Garifuna people, 89–90, 155n8
Garrido, Juan, 82, 90–92
Geenzier, Enrique, 151n10

Gellner, Ernest, 4
gender roles, 140–43
generations, literary, 155–56n2
gente de color/people of color, 10
George (in *De/From Barbados*), 104–6
Gilroy, Paul, 6
gold and silver rolls, 44, 112
gold bracelets (in *Chombo*), 81, 83
Gómez y Ferrer, Juan Gualberto,
  150n5
gorilla caricatures of blacks, 1
"Gratitude" (Maloney), 111–12
Greaves, Lester León, 49, 65
Greene, Julie, 152n3
gringa stereotype, 49–50, 53
gringo-chombo, 57, 63
Guatemala, 90
Guerrero, Lobo (in *Curundú*), 54
Guillén, Nicolás, 19, 115

hair, African: devaluing of, 57, 84,
  88, 134; Nahuatl term for, 155n9;
  straightening and dying of, 63, 107–
  9, 133–35
Haitian Revolution and aftermath, 9,
  89
Hall, Stuart, 5–6, 95, 129, 147
"Hanseatic Republic," 10
Hernández, Gaspar Octavio, 4, 144–
  45; as "Black Swan," 29; on Botello,
  40–41; "Canto a la bandera,"
  30–31; choosing nationalism over
  ethnicity, 32, 40; and "complexity"
  of black beauty, 37; "El culto del
  idoma," 31; Korsi on white women
  and, 34–35; lacking "authenticity,"
  39–40; and Latin American romanticism, 151n10; life of, 29–30; in
  literary canon, 70; "Melodías del
  pasado," 30; and *negrista* movement, 19–20; and *panameñidad,*
  17; racial awareness of, 40–41;
  struggling with blackness, 36–39,
  129–30; veneration of whiteness by,
  32–35; "Visión nupcial," 32–34
"herstory," 138

hispanidad (Spanish nationality), 2, 11
Hispanophone Africana literature, 79
Historia de la literatura panameña
    (García), 42
"El hombre blanco en la poesía
    negra" (Franceschi), 32
"Hombre y mujer" (Wynter Melo),
    140–41
Honduras, 89
Howell, Luisa, 84
Huasipungo, 52, 152–53n14
hybrid cultural identities, 5–6, 112,
    116, 120–21, 127, 130, 144

"I can dance the 'tamborito'" (Rus-
    sell), 121–22
ICC (Isthmian Canal Commission), 44
"Identification" (Jiménez), 109
identity formation and politics: of
    Afro-Hispanics and West Indians, 6,
    147; and Afro-Panamanian identity,
    127; Blades and, 105; Escobar
    and Hernández and, 41; Lowe
    de Goodin and, 94–95; of newer
    generation, 145–46; Russell and,
    124–27, 145; Taylor and, 128–29;
    West Indian female perspective,
    101, 106; Wilson and, 115; Wynter
    Melo, 129
La igualdad (Cuban newspaper), 27
indigenista movement, 59, 153n19
"In exilium" (Wilson), 114–15
"Inmensamente Eunice" (Blanque),
    158n5
Los inmigrantes antillanos en Panamá
    (Westerman), 14
In Search of the Fathers (Zoggyie), 3
Isthmian Canal Commission (ICC), 44
Ivonet, Pedro, 150n2

Jackson, Richard L.: on development
    of black writers, 78–79; on Escobar,
    26; on Hernández, 40; on Wilson
    (Cubena), 72–73, 76, 89
Jamaica, 11, 56, 103
James (in *De/From Barbados*), 104–5

Jaramillo Levi, Enrique, 71–72, 76,
    131, 157n2
Jim Crow laws, 44–45, 152nn4–5,
    153n18
Jiménez, Blas, 107–9
Jiménez Román, Miriam, 116, 121
job applications photo requirement,
    100
José María Sánchez short-story prize,
    138
Jubiabá, 52, 153n15
Juega vivo (Maloney), 107, 112
Juyungo (Ortiz), 155n9
juyungo, meaning of, 90, 155n9

Karafula Barrescoba (in *Chombo*),
    83–84
"Kid Salva Cuatro," 54
King, Martin Luther Jr., 85
Korsi, Demetrio, 34–35, 150n6
Kymlicka, Will, 17

LACES (*Latin American and Carib-
    bean Ethnic Studies*), 3
"Lamentations of an Ex-Slave" (Rus-
    sell), 122–23
Lander family (in *Puente del mundo*),
    151n2
language: of the colonizer, 39, 53,
    115, 123; Creole, 56, 102, 153n16;
    "unharmonious mixture" in Canal
    Zone, 55; West Indians sharing of
    with U.S. imperialists, 53, 55. *See
    also* Spanish language
Last Buffalo (Russell), 123
Latidos (Maloney), 107
latifundio zoneíta, 49, 152n12
*Latin American and Caribbean Ethnic
    Studies* (*LACES*), 3
Latin American romanticism, 151n10
latino, 121
Latino, Juan, 151n8
Laurenza, Roque, 39–40
Law 11 (2005), 100
Law 13 (1926), 14, 85
Law 16 (2002), 100

Law 26 (1941), 14
"Leader" (Maloney), 109–10
Leah (in De/From Barbados), 102, 104
Lesbiaquina (in Los nietos), 87–88, 155n7
Letras de fuego journal, 138
Liequí (in Curundú), 49, 55–56
"Literary Whiteness and the Afro-Hispanic Difference" (Piedra), 151n8
literature. See canon of Panamanian literature
Litó (in Chombo), 80–81
Los de abajo, 52, 153n15
Los del Silver Roll (Maloney), 106
Los nietos de Felicidad Dolores (Wilson), 70, 81, 84–89
Lowe de Goodin, Melva, 32, 94–95, 156n2; Afrodescendientes en el Istmo de Panamá, 101; alignment with African Diaspora, 95; Anglophone Caribbean ancestry of, 96; biographical information on, 101; De/From Barbados a/to Panamá, 102; identity politics of, 145; and preservation of memory, 127; rectifying historical omissions, 103–4
Luis de Mozambique (in La misión secreta), 82
Luna verde (Beleño), 46–47

Maloney, Gerardo, 73; biographical information on, 106–7; "Black Awareness Day," 100; Calypso, 106–7; En tiempo de crisis, 107; films by, 106–7; and inclusive identity, 16, 95–96, 127, 145; inclusive views of, 16; Juega vivo, 107; Latidos, 107; literary generation of, 156n2; "El movimiento," 97; "The New Century Perspective," 107, 111–12; seeking to counter myths, 32; "Staggering Along," 107–8; "Straightening Our Hair," 107, 108–9; Street Smart, 106–12; Tambo Jazz, 106; "Towards Tomorrow," 107, 110–11

Manuelita (in De/From Barbados), 102–4
Manuel Zapata Olivella and the "Darkening" of Latin American Literature (Tillis), 75
María del Pilar (in "La sombra"), 133–35, 142
María la Flaca (in "El viaje"), 136–37
María la Gorda (in "El viaje"), 136–37
María Piedad (in "El viaje"), 136–37
Mariátegui, José Carlos, 153n19
Marley, Bob, 104
Martí, José, 150n2
Martin, Manuelita (in De/From Barbados), 102–4
Martinelli, Ricardo, 1
Martínez Ortega, Aristides, 71
Matilda (in De/From Barbados), 105–6
"Matilda" (Belafonte), 104, 105
McForbes, Charles (in Los cuatro espejos), 57–58, 110, 135
McForbes, Michelle, 155n8
McGuiness, Aims, 47
"Melodías del pasado" (Hernández), 30
melting pot, Panama as, 23
Mendoza, Carlos A., 18, 150n1
Mercedes (in "El viaje"), 136–37
mestizaje (race-mixing) discourse, 2; Afro-Panamanian identity and, 144–45; Federico Escobar and, 27; hair-straightening and, 109; incorporating whites, Amerindians, blacks, 12; Joaquín Beleño and, 60, 67; Juan de Castro on, 12; "Karafula Barrescoba" and, 83–84; Lowe de Goodin and, 94; and marginalization of West Indians, 2–3; and negrista movement, 19; and Panamanian racial classification terms, 12–13, 114; Torrijos and, 98; Wilson's fiction and, 96
mestizaje negativo, 70, 93, 154n1
mestizaje positivo, 154n1

mestizo, meaning of, 12, 120–21
"Mi apellido" (Guillén), 115
Microcosmos (Taylor), 131
Middle Passage, 136
minicuentos, 131
"Mi raza" (Wilson), 115
Miró, Ricardo: as an "authentic" poet, 39–40; and Latin American romanticism, 151n10; "Patria," 30
Miró, Rodrigo: on Beleño's Canal Zone trilogy, 47–48; *Cien años de poesía en Panamá,* 18, 20, 23, 70
mirrors: in *Camino a Mariato,* 133–35; in *Curundú,* 57, 109–10; in "Inmensamente Eunice," 158n5; in "La sombra," 133–35; in "Leader," 109; in *Los cuatro espejos,* 57, 110, 135, 158n6; in *Los viajes de mi cuerpo,* 158n5; in *Mujer que sabe latín,* 158n5
La misión secreta (Wilson), 70, 82–83, 88–93, 138
Miss Anna's Son Remembers (Russell), 118
Miss Soul Queen Contest, 99
modernista aesthetic, 32–33, 37–38, 70
Molinar, Lucy, 1–2, 98
Morejón, Nancy, 136
Moreno, Aníbal (in *Los nietos*), 86
Moreno, Juan (in *Los nietos*), 86–87
moreno/a, meaning of, 12, 35–36, 53–54
Morgan, Henry, 136–38, 158nn7–8
Morúa Delgado, Martín, 18, 150n2
Mosby, Dorothy, 5, 145, 146, 154n2
Moscoso, Mireya, 100
Los mosquitos de orixá Changó (Wilson), 113–15
Motivos de son (Guillén), 19
"El movimiento" (Maloney), 97
"Mujer negra" (Morejón), 136
Mujer que sabe latín (Castellano), 158n5
Mujica, Bárbara, 72
mulato, meaning of, 12, 109

"El Mulato" (Urriola), 18
"La muñeca menor" (Ferré), 132, 157n3

Natasha (in "Desnudez metafísica"), 141–42
National Committee of Black Panamanian Organizations, 7, 100–101
National Conference of Panamanians (1974), 116–17
national independence, theme of, 22
National Institute, 117
nationalism: black, 112, 121, 125, 145; black writers supporting, 17–20; emphasizing culture, 4, 6; of Escobar, 20, 22–23, 47, 70; of Hernández, 30, 32, 40–41, 47, 70; nineteenth-century, 9–13; rise of in Panama, 10–11
National Union of Panamanians, 99
negrista period, 19–20, 50, 60, 150n6
negro: colonial vs. *antillano,* 12–13, 15–16, 94, 148, 149n1; connotations of term, 10, 12; in "I can dance the 'tamborito,'" 121–22; meaning of in Canal Zone, 45
"Negro nací" (Villalobos), 24–26
"Negro nací: Authorship and Verses Attributed to Candelario Obeso" (Prescott), 150n4
"Negros civilizados" (Maloney), 109
Nenén (in *Chombo*), 80–81, 83, 88
neoimperialism, 53, 67
Nevis, 155n9
"New Century Perspective" (Maloney), 107, 111–12
"New Nomads" (Maloney), 110–12
"Nicanor da la vuelta" (Wynter Melo), 139–40
Nicaragua, 90
"nice appearance"/"buena presencia," 100
"Nieblas" (Escobar), 23–29
Los nietos de Felicidad Dolores (Wilson), 70, 81, 84–89
"El niño de harina" (Wilson), 72

Nissán, Rosa, 158
Nkosi, Lewis, 39
No me pidas una foto (Barrow), 100
Noriega, Manuel, 99, 149n6
"No Woman, No Cry" (Marley), 104
Núñez de Arce, Gaspar, 29
Nwankwo, Ifeoma C. K., 3, 104, 156n5

Obaldía, José de, 150n1
obesity, 142–43, 158n5
Obeso, Candelario, 19, 23, 24, 150n4
Ojeda, Martha, 73, 75
Olano, Nuflo de, 82, 90–92
An Old Woman Remembers (Russell), 118
Omi, Michael, 17
one-drop rule in Canal Zone, 44–45, 58, 67, 97
"El Orejano" (Porras), 9, 149n3
Ortiz, Adalberto, 155nn6, 9
Ozores, Renato, 43, 151n2

Palenque magazine, 146, 147, 159n1
Palés Matos, Luis, 19
Pana-Caribbean consciousness, 96–97
Panama, history of: abolition of slavery, 10; black proportion of population, 9; celebrating independence, 30–31; consequences of geographic position, 151n2; drive for independence, 10–11, 22, 150n2; Law 11 (2005), 100; Law 13 (1926), 14, 85; Law 16 (2002), 100; Law 26 (1941), 14; as protectorate of United States, 11; Remón-Eisenhower Treaty, 85–86, 116; Torrijos-Carter Treaty, 69, 70, 80, 85–86, 98. *See also* Canal/Canal Zone
Panama City, 9, 43, 48
Panamá cuenta (Jaramillo Levi), 71–72, 157n2
Panamanian Committee against Racism, 99
Panama Railroad, 2
panameñidad (Panamanianness), 2, 15; vs. *antillanidad*, 51; apply-
ing only to white elite, 47–48; as culture, 17–18; Escobar and, 22, 41; Hernández and, 40–41; promoting blackness over, 125; Rodrigo Miró and, 47–48; West Indians and, 66. *See also* nationalism
Panameñísma Reina Negra, 99
Papá James (in *Chombo*), 80, 88
Papimambí (in *La misión secreta*), 82, 89–91
Parecen noticias parody, 1
Partido Independiente de Color, 150n2
Partido Liberal de Negros (Black Liberal Party), 18, 150n1
Partido Revolucionario Democrático, 98
"Patria" (Miró), 30
Patrióticas (Escobar), 21–23
El peligro antillano en la América Central (Alfaro), 13
Peña, Concha, 40
Pensamientos del negro Cubena (Wilson), 69, 113
Pérez Olsen (in "Un día con los Pérez Olsen"), 142–43
Perla (in *Gamboa*), 61–62, 66
Peru, 153n19
Perús, Françoise, 152n11
Petrablanche de las Nieves de Monte Monarca Moreno, Lesbiaquina (in *Los nietos*), 87–88
photographs on job applications, 100
pichón, 90, 155n9
Piedra, José, 35, 151n8
Poesía panameña contemporánea (Jaramillo Levi), 71
Ponce Aguilera, Salamón, 130
"por encima"/"on top," 49
Porras, Belisario, 9–10, 149n3
postblackness, 129
postracial identity, 129
"pre-*negrista*" writers, 19
Prescott, Laurence E., 150n4
Priestley, George, 98–100, 116
"process of becoming," 129

Protestantism, 2, 11, 13–14, 54–55, 114
Pueblito Afro-Antillano, 146
Puga, María Luisa, 140
Puri, Shalini, 95, 120–21

"¿Quién soy?" (Russell), 119–20, 124

rabiblancos, 98, 156n4
race: ambivalence toward identifying by, 115; ban on political parties based on, 18; darkest Latin Americans in lowest socioeconomic group, 4; failures to acknowledge prejudice based on, 14; Jim Crow and one-drop rule in Canal Zone, 44–45, 58, 152nn4–5; and nationalism, 4; Panamanian racial classification terms, 5, 12–13, 99, 114; patriotic message emphasized over, 18; postblackness, 129; postracial identity, 129; rise of dual racial hierarchy, 46; self-identity terms on census, 15–16, 147–48; vs. social class as cause of poverty, 4, 14; as a social construction, 4. See also blackness
radio and television, 106
Rahim, Jennifer, 106
Raíces africanas (Wilson), 113
Ramón (in Luna Verde), 47–48, 51–53
Red Box (in Curundú), 49, 57–58, 66, 109
reggae en español, 107, 147, 156n8
religion in Panama, 11
Remembranzas y lágrimas (Russell), 118
Remón-Eisenhower Treaty, 85–86, 116
Restall, Matthew, 91, 92
Restrepo, José Manuel, 152n2
"revolutionary books" in Luna Verde, 52
Río Abajo, Panama, 105
Ritter, Pulido, 9
Roatán island, 90

Rodó, José Enrique, 124
Roquebert, Ramón de (in Luna Verde), 47–48, 51–53
Rout, Leslie B., 92
Rubén (in Curundú), 47, 53–54, 58
Russell, Carlos E.: biographical information on, 117–18; "Caliban's Contemporary Caribbean Dilemma," 123–27; countering stereotypes of West Indians, 32; effect of prejudiced teacher upon, 117–18; and identity politics, 95–96, 112; literary generation of, 156n2; as part of Brooklyn diaspora, 117; promoting blackness over panameñidad, 125–27, 145; refusing to relinquish Caribbean heritage, 145; on rejection of by Panama, 121–22

Salvadora Brown (in Los nietos), 86
Salvador Brown (in Curundú), 49, 53–55
SAMAAP (Sociedad de Amigos del Museo Afro Antillano de Panamá), 1–2, 97, 98, 101
Samuel (in De/From Barbados), 102, 104
Sandino (in Luna Verde), 50–51, 53
Santa Ana, Panama, 47
Santa Cruz, Nicomedes, 72–73, 75
Scott, Renée S., 135, 158n5
Seales Soley, La Verne Marie, 69
self-image: of Atá (in Gamboa Road Gang), 63–66; census results (2010), 147–48; of Lowe de Goodin, 94; of María (in "La sombra"), 133–35; of Red Box (in Curundú), 57–58. See also body-image; identity formation; mirrors
Seven Essays on the Interpretation of the Peruvian Reality (Mariátegui), 153n19
Shakespeare, William, 124
short-story genre in Panama, 130
"Silenciosamente" (Russell), 119, 124
silver rolls, 44, 106, 112

slaves/slavery: abolition in Panama, 10; Afro-Hispanic background of, 2, 5, 9, 20, 70, 78; Caliban as, 124; causing loss of language, religion, identity, 122–23; and criminalization of writing, 21; "Escudo Cubena" shield, 79; and Garifuna ethnogenesis, 155n8; Maloney on, 109; necessity to downplay, 21; recalling contributions of slaves, 82–83, 89–93; recalling horrors of, 84, 110–11, 115, 122–23, 136–37; Salvador on, 54; term *negro* and, 10, 12; Wilson's portrayal of, 91–93
Smart, Ian: *Amazing Connections,* 79; on Beleño, 65, 152n9; *Central American Writers of West Indian Origin,* 3, 5, 66, 73, 152n9; on Maloney as "Caribbean Man," 96; translation of *Cuentos del negro Cubena,* 74; and *tremendismo negrista,* 155n6
social protest literature, 32
Sociedad de Amigos del Museo Afroantillano de Panamá (SAMAAP), 1–2, 97, 98, 101
"*sodinu,*" 81
"La sombra" (Taylor), 133–35, 142
Sosa, Juan B., 18
Souls of Black Folk (DuBois), 66
Spain: blacks in, 81, 87, 151n8; importance of Panama to, 158n7; Panamanian independence from, 21–22; Spanish-American War, 124
Spanish language: and citizenship requirements, 14; Cubena and, 113–15; Hernández in "El culto del idioma," 6, 31–32; mixed with English in Canal Zone, 55–56; seen as foundational, 151n1; West Indians seen as threat to primacy of, 11–15
spar, 55–56, 60
"Staggering Along" (Maloney), 107–8
St. Kitts, 155n9
St. Lucia, 105

"Straightening Our Hair" (Maloney), 107, 108–9
Street Smart (Maloney), 106–12
St. Vincent (Antilles), 89–90, 155n8
Sueños compartidos (Jaramillo Levi), 72, 76
suicide, 65, 132–33
Szok, Peter A., 10, 18

Tambo Jazz (Maloney), 106
tamborito, 121, 156n12
Tamtam (in *Curundú*), 49, 55–56, 58
Tarik, 82, 92
Taylor Herrera, Melanie, 128–38; biographical information on, 130–31; family background of, 157n1; not writing overtly racial themes, 146; in *Palenque* journal, 146; selfidentity of, 128–29; works, 131
Tejeira, Gil Blas, 43
television, blacks on, 1, 106
Tempest (Shakespeare), 124
Teresa (in "El viaje"), 136–37
"3 de noviembre" (Escobar), 22
Tiempos acuáticos (Taylor), 128, 131, 132–33
Tillis, Antonio, 75, 107–8
Tokio (in *Tiempos acuáticos*), 132–33
"Torrejitas de maíz" (Taylor), 131–32
Torrijos, Martín, 111, 156n9
Torrijos-Carter Treaty, 69, 70, 80, 85–86, 98
Torrijos Herrera, Omar, 98, 156n9
Toti (in "Desnudez metafísica"), 141–42
"Towards Tomorrow" (Maloney), 107, 110–11
Treaty of Paris (1763), 89
tremendismo negrista, 154–55n6
La trepadora (Gallego), 52, 153n15
"tri-ethnicity," 121
Trinidad and Tobago, 111–12
triple consciousness, 116
"T & T" (Maloney), 111–12
the Twelve, 99

Ugundani (in *La misión*), 90
"undefined Caribbean," 125–26
"Un día con los Pérez Olsen" (Wynter Melo), 142–43
Unión Nacional del Negro Panameño (UNNEP), 97
United States: actions of vs. democratic ideals, 49; blamed for racism within Panama society, 45–46, 67–68; Brooklyn diaspora, 116–18; Canal displaying strength of, 152n3; Canal Zone as synonymous with, 12, 43; democracy ideal of vs. actions of, 49; desires for revenge against, 50; exacerbating pre-existing racism, 67; Filós-Hines Treaty (1947), 48, 152n10; gold and silver rolls in Canal Zone, 44, 112; identified with *terratenientes*, 59; imperialism of, 124–25; invasion of Panama, 99, 149n6; Jim Crow and one-drop rule in Canal Zone, 44–45, 58, 67, 97; Ku Klux Klan in, 72; Panama becoming protectorate of, 11, 43; as part of Pana-Caribbean consciousness, 96; Protestantism associated with, 55; returning Canal to Panamanian control (1999), 70; soldiers' abuse of women in Canal Zone, 52–53; taking over Canal construction, 11, 22, 43; Torrijos-Carter Treaty (1977), 69, 70, 80, 85–86, 98; "triple consciousness" of black Latinos in, 116–20; use of term *latino* in, 121; West Indian migration to, 98. *See also* Canal/Canal Zone
UNNEP (Unión Nacional del Negro Panameño), 97
Urriola, José Dolores ("el mulato"), 18
utilitarianism, 125

Valiente, Juan, 82, 90–92
"Venceremos Brigade," 124, 156–57n13
Venezuela, 153n14

Verónica (in "Hombre y mujer"), 140–41
"El viaje" (Taylor), 136–38
Los viajes de mi cuerpo (Nissán), 158
Villalobos, Joaquín, 24–26
Violeta (in *De/From Barbados*), 102–3
"Visión nupcial" (Hernández), 32–34
Voices from Our America, 155n1, 159n2
Voices from Our America (Lowe de Goodin), 32, 94
La vorágine, 52, 153n15

Wallai (in *Gamboa*), 64
Webster, Johnny, 4
Westerman, George, 14–15
"West Indian Man" (Blades), 104, 105
West Indians, 5; "biological visibility" of, 14; challenging *panameñidad*, 2, 11, 15; *chombo* term for, 80; concerns about loss of English, 123, 126; cultural identity shifting over time, 146; discrimination against, 13–14; disjunction between generations, 102; encouraged to leave after Canal completion, 14; extinction concerns, 127; Hernández "cult of language" essay against, 31–32; history of, 2; identity formation of, 6; maintaining English-speaking Protestant roots, 11–12; maintaining native languages, 31–32; as non-assimilationist, 13–14; perceived as allies of North America, 32, 53; perceived as foreigners, 32, 47–48, 113; population growth of in Panama, 152n13; referred to as *negro*, 12–13; tensions with Afro-Hispanics, 3, 86–93; third-generation, 8; as threat to *mestizaje*, 11; and "West Indian" connotation of blackness, 5; West Indian museum, 146; and "West Indian rage," 73, 127

What Is Eating Latin American Women Writers (Scott), 158n5
whiteness: associated with beauty and virginity, 33–35; and *gringa* sexuality, 49–50; as theme by Escobar, 24–28; veneration of by Hernández, 32–35. *See also* Atá (in *Gamboa Road Gang*)
"whitening," 109
Wilson, Carlos Guillermo "Cubena": addressing African Diaspora experience, 70, 76–77, 78–80; Anglophone Caribbean ancestry of, 96; on black *conquistadors,* 89, 91–92, 138; black nationalism of, 112, 121; on boom novels, 75; on Canal as theme, 69; on Caribbean influence in Panama, 95; *Chombo,* 70, 76, 80–81, 83–84; *Cuentos del negro Cubena,* 69; "darkening" Panamanian history, 93; disagreements with Beleño, 59–60, 86; "Escudo Cubena" shield, 79–80; exclusion from Panamanian literary canon, 69, 70–78; informative content of novels, 77; Jackson on, 73, 76–77; *La misión secreta,* 70, 82–83, 88–93, 138; literary generation of, 156n2; *Los nietos de Felicidad Dolores,* 70, 81, 84–89; optimism toward future, 148; origin of "Cubena" pen name, 79; redeeming literary image of West Indians, 74; shifts over time, 145; "Sinopsis de la poesía afro-panameña," 74; and *tremendismo negrista,* 154–55n6
Winant, Howard, 17
women: abuse of by U.S. soldiers, 52, 61; black women as doubly marginalized, 62; as *chombas,* 60, 154n20; and cooking trope, 132; in "El viaje," 136–38; and female alienation, 131; and feminist discourse, 130–38; and gender roles, 140–43; *gringa* stereotype, 49–50, 53, 61; Korsi on Hernández and, 34–35; and Middle Passage, 136; obesity and body image, 142–43, 158n5; perspective of on identity politics, 101–6; race and body image, 133–35; transmitting history through storytelling, 103; views of in *Curundú* (Beleño), 60–62; West Indian female identity formation, 101, 106
"writing white," 35, 151n8
Wynter Melo, Carlos Oriel: family background, 157n1; José María Sánchez prize winner, 138; "Nicanor da la vuelta," 139–40; nudity and gender roles, 140–42; postmodernist fiction of, 138–43; racial identity of, 128–29, 146; short story collections, 138–39

Zapata Olivella, Manuel, 3, 75, 79
Zien, Katherine, 147
Zoggyie, Haakayoo, 3, 86

Sonja Stephenson Watson is associate professor of Spanish and director of the Women's and Gender Studies program at the University of Texas at Arlington.

www.ingramcontent.com/pod-product-compliance
Lightning Source LLC
Chambersburg PA
CBHW032118020726
47494CB00007BA/2125